ROLL AROUND HEAVEN ALL DAY

A Piecemeal Journey Across America by Bicycle

Stan Purdum

Communication Resources, Inc.
Canton, Ohio

Published by
Communication Resources, Inc.
4150 Belden Village Street
Canton, Ohio 44718

Cataloging-in-Publication Data
Purdum, Stanley.
    Roll around heaven all day : a piecemeal journey across America
by bicycle / Stan Purdum. — 1st ed.
    p. cm.
    Includes bibliographical references.
    Preassigned LCCN: 97-92439
    ISBN: 0-930921-11-9

    1. Bicycle touring—United States. 2. United States—Description and travel.
I. Title.

GV1045.P87 1997   796.6'4'0973
                          QBI97-41156

Printed in the United States of America

10 9 8 7 6 5 4 3 2 1

ROLL AROUND HEAVEN ALL DAY

*A Piecemeal Journey Across
America by Bicycle*

Stan Purdum

Communication Resources, Inc.
Canton, Ohio

Published by
Communication Resources, Inc.
4150 Belden Village Street
Canton, Ohio 44718

Cataloging-in-Publication Data
Purdum, Stanley.
        Roll around heaven all day : a piecemeal journey across America
by bicycle / Stan Purdum. — 1st ed.
        p. cm.
        Includes bibliographical references.
        Preassigned LCCN: 97-92439
        ISBN: 0-930921-11-9

        1. Bicycle touring—United States. 2. United States—Description and travel.
I. Title.

GV1045.P87 1997   796.6'4'0973
                          QBI97-41156

Printed in the United States of America

10 9 8 7 6 5 4 3 2 1

To Jeanine, my partner and friend.

Preface

After I declared my cross-nation ride complete, a non-cyclist friend asked me if it was normal for people to break the ride into segments as I did. Frankly, I don't know.

I do know that every year, a few hundred people buy specialized bicycle maps for routes across America, but how many people complete the journey or ride without interruption nobody seems to know. It's not the sort of thing anybody keeps track of — or could.

That's because trips like mine often originate in private dreams and personal goals. And the point seems to be more in the doing and in the personal accomplishment than in any form of public reporting.

For me, the reality of schedule dictated that I could not complete the trek in a continuous block of time, and, in fact, that I could not close the gaps between the three segments that I rode.

I expected to be bothered by the incompletions and the installment nature of my journey, but I haven't been. What the roads I did ride gave me was more than enough to satisfy the dream that pushed me out on this midlife odyssey to begin with.

Many strangers befriended me as I made my way across the country. I did not always remember to ask their names, so some, including four drivers who provided rides in their vehicles during times of either mechanical or human breakdown, must go unthanked by name. They have, however, spurred me to be quicker to offer a helping hand to others, and I hope that will be some small measure of thanks for them.

Thanks also go to Randy, Shelley, Aaron, Adam and Jesse Croft; Jack Croly; Carolyn Duncan; Tina Faiszt; Jane, Jacque, Tyesha and Jim Gilmore; Dick and Eli Krahenbuhl; Katy Lopeman; Peter and Phyllis Lowe; Mike and Chris Sackett; John and Mary Sheldon; David Stanley; Wes and Dawn Stumbo; and Skip Volkmann; as well as to bike mechanics in Baker City, Oregon, and Carbondale, Illinois.

It was my special joy to share the road for portions of my trip with my brother Scott Purdum, my daughter Rebecca Purdum and the fellow rider I met by pleasant happenstance, David Barnas.

Although my physical journey eventually came to an end, the memory of the road became this book, thanks in large part to the encouragement of my publisher Randy Coy, the careful work of my editor Timothy Merrill and the astute observations of friends who read the manuscript at various stages along the way. They include John Burns, Carol Coy, Sherry Lowry, John Marotta, David McCoy, David Noble and Maribeth Wilmer.

The book became a reality because of the work of the members of the publishing staff: Connie Avdul, Amy Craver, Jennifer Fisher, Robert Fisher, Joni Hendricks, Sherry Mancini, Tammy McNamara, Lisa Michalek, Kym Sheetz, Heidi Staples and Jane Wagner.

Finally, family members were a valued part of this adventure, lending moral support, prayers and assistance. My appreciation and thanks to Don and Ruth Lewis, Noreen Purdum, and Norman and Geraldine Purdum. Above all, my thanks to my wife Jeanine, who carried a double load so I could enjoy the freedom of the road.

That lucky old sun has nothing to do,
But roll around heaven all day.

— B. Smith and H. Gillespie

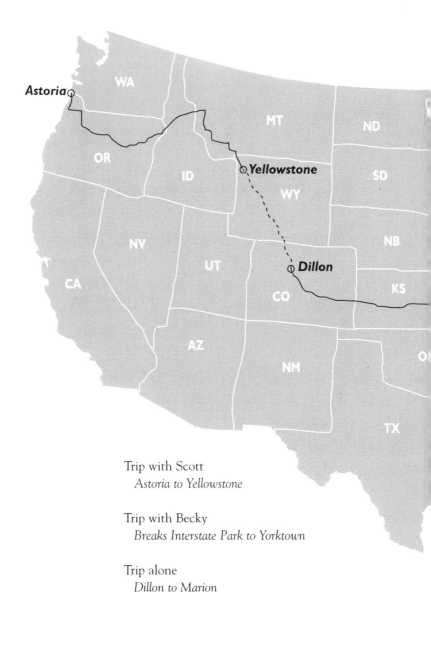

Trip with Scott
Astoria to Yellowstone

Trip with Becky
Breaks Interstate Park to Yorktown

Trip alone
Dillon to Marion

Route not covered

The names and certain characteristics of some people
described in this book have been changed.

Part 1

Chapter 1

ANTICIPATION

We made our first wrong turn before we even left Astoria.

I had the map, which I almost immediately misread, causing us to blunder our way up a very steep hill (each loaded with about 40 pounds of gear) and then roll down the other side — right back to the street we'd started the climb from. "I assume that little excursion was to condition us for climbs to come," Scott commented dryly.

I felt a little chagrined; I'm the one who enjoys map reading, and I prided myself on being good at it. At the moment, however, I was too excited to be much bothered either by the mistake or by my brother's good-natured ribbing. The bicycle ride across America I'd been planning for two years and dreaming about since I was a child, was at last beginning.

The notion to ride a bicycle across America initially occurred to me when I was 12, shortly after purchasing my first bike, a single-speed heavyweight with 26-inch balloon tires. It cost about $45, the sum total of my savings. During the long summers of my childhood, I rode with various companions to locations within a 15-mile radius of our town. Frequently, when it came time to turn around and wheel home, I'd imagine what it would be like to continue pedaling beyond the horizon. I promised myself that someday I would find out.

That notion simmered on a back burner of my life for nearly three decades. But finally, the year I turned 48, it hit me that
if I were going to fulfill that promise and actually pedal across
America, I'd better get on with it. The prospect of soon being
a half-century old reminded me that some dreams can be put
off too long. I decided that during the summer of my 50th year,
I would begin the journey and pedal as far as I could in the time
I had available.

My wife hated the idea.

Even now, as I began the ride, I knew Jeanine worried
about me — that I'd get sick or hurt or mugged or simply that
I had overestimated my abilities. She had relaxed a little when
Scott agreed to join me for the journey, but she remained
uneasy about it.

But beyond safety concerns, she wasn't crazy about the fact
that I would be away from the family for my entire vacation
allotment, nearly four weeks. Although I had occasionally
taken a week off without the family before, this would be the
first time in the 29 years of our marriage that my plans included no time off together. (I was also using our entire vacation
budget.) Two of our three children yet lived at home, and
although they were teenagers, they still needed some supervi-
sion and chauffeuring, which Jeanine would have to handle
while also maintaining her job responsibilities. As the director
of nursing at a facility for children with mental retardation,
Jeanine was used to handling tough assignments. But with the
facility being located 100 miles from our home, juggling both
her own and my usual parenting tasks was asking a lot of
Jeanine, and I didn't feel great about it. She was using some
vacation days to cover a portion of my absence, but it wasn't
going to be a holiday for her.

In the end, she put her objections aside and accepted my
expedition, if not wholeheartedly, at least without rancor. She
even helped with some of the getting-ready tasks. And for

Christmas, Jeanine bought me a new tent to use on the trip.

Taking the time away from work was only marginally more comfortable. I'm the editor at a publishing company where the staff roster is small, and none of our jobs are duplicated. With me gone, other staff members would cover my responsibilities, but not easily. Seldom had anyone taken more than two weeks off in a row before.

Nonetheless, my employer and coworkers were pulling for me. They even hung up a map and urged me to call in trip updates occasionally. The staff artist designed a little "biker guy" to place on the map and move from location to location as I progressed.

With job and family arrangements made, I still had to select a route, purchase and test equipment, and get myself ready physically. In the 12 months before my departure, I rode 2,000 miles, including a five-day tour across Ohio. For some of these rides, my daughter Becky joined me, but for most, I rode alone. I got to know the roads within a 30-mile radius of my home very well. I also dieted and lost 25 pounds — which left me still 20 pounds over my ideal weight.

For the route, I selected the original itinerary of the cross-nation bike tour established for the American bicentennial celebration in 1976. Laid out by Adventure Cycling Association, the course, some 4,200 miles long, is known as the TransAmerica Bicycle Trail. I purchased the maps from the Association, planning to begin from the West Coast. I figured that if we rode 80 miles a day, we would reach Pueblo, Colorado, before our time ran out. When I told Scott of this mileage goal, he looked dubious. "We'll have to see," was all he would say.

But now all that preparation was behind me. We started our ride where the TransAmerica Bicycle Trail begins: in the parking lot of the Columbia River Maritime Museum in Astoria, Oregon. Don Lewis, my father-in-law, who lives in Oregon and had driven us from the Portland airport to Astoria, said, "You should visit the museum; it's worth seeing."

I glanced at Scott and from his expression could tell that he had no more interest in touring a museum at that moment than I did. Our trip was about to become a reality, and we were impatient to begin. The call of the road had been gradually increasing in intensity since I started planning this journey, and now that we were actually at the origination point, that call had suddenly taken on the urgency of an impassioned lover's entreaty. I could no more disregard it than a just-home-from-the-sea sailor could ignore a pretty girl with a come-hither look in her eyes. Besides, it was already late in the afternoon and we still needed to uncrate and assemble our bikes.

So we made our excuses. Don helped us put the bikes together. When we finished, he took our picture, then watched as we headed down the main street toward our wrong turn.

Back down the hill now, Scott and I stood straddling our bikes while I studied the map. It folded to 30-40 mile sections, and each section was sized to fit in the window on the top of a bicycle handlebar bag. "Well, here's the reason we took the wrong street," I said. "This part of the map is not oriented with north at the top!"

"Sure, sure, Stan. Blame it on the map." Scott grinned and continued in a mock-aggrieved tone. "Here I trust myself to my big brother and the first thing he does is lead me astray."

"Well, look for yourself." I pulled the map from the window and held it out for him to see. "If you'll notice, the orientation differs from section to section, according to which arrangement allows the most route mileage to be viewed."

"You're right," Scott agreed. "Of course, you'd have known that if you had bothered to read the instructions that came with the map."

"Okay, okay. I give," I said, warming to the brotherly banter. "I blew it. But you just wait and see if this isn't the ride of your life."

Chapter 2

COAST

Astoria, located at the northwestmost corner of Oregon and on the mouth of the Columbia River, was named for John Jacob Astor, who, in 1811, sent two expeditions to the region to establish a fur-trading post. Lewis and Clark had been there six years before that. Over the next weeks as we cycled the TransAmerica Trail, we were to discover we often traveled on or near ground traversed by the Lewis and Clark Corps of Discovery.

A city built on the side of a hilly peninsula, Astoria offered us an impressive view of the toll bridge that crosses the embouchure of the Columbia River into Washington. After pausing for a look — and to check the map one more time — we headed out of town, now on the right road, crossing Youngs Bay on a narrow bridge.

Just seven miles into our ride, we came to the Fort Clapsop National Memorial, which marked the site of the Lewis and Clark expedition's winter headquarters. With the road still singing her siren song, we didn't feel too disappointed that the park was about to close, leaving us no time to visit the recon-structed fort.

As we pedaled southward along the smaller Lewis and Clark River, we passed through a rural area where some of the homes were rundown and in disrepair. Coming from the

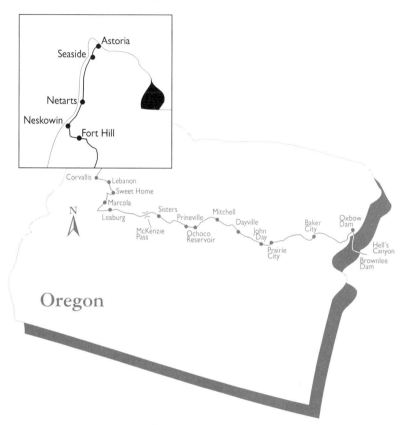

Midwest, we expected scenery very distinct from that which we usually rode through. This land was different, but Scott commented, "Poverty looks pretty much the same, no matter what landscape it sits in, doesn't it?" Glancing at the ramshackle houses, I agreed with his assessment.

Several of the surrounding hills displayed the aftermath of the logging method known as "clear cutting," where virtually every tree on a given patch of land is felled. However, rather than entire mountains being denuded, the clear cuts were confined to strips of each summit, with untouched acreage in between. The result looked rather like the partially shaved heads on a cluster of punk rockers.

After 26 miles, we rejoined the coast at the community of Seaside, where we stopped at an RV park for the night.

The campground provided the first test of how we would deal with a unique problem we faced as tent campers. Scott suffers from sleep apnea, a condition that presents no problems when he's awake but causes him to stop breathing as often as 50 times an hour during sleep. After each breathing pause, he awakens slightly, meaning that he never falls into a deep sleep and is therefore very tired the next day. The solution is to wear a breathing mask connected to a "Continuous Positive Air Pressure" (CPAP) pump, a device powered by electricity that keeps his airway open all night.

Typically, RV parks welcome tenters but usually relegate them to areas with no hookups for electric, sewer and water. In full-occupancy times, campground managers are understandably reluctant to assign tenters, who generally pay less, to full hookup sites. So when we requested a slot with electricity, we were not surprised that the woman behind the desk gave us a "you've-got-to-be-kidding" look.

Scott, however, briefly explained his problem and the woman became immediately cooperative, assigning us to a grassy spot behind the shower house where an electric outlet clung to the wall. Subsequent experience confirmed that as long as Scott was willing to tell his story, most campground operators did their best to accommodate us and seldom even charged for the electric hookup.

From a public phone, we both called our wives, to assure them that we'd arrived in Oregon safely.

Noreen, Scott's wife, would be alone for their 24th wedding anniversary, which would occur while Scott and I were on the road. But she, too, had come to accept her husband's absence. Before we left Ohio, she slipped me an envelope containing an anniversary card to give Scott on their special day.

———•◦•———

Our route the next day was almost entirely along the coast, which presented us with one breathtaking vista after another of the Pacific Ocean. Especially spectacular were the frequent huge, craggy rocks, some more than 100 feet high, that stood in the water several yards offshore like sentinels for the coast-line. Called "sea stacks," they had once been part of the main-land itself, but had been isolated by millenniums of beating waves that severed their connection.

At one vantage point, a local resident astride a bike inquired about our journey. "This is a beautiful state," Scott said. "It's my first time in Oregon." He pronounced the state name as "Or-a-*gon*."

The local cyclist smiled and shook his head. "I can tell that," he said. "If you lived here, you'd say it 'Or-a-*gin*.'"

Highway 101, the westernmost road in the lower 48, is a heavily used artery, so we were delighted to discover that for much of its distance, wide, paved shoulders had been provided and labeled as bike paths. On many roads, even if the shoulders are blacktopped, so much debris has been kicked onto them by passing vehicles that it's perilous for cyclists to use them. On this coastal highway, however, the verges were reasonably clean.

Provisions for cyclists even extended to the narrow tunnel south of Arch Cape. There, we pushed the roadside button to activate flashing lights on a sign that warned motorists that bicyclists were in the tunnel. As a further precaution, we turned on our blinking taillights. There were no road shoulders in the tunnel, and we didn't like the prospect of meeting a car in there driven by someone whose eyes had not yet adjusted to the dark. We wasted no time getting through it.

Late in the day, we cycled the perimeter of Tillamook Bay, leaving Highway 101 where it took a more inland route. As we swung back toward the sea, we were smacked by a very stiff headwind blowing in from the water. We slogged along, expending at least double our usual energy. Clearly, my 80-miles-per-day goal wasn't going to be met this day, and I wondered if that objective would prove overly optimistic for most days.

Stifling the concern, I looked hopefully toward the end of the bay, assuming that when we again headed due south, we'd be dealing with only a crosswind. Once we turned the corner, however, we found that although the highway was protected from wind by forest, it climbed steeply upward. After attempting to pedal the hill, we both gave up almost simultaneously, dismounting and walking the bikes to the top. We were further humbled when, as we neared the summit, three young men with bicycles loaded as heavily as ours blasted by us as they hammered up the incline. "I bet they weren't bothered much by the headwind either," Scott observed.

Days later, when we'd ridden much steeper and longer mountainous roads, we would look back at this hill as a "beginner slope," but early on, before we had become fully conditioned, it seemed tough.

It's a problem trying to train in the Midwest for a tour in the far West. My 2,000 miles of cycling during the preceding year were all in Ohio, where there simply are no real mountains. Scott's schedule yielded even less time for pre-trip training rides, so he still had a bit more "spare tire" around his middle than I now had.

Still, in most ways, Scott and I are ideal companions. He's as adventure-hungry as I am, has like interests, and usually rides at about the same pace as I do. He also shares my offbeat sense of humor and has similar thought patterns. (Sometimes it's almost spooky. On the coastal hill, we each gave up the attempt to pedal at virtually the same second, both uttering the exact same words: "Oh, the heck with it.")

We've enjoyed several previous adventures. Our earliest bicycle ride together took place right after I got my first bike at

12. Scott was 6 and didn't yet have a two-wheeler of his own, but he eagerly begged to join me on a cycling excursion. So I carried him "double" on a round trip of 14 miles. He sat sideways on the top tube while I pumped for both of us. When we returned home, he claimed the ride hardly tired him at all!

As adults, we once rode a 450-mile tour together from mid-Kentucky northward through Ohio and into lower Michigan.

But that had been five years earlier. In preparation for our present journey, we managed only a couple of training rides jointly. One of these was in Ohio's Holmes County, an area that provided challenging hills. That county also contains one of the largest concentrations of Amish people in America. The convoluted terrain gave us a good workout, enough that Scott commented that the horses that draw the Amish buggies briskly up and down the slopes must have exceedingly stout hearts.

During that ride, we camped out to test our new gear. The additions we made to our kits after that cool spring nighttime were stocking hats to cover our heads while sleeping. We appreciated those hats now as we spent our second night on the coast. The campground at Netarts is set in a cove, and although we couldn't see the ocean from our tents, we could feel the chilling breezes.

The park catered to RVs, and each established site had full hookups and a graveled parking spot. Where the manager put us wasn't actually a site, simply a grassy spot behind his house. But we much preferred sleeping on grass to sleeping on gravel, and Scott was glad for the 50-foot extension cord the manager loaned him to power the CPAP. We plugged it into a barely attached porcelain socket in the nearby rickety woodshed, carried our gear into our tents, and settled in for the night. We had ridden 63 miles since dawn.

Then I did something stupid. Among my new gadgets was a candle lantern. This is a small metal cylinder surrounding a plumber's candle. A glass chimney topped with a metal heat deflector telescopes out of the cylinder. I set the device up, lit it, and read by its light for about 30 minutes. When I was ready to sleep, I blew out the candle and without thought, pushed the upper section back into the lower portion. In an instant, pain shot through my thumb as the hot deflector seared it, raising an immediate blister.

In agony, I flipped on my flashlight, pawed hurriedly through my panniers (saddlebags), and dug out my drinking cup and a water bottle. Sloshing water into the cup, I plunged my thumb into it, and sighed as the cold began to draw the sting out. Twice in the next 20 minutes I changed the water as it became too warm. Finally, the pain subsided sufficiently to let me sleep.

The next morning, Scott saw me bandaging my thumb and asked what had happened. (With his CPAP running, he hadn't heard me yelp.) When I explained, he shook his head and said, "Stan, Stan, Stan. What am I going to do with you? Your second night out and you get a second-degree burn."

"Yeah, but now that we've had an injury, maybe that will be the last of our health worries on this trip." Little did I know then that an illness I would face later on would make this one mishap pale in comparison.

A couple of miles into our ride for that day, we encountered our first real mountain. This involved a five-mile climb, which, being yet early in the day, we managed mostly to ride, though with lots of puffing. The descent was about the same distance, but we rolled down effortlessly at 35 miles per hour. At that speed, the rushing wind caused my eyes to tear, despite the protection of my glasses. On other descents I have occasionally ended up with bugs in my teeth, and once a bee flew into my mouth and stung my tongue. (I'm now careful to keep my mouth shut.) But this time the primary sensation was pure exhilaration, a natural, joyful high. I felt as if I could have cruised on like that forever.

Near the bottom, the road passed through fields of sand dunes that extended for miles, right up to the ocean itself. The dunes are a land feature unique in the United States to Oregon.

North of Neskowin, the coast highway rises a few hundred feet to where a roadside parking area offers a scenic overlook of the ocean. There we found the trio of cyclists who the day before had passed us on the hill like an express train with a full head of steam. This was the first we'd seen them since. In their early 20s, the three were college friends riding a five-day loop with the Oregon coast as one arc of the circle. Learning that we were on a cross-country ride, all three stated that they'd like to do the same someday, a refrain we were to hear again and again from other short-trip riders.

We noted with surprise that one of the three did not have a "granny" — the third and smallest chainring on the crankset of most touring and mountain bikes. It's the granny that provides the lowest gears for climbing. They had flown by us powering uphill, and one didn't even have the right gears! "Do you miss the granny?" I asked him.

"So far, I've managed the hills okay without it," he said.

"Uh, yeah. I noticed that," I said, feeling old and sluggish.

Maybe he sensed my dismay, because he added, "But I'll have one before I do something like this again." (Sure, like maybe when he's 50 and overweight!)

After they rolled out, an older man got out of a motor home, asked about our trip, and then requested advice on what sort of bicycles to purchase for himself and his wife. We told him what we knew, but sensed he was more interested in the simple opportunity to chat with someone doing something "adventurous" than in buying bikes.

Scott's bicycle was actually designed for touring. It came equipped with a granny ring and a wide range of gears to accommodate varying terrain. My bike was an old, inexpensive 10-speed that I had regeared — it now had 18 gears and higher-quality wheels. You can easily drop $1,000 on a high-end touring bike today, so instead, I simply upgraded components on my old bike as they needed to be replaced. By this time, the bike frame itself and the shift levers were about all that remained of the original equipment.

Midway through the day, after a two-and-a-half-day total of 120 miles on the coast, we turned inland, leaving the ocean at the town of Neskowin. Within minutes, we moved from the coastal climate and environment to one of forest and mountains and began climbing the Coast Range, a belt of mountains that parallels the shore. As mountains go, the Coast Range is relatively low. Most summits are 4,000 feet above sea level or less, and the average is only 2,000 feet. Leno Hill, the pass our route traversed, is a mere 820 feet in elevation, but since we started from sea level, it seemed a significant climb. Scott especially had a tough time, feeling suddenly drained of energy (an experience cyclists call "bonking"), although he managed to achieve the pass without walking his bike. Still, Scott turned in abruptly at the very first restaurant we saw after Leno Hill, without our usual consultation about where to eat.

At a rest area before the top, a Federal Express driver who'd pulled in ahead of us, asked us questions we were to hear repeatedly throughout our journey: Where were we riding from? How far did we plan to go? How many miles did we ride each day? How much conditioning did we do for this trip? Scott's standard reply to the latter was "Not enough!" Unless a person is free to ride long hours day after day, some conditioning inevitably remains for the trip itself.

After learning of our route, the FedEx driver suggested a shortcut and even dug through his case of maps to show us the way. Because of his obvious interest, I wondered if Scott and I were planting a dream in him.

Our camping spot that evening was dictated by the need for electricity. After a reviving supper, we both felt eager to ride further, but a look ahead on our map revealed no campgrounds beyond the one near at hand at Fort Hill. Had we not needed to be plugged in, we'd have no doubt gone on and simply camped free with permission on private land or behind a church.

As it was, because we slept in separate tents, the manager of the only half-filled campground charged us two dollars extra. It made no sense to us; we used only one site and no more of the park's resources than if we'd shared a single tent, but we didn't argue. The woman at least supplied an extension cord for Scott's CPAP.

After we settled in, I totaled up our mileage for the day: 67. A respectable distance, surely, but not the 80 average we needed to make Pueblo by trip's end.

Chapter 3

BROTHERS

Just west of Salem, we turned southward again, heading down the Willamette Valley — a farming region — toward the city of Corvallis. On the coast, we'd been cooled and sometimes almost chilled by sea breezes. The journey over the Coast Range had been comfortably warm. In contrast, the Willamette Valley was hot, hitting 90 degrees by midmorning. But with the wind at our backs, we fairly flew along.

The farming economy of the valley is based on vegetables, dairy farming and wheat. In fact, in the early days of settlement in the area, wheat served as legal tender, worth $1 a bushel. Later, as gold seekers rushed through the valley on their way to California, the value of a bushel rose as high as $6.

In Monmouth, we stopped to get fresh batteries for my cyclometer, which had ceased functioning. As we pushed our bikes along the sidewalk, a man waved to us vigorously from a car and then pulled into a parking slot. Other drivers had waved too, so we didn't think much about it and continued toward the store. But then a voice called out and when we turned to look, we saw the same man hurrying toward us. He was a retired United Methodist minister, he said as he introduced himself, and had noticed the UM emblem on Scott's T-shirt. My brother is a UM pastor and I, although now working in a different field, am ordained in the UM ministry as well.

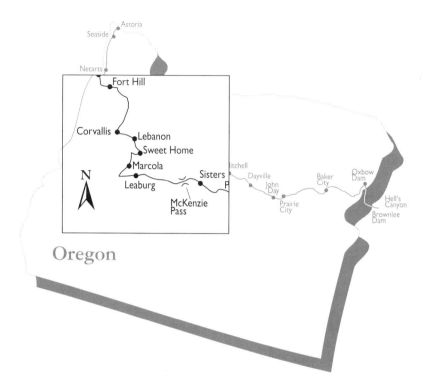

"Where are you from?" he asked.

When we told him, he was eager to hear about the work of the denomination in our state. He named a couple of pastors he thought now lived in Ohio, but we didn't know them. Although retired, this energetic man was on his way to a local church to help out with the vacation Bible school program. If we could wait until he finished that, he said, he'd buy us lunch.

In other circumstances, we'd have liked to talk further with him, but we had already eaten and my father-in-law expected us at his home by nightfall, so we declined and went on our way.

Although Don had driven us to Astoria, he lives farther

inland. This day's portion of the TransAmerica Trail passed close enough to his town to make stopping there feasible, and we were looking forward to visiting with him and my mother-in-law, Ruth.

Back on the road, I found that the new batteries didn't help. My cyclometer was dead.

Cyclometers combine the functions of a clock, an odometer, a speedometer, a trip-mileage counter and an elapsed-time recorder. Some also show maximum speed, average speed and altitude. For long-distance riders, the most important of these functions is the trip-mileage counter, which is reset for each day's journey. Keeping track of the daily mileage is for more than pride of accomplishment. Knowing how many miles have already been covered helps riders estimate how close they are to intended destinations and whether they are likely to have enough energy remaining to press farther. Since exhaustion can set in without warning, most cyclists soon learn their normal mileage limits. The cyclometer is a useful tool for distance riding, and fortunately, Scott's still worked fine.

At Corvallis (from the Latin for "heart of the valley"), we departed from the mapped route to head for Lebanon, where Don and Ruth make their home. Our bike maps showed little beyond the bike route itself, so we selected what, according to a state highway map, appeared to be a secondary highway, Route 34. It didn't take us long to discover that this road had been widened to four lanes and was heavily traveled. Vehicles of all sizes roared past us at high speed, while we plowed through the gravel and assorted trash that had accumulated on the paved shoulder. The frenzied traffic precluded riding side by side, so I took the lead.

Since leaving Corvallis, Scott seemed to be riding more slowly. After a few minutes, I noticed he was falling behind, so I dismounted and waited for him to catch up. "Are you okay?" I asked, shouting to be heard above engine roar and tire whine.

"Yeah," Scott said. "I'm just a little tired. I'll be fine, but I can't push as hard right now. You go ahead; I'll catch you eventually."

I didn't care much for that idea, so I slackened my pace. But no matter how slowly I pedaled, the distance between our bikes widened. I was concerned that Scott might not be feeling well. I also worried that if a real difference in our riding energy persisted, the journey might become an ordeal for both of us. I knew of friendships that had been strained by differing goals and abilities when traveling together on bikes, and I didn't want that to happen to us.

For now though, I figured that as long as I could see Scott in my rearview mirror, he was okay. Anyway, the debris on the shoulder demanded most of my attention. Our bikes are the skinny tire type, and won't tolerate as much abuse as wide-tire mountain bikes, so I had to do a lot of dodging and weaving, while making sure I didn't veer into the all-too-close rush of vehicles.

When I next glanced in my mirror, I couldn't see Scott. I stopped and waited. Still no Scott. I waited another minute. No matter how languidly he was riding, he should have overtaken me by this time. A few nasty possibilities came to my mind. Had he been sucked into the significant wake of air trailing behind a passing semi? Had litter on the shoulder directed his wheel into the traffic path? Had he gotten sick? Broken down? With my concern mounting, I decided to retrace my route and look for him. The stream of traffic was too constant to permit crossing the highway, so I pedaled back against the traffic flow.

My anxiety increased when I didn't come upon him quickly. Surely I hadn't gotten this far ahead, I thought. I scanned the road shoulder ahead, but saw no sign of him. I pedaled faster.

Finally, after nearly a mile, I spotted him. His bike was upside-down, wheels pointing skyward. Scott knelt beside it, leaning as far from the roadway as possible, doing something to his front wheel. "Flat tire," he said as I drew up next to him. Then looking at me, he asked, "Were you worried?"

"Yeah," I confessed. "I guess I'll never stop being your big brother."

Flats are a fact of life for cyclists, and Scott had lots of experience fixing them. It took only five minutes or so for him to remove the wheel, insert a new tube, pump it up, and put the wheel back on the bike.

I, too, have changed a lot of flats, but the most memorable time was one of my very first flat tires. I was about 14. There was a lake with a public beach some 10 miles from home, where a couple of my friends and I rode from time to time to swim. One day, neither of my buddies was available, so I made the trip alone. The ride there went fine, but as I began the return trip, my front tire went flat. I had a patch kit along, and there was a gas station at hand with an air pump. But though I located and patched the puncture quickly, the tube would not hold air. When I stuck the tube into the garage's pail of water, the escaping bubbles seemed to indicate that the patch was not holding. Three times I tore it off and glued on a new one, but without success. Finally, defeated, I rode the whole trip home on the flat, ruining the tire.

At home, I examined the tube once more. This time, I noticed that whatever object had penetrated the tube had gone completely through, making an entrance hole on the bottom face, which I'd fixed, and an exit hole on the top face, which I'd failed to observe. There had been nothing wrong with my patch job! From that experience, I learned the importance of studying a problem for a moment before simply repeating a repair that hasn't worked. Occasionally I've even remembered to apply that bit of wisdom to the difficulties of my life, and usually have been well-served when I did.

Scott returned his bike to the upright position and mounted up. As we resumed riding, I determined not to outdistance him, but found him now riding stronger anyway.

The road did not improve and soon narrowed back to two lanes, but now with no shoulders. Traffic continued to whiz by steadily, and we clung precariously to the edge of the road just inside the white line. Then my rear tire began losing air. As there was not much room to pull off, I inflated it quickly with my frame pump and hoped it would get me to Lebanon.

About five miles before the city limits, we came upon a side road where a man, standing beside his car, waved us over. "Welcome," he said, pointing with a smile to Route 34, "to the worst road for bikes in America." When we acknowledged that he was no doubt right, he introduced himself as "Skip." "When I saw your gear," he said, "I figured you weren't from around here and didn't know about the back road."

"What back road?" I asked.

Skip pointed southward. "There's a quiet country road just about a mile that way. It parallels Route 34 almost all the way from Corvallis." Skip lived in Lebanon and worked at Hewlett-Packard in Corvallis, he explained, so he made the round trip daily. But he was a cyclist and often rode his bike to work, so he'd searched out the less-traveled roads.

Like us, Skip was a bike tourist, but unlike us, he had ridden 30,000 touring miles, 6,000 of them with his wife. "You're welcome to stay at our house tonight," he said. We would have accepted gladly had we not already had people to meet in Lebanon.

Before we parted, Skip told us how to get to the parallel road for the remainder of our ride into town. I pumped up my rear tire once more, and we were soon at our destination, where we were warmly received by my in-laws and their other guests, Jeanine's aunt and uncle. That night, Scott and I "camped" in their living room, and Ruth did our laundry.

We had logged just over 70 miles that day, again shy of my 80-miles-per-day target, but it was a hopeful sign that we both felt able to continue. We'd stopped simply because we had arrived at our destination.

As we pedaled out of town the next morning, I thought about how contented Don and Ruth seemed spending most of their adult lives in the same small community. Actually, I envied their contentment. They had moved to Lebanon years ago when Don took a job in the lumber industry, purchased a small house, and apparently never saw any need to go elsewhere.

Don had taken Scott and me out for breakfast that morning, and in the diner, Don was cheerfully greeted by name by the waitress and several patrons. Lebanon is small enough that residents can know and be known by fellow citizens. I loved that small-town feel, an atmosphere I had experienced myself in two locations, communities where I felt very much at home. But in both cases, as well as in several other places where Jeanine and I had lived for shorter periods, I eventually grew restless, eager for new job challenges. And although Jeanine never actually refused to relocate with me, she hated each uprooting, so that every move was accompanied by some weeks of tension. Finally, I promised to stay put — and have, for five years thus far — but our current community lacks the small-town atmosphere that I enjoy. While I was growing up, my parents' work required frequent relocations, so we lived a nomadic lifestyle and never remained in one place long enough to belong. But I seldom thought of that as a loss.

Robert Frost might have understood my gentle melancholy as we rode out of Lebanon. He wrote about the second-guessing regret of "The Road Not Taken." I'd chosen the path of adventure and change, but sometimes I wondered how it would have been on the other track, the one that led to a sense of place and rootedness. But the pensiveness didn't linger; I knew that if I had my life to live over, I would take the same road again.

Rather than backtrack to the TransAmerica Trail, we

chose an alternate route that Don assured us was not heavily
traveled and that would eventually put us back on our planned
course. Not only was he right, but his route — by way of Sweet
Home and Marcola — took us through an exceptionally scenic
area. Close at hand were quiet pastures and fields, but hover-
ing just behind them loomed pine-forested hills that gave the
whole panorama a hidden-valley ambiance. My enjoyment of
the view reminded me of some lines I'd read a couple of years
earlier. One day in 1836, after walking the land around his
Massachusetts town, Ralph Waldo Emerson returned home
and wrote:

> *The charming landscape which I saw this morning is*
> *indubitably made up of some 20 or 30 farms. Miller*
> *owns this field, Locke that, and Manning the woodland*
> *beyond. But none of them owns the landscape. There is*
> *property in the horizon which no man has but he whose*
> *eye can integrate all the parts, that is, the poet. This is*
> *the best part of these men's farms, yet it is to this their*
> *warranty-deeds give no title.*

I did not own the land we now wheeled through either, but
for a short time, the landscape was mine.

The morning temperature rose well into the 90s, and our
last climb shortly before Marcola sapped us both. Lunch in
that town helped, but afterward we were still hot, so we
flopped down in the shade in the local schoolyard and slept for
about an hour, hoping the air would cool.

It didn't, but the naps restored us, and we resumed the
journey. By late afternoon, we rejoined the mapped route just
north of Springfield, again heading east and now in the region
of the Cascade Mountain Range. The farms of the Willamette
Valley had given way to a more mountainous terrain, and the
visible industry now had to do with logging and recreation.
The route paralleled a river on the floor of a valley, with mountains visible on each side. The name "McKenzie" appeared fre-

quently: It was the name of the river, the valley, a community ahead (McKenzie Bridge), the mountain pass we journeyed toward and even a large, prominent building built on the hillside (McKenzie Estate).

At our supper stop, a café called "Tina's Lucky Logger," I asked our waitress, an aging but trim bleached blond in tight black jeans, the origin of the ubiquitous McKenzie name. She said, "Well, I don't know about that, but there's a town up the river called 'Finn Rock.' They say the Finns were the biggest liars on the river. My name used to be Finn — but I'm not related to them." Then she aimed a conspiratorial wink at Scott as she headed for the kitchen.

We later learned that the name referred to explorer David McKenzie, who was a member of the 1811 expedition sent by John Jacob Astor to establish the fur-trading post at the mouth of the Columbia. McKenzie is also credited with being the first white to explore the Seven Devils region of the Snake River.

We camped that night — free of charge — in a county park on the bank of the McKenzie River, near Leaburg, with 68 miles completed. It was the first time we'd been unable to locate a place for Scott to plug in. Scott resigned himself to a less-than-restful night.

Come morning, we dined on cinnamon buns and bananas at the little market in Leaburg. Actually, it offered much more than groceries: video rental, fax and copier service, hot food, gas pumps and the town's post office. With a steady stream of customers for all these services, the lone woman operating the place was very busy.

Later, we passed several groves of filbert trees with such dense foliage that the ground below was in perpetual shade. Filberts, also known as hazelnuts, are an export crop from Oregon.

Our lunch stop: the café at Blue River. On the wall of the men's room someone had scratched, "Rednecks are inbred cowfolks." At least that's what I assume the scribe intended. What he'd actually written was, "Rednecks are inbreed cowfolks," which probably said more about the writer than about either rednecks or cowfolks.

We'd been gradually climbing all morning. After about 40 miles, we arrived at Route 242, the road to McKenzie Pass — 5,324 feet high — the point where we would cross the Cascade Range. A sign at the nearby ranger station declared that we were now a little over 1,400 feet above sea level. The map indicated that from where we stood to the top was 22 miles. The map also noted that Route 242 closed in winter — a further indication of its rapid gain in height. On level ground, we can almost always pedal 22 miles in an hour and a half or less. We knew, of course, that climbing took longer, but it was only 2 p.m.

"Let's do it," I said. "There's plenty of daylight left. We'll have lots of time to reach the top, and from there it's only 11 miles — all downhill — to Sisters." The town was named for the three mountains visible from the town.

"I'm not so sure," Scott said. "That's a long way up. There's a campground a mile away. We could camp now and tackle this climb when we're fresh in the morning."

"But we don't want to stop this early. Even if it takes us twice as long, we'll still be on top by five."

"Okay, I guess, but I'm not sure this is wise." Scott's hesitance and reluctance surprised me.

My estimate of "twice as long" proved to be hopelessly optimistic. The climb to the pass was the hardest we had ever done. The road presented us with long, steep climbs followed by series of switchbacks almost as steep, and always the road continued relentlessly upward, constantly surrounded by lush forests. I was riding comfortably, but after the very first mile, Scott started falling behind. I stopped and he eventually caught up, but after we resumed, he lagged farther and farther, going so slow that I found it wearying to hang back with him.

Eventually, he told me to go ahead and just wait for him at the top. Unwilling to split up, however, I continued to stop every mile or so. Each time he caught up, Scott looked a little more weary. We rested for a few moments and then tackled the next mile. I began to resent that Scott had not accomplished as much training and weight loss as I had in preparation for this trip.

About halfway up, a lone westbound cyclist stopped to tell us that we still had a lot more upgrade to cover. Moreover, this young rider from New York said, his cruise downhill — our uphill — was the longest he could recall from anywhere on his entire cross-country excursion. The news seemed to hit Scott hard.

After hours of alternating between climbing and rest stops, we were still five miles from the summit. And Scott, who had not slept well, now found himself in such physical distress that he could do little but sit beside the road, immobile. I checked the time frequently, now concerned that although daylight remained until nearly 9 p.m., darkness would overtake us on the mountain. My worry level shot up, dwarfing the concern I'd felt when Scott dropped out of sight on Route 34. He was so depleted and disheartened that I began to think he'd withdraw from the trip — assuming we made it over the top.

Finally, Scott stood up and started walking his bike, so I fell in beside him and we moved slowly upward, noticing that in shady spots, snow piles remained.

A couple of miles from the crest, the highway leveled sufficiently for Scott to ride again, which he did, slowly and in obvious exhaustion.

Our reward was some of the most unusual scenery we would see. The area had once had active volcanos, and lava fields covered several square miles of the top in a haphazard jumble of jagged black rock, giving an eerie feel as the late-day sun slid toward the horizon.

We reached the pass at 8:10 p.m., and while Scott rested near the road, I hurriedly climbed the observatory that had been built using volcanic rock. Several mountaintops, including Mount Hood, North Sister and Middle Sister, were visible.

At 8:20 we began our descent, which, fortunately, was almost as steep downward as our climb upward had been. We did little more than hold on and brake occasionally as we shot downhill. A mere 35 minutes later, in semi-darkness, we rolled into Sisters. Because of Scott's exhaustion and my own weariness, we took a motel room for the night.

In the lobby, while I checked us in, Scott collapsed onto a couch. The woman behind the desk asked if we'd just ridden over the pass. "Yeah," I said, my resentment erupting, "but my brother wimped out." Scott said nothing, but I immediately wanted to call back my words. They were unkind and undeserved. Before we even started the climb, Scott had expressed his misgivings, but I'd pushed him to go on. He'd done the best he could, and I had no cause to berate him. I felt like a cad.

When we got to the room, I apologized. "Doing this together is more important than just making miles," I said. "I really enjoy your companionship and I'm sorry for what I said."

"Don't worry about it," Scott said graciously. "It's not a problem."

When I calculated our distance for the day, I found that we had logged 76 miles, our best mileage so far. But in light of how my drive to cover ground had caused me to push Scott beyond his limits, I discarded the 80-mile daily goal. We would cover what we could and enjoy ourselves.

As it turned out, that climb was a turning point for Scott. From the next morning onward, his riding strength improved, and we soon found ourselves about evenly matched in endurance.

Chapter 4

IMAGINATION

Although I have only occasionally been privileged to be a wanderer, wanderlust is unquestionably one of the energies that have driven my life. Raised to be a "responsible" person, I have repeatedly squelched the yen to be footloose, turning my attentions instead to the routine endeavors of raising a family and making a living. And for a time, the satisfactions of those enterprises compensated for the unanswered call of the road.

I had also assumed that maturity would silence the vagabond within me, but I was mistaken. If anything, aging added a note of urgency to its voice. Once I reached my fifth decade, its cry could be quelled no longer.

As a boy on a bike cruising the roads near my childhood home, I could see only as far as the next bend, but in my mind's eye, the highway unrolled to a distant and yet-to-be-explored horizon.

My imagination was spurred in part by a love of maps and what they represent. From the time when I first learned what a map was, I burned with a lust to match actual geography with the lines representing highways, and even more, with the blank spaces between the major thoroughfares. I still want to "own the map" — travel the terrain, see where highways actually intersect with byways, find out where side roads go, visit tiny time-forgotten hamlets, and, in general, take the roads less traveled.

The bicycle has been my frequent, and to my thinking, best implement for scratching my explorer itch, but there have been others: the car, a string of unreliable recreational vehicles, a canoe and my feet. As a young teen, I lived about four miles from a large natural park. Maps of the park showed its roads, picnic areas, buildings, waterways and natural attractions, but for some reason, none of the park's trails. As soon as I obtained a park map, I knew I would not be satisfied until I had filled in its substantial blank areas. Over two summers, I spent numerous contented hours following every trail, figuring out my own links between them, and penciling them in on my copy of the map.

My passion to own the map is a lonely one. Though my wife and children have learned to suffer with only minimal grumbling through my innumerable "shortcuts" when driving, they do not share the joy. And they have never understood why, when arriving at an amusement park or other attraction where a map is issued, I want to walk around and get oriented to the guidesheet before queuing up for the rides. Frankly, I don't understand it either, but there it is.

Owning the map is a fairly specific sort of exploration, in no way linked to the desire to be the first to set foot in fresh territory. Even if I had been alive during the discovery of new lands, I doubt I would have been among those who made the initial forays. But I might well have come in the second or third wave, after the first cartographers had done their work.

There's something concrete about a map, something that anchors landscape in my mind. Nonspecific directions ("It's the second or third road to the right, about halfway down on the left side. You can't miss it.") always leave me a bit uneasy (and I've proven that I *can* miss it). But draw me a map and I can get anywhere.

Owning the map is clearly not "possessing" in the usual sense. It is not holding title that counts, but knowing — from firsthand contact — *what's there.* In *Don Quixote*, Cervantes wrote, "Journey over all the universe in a map, without the expense and fatigue of traveling, without suffering the inconveniences of heat, cold, hunger and thirst." His words make no sense to me. A map is not a parking permit, but a ticket to ride.

Many of my youthful ideas have not survived into adulthood, but the vision of a cross-nation bicycle journey, although not always in the forefront of my attention, never fully left my imagination. Eventually, notion and imagination impelled me to make the journey a reality.

Chapter 5

DESERT

Up before Scott, I phoned home, three time zones away. I didn't yet feel homesick — the joy of the journey and Scott's companionship helped to keep loneliness at bay — but it was good to hear Jeanine's voice. We had occasionally been apart for a couple of weeks at a time: twice when Jeanine went to Haiti as a nurse with church mission teams and once when she toured orphanages in Kazakstan. She had gone there to evaluate how U.S. health care institutions could help facilities in that former Soviet land, where decades of atomic testing had taken place in the atmosphere without evacuating the population. During those absences, I'd been the one to stay home and manage the household, but we were always glad when the time came to be back together. Our kids were always glad when Mom came home, too. They acknowledged that "Dad did okay," but they made it clear that I was the "B team."

As we talked now, I told Jeanine about our experience on McKenzie the day before, and she brought me up to date on the news from home.

Since my last call, our daughter had spent her first day as a volunteer at a horse stable that served disabled riders. Becky had signed on as an unpaid helper before I left, but her first time up came after I was on the road. Becky assisted with caring for the horses and walking beside those riders who were not steady enough to guide the animals on their own. Since it was her first time working with horses, I'd been concerned that she might get hurt. I wasn't afraid of horses, but the notion of my little girl playing with big animals awakened my fatherly concern. Jeanine's report, that Becky was doing "just fine," was welcome news.

Jeanine asked about my thumb. I was glad to report that it was healing nicely. Fortunately, the burned area was just below where my thumb normally gripped the handlebar, so the riding itself had not caused further damage. "Take better care of yourself," she said. "I want you back in one piece when this trip is over."

Because of the grueling climb the day before, we decided to rest by hanging around Sisters for a while. Tourism appeared to be Sisters' main industry, and the town catered to tourists by its yuppie feel, by the prices charged at the dining places and accommodations, and by the craft and specialty items offered in its shops. Sisters compared to the little workaday towns we'd already visited like a dance-hall girl in a gaudy dress compares to a ranch wife in chambray and denim. We dawdled over breakfast, then wandered through several of the stores, examined new equipment in the town's two bicycle shops, and walked most of the town's streets. We had planned to stay at least through the morning, but by 11 a.m. we had had enough and itched to get back on the bikes. Soon we were pedaling eastward once more.

Sisters is the beginning of yet another distinct geographic region of Oregon: high desert. In contrast to the forested green of western Oregon, the desert landscape we traveled through now looked barren. The change had been most dramatic the day before as we moved from west to east over McKenzie. Although my concern for Scott and the work of climbing had taken most of my attention, I had still noticed a significant change in the flora from one slope to the other. On the side we ascended, heavy forests of evergreens (western hemlock, western red cedar and Douglas fir according to the text on our map) dominated the land, growing so dense that the ground below was in perpetual shade, and was constantly moist. The map stated that the western slope receives as much as 100 inches of precipitation annually.

As we got higher, the land took on an alpine appearance. Then, heading down the east slope, we again saw trees, but these were more often ponderosa pine. Even the fading light of evening penetrated the sparser canopy of these treetops, and the ground cover was much dryer looking. Rainfall on the east Cascades is about five inches a year.

Now in the high desert itself, I studied the sweep of the land. Clearly, the region was dry, but sagebrush, desert grasses and occasional pine trees dotted the land. This desert was not nearly as barren as it had seemed on first glance.

I thought about a man we had talked to in a café on the green side of the Cascades. "There's nothing to see after you cross the mountains," he had said, in the dismissive style of someone who can no longer see his environment with the eyes of a wayfarer. Of course, if he meant that there were no amusement parks, shopping malls or "scenic wonders" on the scale of the Grand Canyon, he was right. But a certain magnificent splendor permeated this semiarid land.

In terms of effort, we pedaled through this landscape easily. After yesterday's mountain, today's rises were comparatively gentle.

The road from Redmond, where we stopped for lunch, to Prineville, wound through a narrow valley between high bluffs and was especially beautiful in its desolation. I kept expecting to see a stagecoach bounding along in the distance, watched by Indians from the precipice above.

Prineville, with a population of 5,400, was one of the larger communities we visited. We learned from our bike map that it was the first settlement in eastern Oregon and sits 20 miles northwest of the state's geographic center. The town had earned a post office in 1871, but it was the discovery of gold nearby two years later that gave the place a growth boost. However, being 120 miles away from the nearest railway and telegraph lines, Prineville remained an isolated community. The city rectified this situation in 1918 when it financed and built its own rail line. Today, that line connects with a major railroad near Redmond and is the only city-owned railway in the nation.

In terms of our journey, however, Prineville came too soon for our evening stop. But the next town was too far distant to be reached in the remaining daylight. The bike map showed some campgrounds a few miles farther on at Ochoco Reservoir, and provided phone numbers. A call verified that one of them had electric hookups, so we decided to continue.

Before we left town, Scott purchased and mailed an anniversary card to his wife, timed so that she'd have it by their special day.

On the banks of the reservoir itself — a sparkling blue-water lake that looked oddly out of place pooled against the dry hills — we found a scenic and low-cost state park campground that, regrettably, had no electricity. That park looked even better when we saw the private campground, a rundown place with a collection of old trailers and RVs. It did have a tent area, but the manager explained that we had to pay the same price as the RVs since we would be using a trailer site. This was the only place on the entire trip where we had to pay the full hookup fee, and we felt annoyed about it since the park was so shabby compared to the state park across the highway.

The manager pointed at two side-by-side sites and told us to select either. As we began setting up on the first, an elderly woman came out of the adjacent trailer, explaining that she was the mother of the woman who owned the campground and was only visiting. She was concerned about her daughter's tiny dog, which we could hear yapping in the trailer. "Good thing it's not my dog," she said. "I'd kill it." But as we began to set up our tents, she brought the dog outside and fussed over it. To Scott she commented, "I hope the dog doesn't pee on your tent. That's about where he usually goes."

We moved at once to the adjoining site.

When we checked in, the manager mentioned that there were a couple of other riders already in the tenters' section, so after we were established and showered, we looked them up. With two bikes leaning against a fence near their tent, they were easy to spot. They were a young husband and wife from California. They explained that they had been on the road for only a few days but looked forward to four months of travel. He had curly, dark hair and a serious look. She was blond, sturdy and the more outgoing of the two. They planned to cycle the west, bus across some of the flatter Midwest states, and resume riding farther east. Their plans were not firm, she said, but they hoped to bike the Blue Ridge Parkway in Virginia later on.

Back near our tents, another cyclist stopped, heading from the showers. He was camped in the state park but had paid to shower in the private park. When we learned that the state park was showerless, our site began to look a little better. "I'm riding with my wife," he said. "We're on a tandem bike." They'd started at Portland, and were heading, by a circuitous route, back home to North Dakota.

With our dallying start, Scott and I had covered only 50 miles, but since I'd let go of the 80-mile goal, I felt okay about the distance.

———

We were the first of the cyclists on the road the next morning, but even though the highway was relatively flat, I found myself struggling to keep up with Scott, working as hard as if we were climbing. That flustered me. I had been fine when I got up and still felt good, but there was no question that I was laboring now. Scott slowed a bit to accommodate me, but I panted along even at that.

After several miles, we stopped to remove our long-sleeve jerseys and tights, and soon the couple on the tandem caught up. An attractive pair, they introduced themselves as Shannon and Stacy, although as both were unisex names, we couldn't recall later which was which. Thin and built like a midheight basketball player, the husband contrasted with his petite wife.

Actually, the confusion about the names of fellow riders wasn't surprising. Although there's an almost instant camaraderie among cycle-tourists when they meet on the road, the exchange of names, if it happens at all, is usually an afterthought, and last names are rarely given. This has nothing to do with secrecy or rudeness. Rather, sharing route information, ride experiences, anecdotes about equipment and sights not to miss take priority.

We left Shannon and Stacy removing outer layers of clothing, and we soon began the climb toward Ochoco Pass. I was alarmed that I needed to shift to my lowest gear almost immediately. Scott slowed to stay with me, and soon the Shannon/Stacy duo overtook and then passed us, climbing smoothly. I noticed that the young woman, mounted on the rear or "stoker" saddle, seemed hardly to be exerting herself at all. Meanwhile, I continued to labor, baffled that I had to work so much harder than Scott.

Eventually we came to a dip in the climb, which should have provided me some relief. It did not. What was going on? At this rate, I'd be wiped out for the day by 10 a.m.

Finally, I became suspicious that the problem might not be my energy level after all. When I stopped and examined my bike, I noticed that one of the shock cords I used to attach my tent and sleeping bag to the rear rack was not hooked to the bike frame, but to the rear brake, which the cord had pulled against the wheel rim. I'd ridden for nearly 10 miles with one brake half on!

After I moved the cord to its correct position, I rode as easily as if a ball and chain had suddenly been removed from my leg.

Unlike the torturous climb to McKenzie Pass, the ride to Ochoco Pass (4,720 feet) was relatively easy, mostly because the campground where we started the day was already at 3,000 feet, and the incline to the pass stretched over several miles.

The next few miles demonstrated how cycling can go from ecstasy to agony within minutes. The descent from Ochoco Pass was fast and steep, a thrilling high-speed plunge to a deep canyon. We fairly flew to the bottom, but then we began climbing almost at once as the road threaded its way toward Mitchell. It was now high noon and so hot that the remaining water in our bottles was no longer refreshing, and we were hungry besides. The desert canyon we labored through trapped and compounded the heat. If I looked for stagecoaches the day before, here I kept expecting the 20-mule team. The last three miles to reach the town felt like 10, and we rested often as we crawled toward it.

The main street of Mitchell, population 200, is a mere two-block string connected to the main highway at its two ends. Still, the town boasted two cafés, and we cooled down over sandwiches in the first one we came to. Afterward, because the map showed that the next 40 miles were uninterrupted by services of any sort, we purchased some canned food for supper in a little grocery store. The clerk had to total our groceries manually; the electricity was out in the entire town. "We heard that someone shot out an insulator on a pole somewhere up the line," he explained. "It's happened before."

His words reminded me of the gunshots we had heard echoing a couple of miles back. While I assumed the sounds were simply from someone target shooting, they made me uneasy. With no one else in sight, we were all too vulnerable in the rocky expanse of the canyon. We were both glad when the shots receded into the distance.

Being in Mitchell reminded me of a tale I'd read on the back of our bike map. There had once been another settlement five miles east of Mitchell that was actually the first permanent community in the area. Established in 1863 as a stagecoach station, this stop was staffed by two bachelors, C.A. Meyers and "Alkali Frank" Hewot. When the number of travelers using the station increased, the two men decided that the place needed a "woman's touch," and each bachelor proposed that the other man take a wife. Since neither was willing to become a victim of matrimony, they settled the matter in true Western fashion — with a card game. After the game, the loser, Meyers, headed for California to secure himself a wife. The map didn't report whether or not he succeeded.

A small city park, where camping is permitted, sits at the east end of Mitchell's main street. There we found Shannon and Stacy, their tent already erected. The road out of town began with a seven-mile steep climb. They'd decided to postpone that until the next morning, they explained, hoping for cooler air then.

Perhaps we would have been wiser to do that, too, but it was only 1 p.m., and we were reluctant to stop so early. The sports thermometer attached to my handlebar bag registered only 95 degrees, but the exertion of the steep upgrade, total lack of shade and absence of any breeze made the climb desperately hot. We rode as much as we could, but ended up plodding up the last three miles pushing our bikes.

Finally over the top, we once again experienced an instantaneous reversal, exchanging the torture of the climb for the rhapsody of a prolonged downgrade — 33 miles in fact, from the top of the Mitchell hill to Dayville, the next community. As we glided down, the breeze from our movement through the air cooled us off. The scenery was exceptional. We wound through empty canyons, stark bluffs and quiet lands broken only very occasionally by a distant ranch compound. There was almost no traffic at all. As we continued deeper, the canyon walls on each side rose higher, splayed with understated mixtures of reds, browns and other earth tones. For two boys from the flat Midwest, the surroundings were a visual banquet.

I wanted the ride to go on forever, and I found myself humming the refrain to an old Louie Armstrong tune:

That lucky old sun has nothing to do,
But roll around heaven all day.

The canyons ended at Picture Gorge, so named for pictographs painted on the rocks as long as 8,000 years ago. Because of the lateness of the day, the visitors' center, where we would have been able to see the pictographs, was closed, but nature's extravagant display of color and grandeur in the gorge compensated us more than enough for what we missed. We stuffed ourselves with visual delights until surfeited.

Dayville boasts 206 citizens. Although the town offers a commercial campground, the word we had received from the New York rider and other westbound cyclists we met earlier was, "Stay at the Dayville Church." The map explained that the congregation runs a hostel in its building and instructed riders to contact Millie Grindstaff next door to the church to make arrangements.

We found Millie to be the proverbial "little old lady." A younger woman in the house told us we were welcome to pitch our tents in the churchyard — or sleep in the sanctuary if we preferred — cook in the church kitchen, and use the shower in the church restroom. The church charged nothing for all of this, but there was a basket available for contributions. When we explained Scott's sleep apnea, the woman cheerfully loaned us an extension cord to run from the church to Scott's tent.

I suppose the contributions do help the tiny church with its budget, but the congregation also has gained a sterling reputation on the cyclists' grapevine for its gift of hospitality.

Shortly after we set up, the California couple we met the day before rolled in, followed moments later by two women in their early 20s unencumbered by panniers or other gear. A car, bearing their husbands and their equipment, pulled in soon afterward. While the women showered, their husbands set up camp. Later, as all three groups of riders sat in the church fellowship hall, the two women explained that they had driven a support vehicle for their husbands' bike trip earlier in the year, and now the men were returning the favor. Residents of Oregon, these two couples enjoyed exploring their state at a self-propelled speed.

Looking around the room, it struck me that under usual circumstances, Scott and I, who were old enough to be the fathers of any of the others, would not be invited to share companionship and conversation with so young a group. But we found that evening, as we were to discover whenever we met other cycletourists, that the endeavor itself provided common ground.

The young men especially seemed to enjoy the conversation with the whole group that evening. But when one of the wives said, "I'm ready to go to sleep," her husband immediately replied, "Oh, okay," and jumped up at once to go with her. Ah, to be young.

The California husband mentioned that he'd quit his job as a personnel director at a university to ride this journey. He was taking the four months to figure out what he wanted to do next. As we met other cyclists later, we noted that several seemed to be on personal pilgrimages. That night, in the little travel journal Scott's wife had given him for our trip, Scott read this by Henry David Thoreau: "A traveler is much reverenced as such. His profession is the best symbol of his life. Going from — toward; it is the history of every one of us."

The next morning started our ninth day on the road.

When planning the trip, I had expected to be out of Oregon by this time, but we were having such a good time in the state that the distance covered now mattered less than ever.

The two women were the first out, leaving their husbands to strike the tents and pack their equipment. Planning to go only as far as the town of John Day, the women were on the last leg of their ride. The California couple decided to remain in Dayville until the next morning; they, too, had climbed the steep hill out of Mitchell in the heat, but they'd ridden all the way and now felt the need of some recovery time. We did not see them again.

Before Scott and I reached John Day, the two women, their trip completed, passed us in the car with their husbands, heading back the way they'd come. They tooted and waved encouragement.

The sky had been threatening all morning, and the temperature was the coolest we had encountered since the coast. About two miles west of John Day, rain began to fall. We hurried into town and ducked into a restaurant for lunch, but the rain continued even after we'd eaten.

The town was named for a Kentuckian. John Day came to the Oregon Territory with the Astor party in 1810. With winter approaching, the group ran out of food near the Snake River, and Day ran out of steam. Too worn out to continue, Day and a companion, Ramsey Crooks, remained near the Snake, while the balance of the party pressed on. Day and Crooks survived on scraps, pelts and even fish bones. When the two finally made it to the Columbia River, they were captured by a band of Indians, beaten and robbed of their clothes. Finally the rest of Astor's company found the two — naked, starved and screaming to be saved. By fall, when he came back up the Columbia with a trapping party, John Day had lost his mind. He died within months.

While my sanity remained intact in the town bearing this

hapless man's name, I did have a potentially troublesome run-in with the automated teller machine at the John Day bank. Rather than carry large amounts of money or bother with traveler's checks, Scott and I had both decided simply to make periodic cash withdrawals from ATMs. Accustomed to finding these money machines in virtually every town in Ohio, we were surprised that many of the very small communities in the West had no banks, let alone ATMs. Fortunately, John Day, with its 1,800 souls, was sufficiently populated to have both. When I inserted my cash card in the bank's ATM, however, a notice appeared on the screen stating that my account could not be accessed. As it was Sunday, the bank was closed, so I had nowhere to turn for assistance. I hoped the problem was with the ATM system and not with my card or my account. I still had a few bucks in my pocket, but not enough to get me to our destination.

The rain fell steadily and harder, so we took advantage of the time to do our wash in a nearby laundromat. Limited space on the bikes meant that we carried a minimal wardrobe, so that even by combining our wash, we had only a small amount of garb to launder. Our usual uniform was T-shirt, bike shorts and white socks; we each carried only a few changes of each. In addition, we carried a pair of tights each, a long-sleeve jersey, a wool sweater, a wind jacket and a cyclist's cap. We both added a pair of street slacks and a flannel shirt, reasoning that if the jersey and tights got wet on a rainy ride, we would want something dry to change into come evening.

While waiting for the washers to do their work, I wandered over to the grocery store across the street to buy a few supplies, and while there, found that they, too, had an ATM. To my relief, this one spewed out the requested amount of money when I tried my card.

By the time we finished our laundry, the rain had ended, but the cool remained. We resumed our journey.

We stopped for the night at Prairie City, even though we had both energy and time for continuing (we'd had a tailwind all day) and had completed only 49 miles since Dayville. Three successive mountain peaks lay ahead, with camping available in the dip between the first two. But when we inquired about that in Prairie City, we learned that the camping area was merely a clearing across the highway from a café, with no electric available. Instead, we stayed at Prairie City's campground, on the grounds with the town's museum.

We were directed there by the attendant at the town's only gas station. As we walked into the station, the large man in bib overalls waved a friendly hello from his rocking chair as though he'd been waiting all day for our arrival. In short order, he supplied the information about the no-electric campsite ahead, recommended the local campground instead, inquired about what each of us did for a living, told us that the removal of one of his lungs kept him from vigorous exercise (like biking), and suggested we eat at the restaurant across the street, the "home of the best hamburger in Oregon."

It struck me that the attendant was the first stranger, aside from the United Methodist minister, who'd asked about our employment. Even at the Dayville Church, where we'd spent the evening with other riders, occupations came up only in the course of conversation, not because anyone asked. Evidently, the riding itself captured most people's interest enough to render normal get-acquainted questions superfluous.

When we tried the restaurant, we found the burgers if not the best we'd ever eaten, at least among the biggest.

Chapter 6

WIND

"May the wind be always at your back." So goes one verse of a well-known old Irish blessing. And, as any bicyclist knows, it's more wishful thinking than prophetic benediction.

Headwinds, which slow forward progress and tire riders quickly, are a fact of life for those who bike. (Of course, this blessing was clearly not written for cyclists. Its opening salvo is, "May the road rise to meet you," which is hardly the prayer of any rider who has pumped up a 7-percent grade!)

A ride with a strong tailwind, however, is a joy. With a good breeze pushing, even an inexperienced rider can log an extra 10 miles a day. And the hope of going with the flow is the reason most transcontinental bike trips begin on the West Coast. Supposedly, the jet stream causes surface air to move more often from west to east than the opposite way.

In practice, however, the wind often seems to be headed whichever way the rider isn't. But from time to time, the wind does come from behind, gracing whatever riders it chances to catch with a friendly shove and a light heart.

On tailwind days, I feel as if I can ride forever. I remember the exhilaration of early rides that hooked me on biking to start with. I get that "all's-right-with-the-world" attitude, start noticing the scenery instead of the tarmac, and even begin to count myself blessed.

And well I should. Tailwinds, happy days, times when all plans turn out as desired are rare enough to make each occurrence a jewel. We're all wise to revel in them and store up their memory for headwind days.

The danger from tailwinds is when they lull riders into thinking they can ride forever, a common experience on out-and-back trips. If there's a tailwind on the outbound leg, the temptation is to go too far. Then the return journey is an overlong struggle with wind in one's teeth, desperation in one's heart and the word "fool" stuck in one's craw.

On second thought, though, the power of tailwind optimism outweighs the risk. Seeing what is possible when everything goes right causes us to challenge ourselves and extend our reach toward higher goals — a worthy benefit in any field of endeavor.

Headwinds either discourage would-be riders or build perseverance and character in those who keep cycling.

Tailwinds help us to glimpse the vision, attempt the impossible, and plan transcontinental bike trips. And in the long run, the ability to dream is as important as the ability to face adversity.

Chapter 7

REPAIRS

The next day was July 3rd, Scott and Noreen's anniversary. The moment we were both up, I presented Scott with the card Noreen had entrusted to me. It surfaced only slightly soiled and mildly dogeared from being scrunched in the bottom of my pannier for several days. Scott read its message, which he declined to share, and looked pleased.

A clear sky and cooler temperatures bode well for more comfortable climbing. Although we were soon wet with sweat under our tights and jackets as we ascended the first of the three mountains, the rapid glide down the mountain proved so chilling that we had to stop and pile on additional clothing. The wind striking my chest proved so cold that I removed the map from the handlebar bag and slid it up under my jacket for additional insulation. Our frigid hands made us wish that we had brought full gloves in addition to the fingerless riding gloves we wore in summer.

Eventually we came to a café and store. Thoroughly chilled, we decided to eat lunch even though it was still early. The café had not yet opened, so we hurried into the store, where we were able to buy hot drinks, microwave food and gloves from a disgruntled man who obviously considered customers an inconvenience. When we lingered over our sandwiches, he said, pointedly, "Will there be anything else?" We

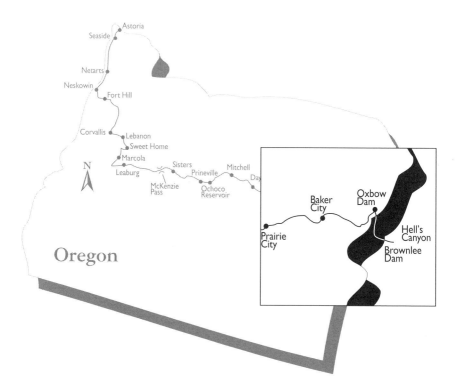

got the message and moved to the bench outside.

Finished eating, Scott and I tackled the second of the mountain passes. Just after we topped it, we met a rider coming up the other side. Brendan Ryan, from Dublin, Ireland, was 65 and in his 10th week of a coast-to-coast ride from New York to Oregon. Tall, and almost gaunt, his red-going-gray beard and ruddy skin stood out against his light-colored clothing. Unlike almost every other rider we met, Brendan wore no specialized biking garb at all. He sported a baseball-type cap, an ordinary button-up jacket, jogging pants and tennis shoes. Considering the impressive amount of territory he'd covered, the lack of bike clothes obviously wasn't much of a handicap to him.

Brendan had previously biked most of Europe, he explained, and had long wanted to see the "States." We decided that with that much time away from home, he must either be single or have a sainted wife.

Ever since we left Lebanon, I had had intermittent problems with the shifting of the chain on my front chainrings. The chain moved down to the granny without problem, but when I attempted to shift back up, the chain just skittered across the teeth of the middle and large rings. Eventually the big ring picked it up, and then I could shift from the big ring to the middle one, but by that time I'd lost most of my momentum. As we worked up and down the three passes after Prairie City, the problem worsened; now not even the large ring would catch the chain when it was coming off the small one. I was finally forced to abandon use of the granny altogether, which denied me my lowest gears. Fortunately, the journey after the third pass was relatively flat, and we were able to reach Baker City, our minimum destination for the day.

Although we'd ridden bike tours in the past, none had been over as demanding terrain as this journey, and we were both surprised by how the daily pedaling stressed the equipment. Climbing steep grades especially took its toll. As I downshifted under load, I'd hear the chain bang into place. I knew the action had to be hard on the drivetrain components.

The bike map listed three bike shops in Baker City. But because we didn't know the streets, we inquired at the first gas station we saw and were directed several blocks down the main street, where we found no shop. Evidently the shop that had been there had gone out of business. Eventually we stumbled onto another shop, not listed on the map, but after listening to the owner talk about replacing parts willy-nilly, we beat a hasty retreat, realizing he was the bike-industry equivalent of a medical quack. Finally, a local rider directed us to a good shop, *right across the street from the gas station where we'd begun.*

My chain problem was unusual and a bit puzzling. The store's closing time came and went, but the shop owner stayed open to help us. In contrast to the man in the first bike shop, this man began by simply adjusting the existing parts. Only after assuring himself that the problem was more than maladjustment did he consider any new part. Then, by changing one component at a time and testing as he went, he eventually sorted it out. In the end, he had to replace the chain, the middle chainring, two rings on the back gear cluster and the front derailler (the mechanism that lifts the chain from one chainring to the next). Of these, all but the middle chainring had a lot of miles on them before we began the current trip. As each part was replaced, the shifting problem diminished, but didn't cease completely until all the new components were in place. When he finished, he charged a surprisingly reasonable price for the new parts and his labor.

Actually, we were not surprised by the extra service from a bike shop. A lot of such stores are operated by people like this man, who are themselves cyclists. They know what it's like to be on the road with a broken part and will often go to great lengths to help. On a bicycle trip in Ohio with Scott a few years earlier, a grinding noise began emanating from Scott's bottom bracket. (The bottom bracket is part of the bike frame that the pedal-and-crank assembly passes through.) We tried to repair it ourselves, but found both ball-bearing sets shot. Putting the bike back together as best we could, we headed for Chillicothe, the nearest town large enough to have a bike shop. Scott's bike complained all the way.

The shop we found turned out to be, like the one in Baker City, a one-man operation; the young owner was also the mechanic and salesman. When he learned of our difficulty, he dropped everything to repair Scott's bike. He rebuilt the bottom bracket, installing a new spindle and bearings, a process that took nearly an hour. I envisioned a sizable bill.

At one point, he needed a lubricant he'd run out of. He excused himself to run to another store, leaving us alone in his shop with all those bike accessories — and his unlocked cash box.

When he'd finished, he charged us only $15, including parts.

Bike people such as that proprietor and the one in Baker City are part of the reason cyclists often develop profound loyalties to certain shops and will purchase bike components at their favorite shop even when they can find them cheaper elsewhere.

But back to the Baker City shop. While the proprietor worked on my bike, a young man came in looking for a bike part, and from his conversation, it was clear he and the shop owner were friends. Seeing our gear, he asked the usual questions, introduced himself as "Wes," and invited us to camp for the night in his yard.

"Do you have a note from your wife saying it's okay to bring strangers home?" I asked.

Wes grinned. "I don't need one. She'll be pleased because she knows she'll get some quick housework out of me before you arrive." We accepted the offer.

Before leaving the shop, I asked the owner where we could get a good meal. "Well, I don't know that you can, in Baker City," he said, "but there are lots of places if you can settle for a mediocre meal." Then he directed us to a local restaurant where our supper was about as good as the food at most of the places we had eaten on the trip.

After Wes had left the bike shop, the proprietor described him and his wife Dawn as a "neat couple," declaring them both cycling enthusiasts. They were all of that, plus charming hosts. Wes and Dawn Stumbo each owned a road bike and a mountain bike, two of which leaned against the wall in the kitchen of their snug house. The pair spent time in both versions of the sport. Shyly, though, Dawn mentioned that she'd probably have to cut back on riding soon, as they hoped to start a family.

In the meantime, however, Dawn managed the gift shop at the Oregon Trail Interpretive Center, located a few miles east of town. (By the time we reached Baker City, three people had told us to be sure to visit the Center.) Dawn rode her bike to work a couple of days a week "to stay in shape."

We talked late into the night. When we mentioned the grouchy man at the store where we had stopped earlier in the day, Wes, who traveled that area as an engineer with the Forest Service, said, "Don't take it personally. That guy hates everybody. When someone comes into the adjoining restaurant wearing a Forest Service uniform, he purposely burns their food."

———•◆•———

In the morning, Dawn provided breakfast and gave us homemade cookies for the journey before she mounted her bike for the ride to work. We promised to see the Center before we exited the area.

Judging by our outbound journey, Dawn had to be a strong rider. Her route first climbed Flagstaff Hill, a significant and lengthy incline. Then, she faced a tougher challenge: the mile-long driveway to the Center itself, which was located on a high bluff. Wes, who as an engineer no doubt knew what he was talking about, had casually mentioned that the driveway included *10-percent grades*. Scott and I, laden as we were, found it impossible to pedal all the way up; we had to dismount and walk the bikes.

When we saw Dawn in the gift shop, dressed for work and looking as if she hadn't exerted herself at all, I said, incredulously, "Did you ride all the way up?"

She nodded. "At first I used to walk parts of the drive, but I finally decided that if I let myself walk at all, I'd never ride it, so now I don't stop at all."

I was impressed!

The Interpretive Center offered an exceptionally well done and informative collection of displays and artifacts from the pioneer era. But equally impressive, I thought, were the plaintive wagon tracks still clearly visible on the prairie below, more than a century and a half after the last prairie schooner had passed. The Center was well-placed near Baker City, for that community was the first in northeast Oregon to be established along the Oregon Trail. It became a major trading center and, after mining flourished in the region, earned the title, "Queen City of the Mines."

Leaving, Scott said, "Well, visiting this Center will make Noreen happy. Every time I call home, she asks, 'Have you done anything yet?' Now we've 'done' something." Both of our wives had trouble comprehending that riding itself was "doing something." But for us, it was a "something" that brought exquisite pleasure.

Planning specific things "to do" and sights "to see" was the antithesis of what this trip was about. Although we'd never discussed it, it was clear that Scott, like me, began each day of our ride without specific expectations of what we would receive from the day's journey. Every day was itself a gift, and we hadn't been disappointed in any of them so far.

The journey from the Center to tiny Richland was a dream ride: a gradual downgrade following the turbulent Powder River between darkly beautiful mesas of the high desert, on a landscape rimmed in the distance by snow-capped peaks.

Eventually our stomachs began to call for food, and we began anticipating the next small town. Unlike many cycle-tourists, Scott and I carried no stove or cooking gear. Neither of us really enjoys camp cooking, but more importantly, we wanted to use our energy (and the available daylight) to ride, not to perform culinary and cleanup duties. We ate our meals in restaurants or grocery stores. Unfortunately, in many small towns, the local cafés offer menus of monotonous similarity. Usually there's one fish and one chicken sandwich (both deep-fried) and then six or seven variations on a hamburger, and all served with french fries.

But now we noticed a building on the left with tables and a pop machine on the porch. Several people sat at the tables, dining off paper plates. The map had not shown a restaurant here, but we pulled in, salivating at the aroma wafting from the cuisine. "Do we order by the plate?" we asked the woman who seemed to be in charge.

"You don't order at all," she said. "This is a private home and we're having a reunion."

We were chagrined. We had crashed a family party! I mumbled something about being misled by the pop machine. "Oh, that *is* for the public," she said. "Help yourself." We inserted coins and then took the cans across the road, where we drowned our annoyance in colas.

Later, at a café in Richland, our disappointment at not getting a meal at the pop-machine home was mollified when we discovered that for once, we could order a swiss-steak dinner with mashed potatoes and a vegetable.

Tiny Richland earned its name from the fertile land that surrounds it, a dramatic change from the high desert we passed through earlier. The area yields wheat, potatoes and other crops.

The warm sun on the hamlet's sleepy main street called us to linger, so after lunch we adjourned to the park on the edge of town and slumbered in the shade for an hour.

As it turned out, even that rest wasn't enough. Almost immediately after Richland, the road climbed a butte abruptly. Uncomfortably hot, we walked almost half of the steep 12-mile grade. The climb was so debilitating that although the rest of the day's journey was mostly downhill through coolly forested land, the road seemed more of an obstacle between us and the campground than a journey to be savored.

Finally there, we camped at Oxbow Dam in a campground owned by Idaho Power, in view of the state of Idaho across the Snake River.

As soon as I awoke the next morning, I knew it was not going to be one of my better riding days. I felt neither rested nor eager to be underway. I simply had little energy. The first thing we encountered was a sudden but short hill. Sweat oozed out of me before I achieved the top. The next part of the day's journey, a 12-mile level stretch through Hell's Canyon along the Snake River was without significant wind and should have been easy, but I found it as tiring as if we were battling a headwind. I reveled in the postcard beauty of the canyon, but every turn of my crank was an effort.

In midmorning of our 11th day, we crossed the Snake below Brownlee Dam, and, after 707 miles in Oregon, entered Idaho.

Chapter 8

ATTIRE

I bought my first pair of tights without telling my family that I'd made the purchase. I ducked into the bedroom, climbed into the tights, and then stalked to the family room without a word. My wife and daughter both burst into laughter. My teenage son, speaking without the hysteria infecting his mother and sister, but with obvious intensity, made an unflattering comment about my sartorial taste and asked me to make sure none of his friends were visiting when I was dressed for biking.

But as tights are the most sensible choice for cold-weather cycling, I've persisted in wearing them, surrendering to the collective wisdom of thousands of cyclists. Jeans are too bulky and impede easy movement; sweat pants turn into a cold, sodden mess when they get wet and don't repel wind well in any condition; and other street pants flap in the breeze and feature chain-snaring cuffs. Tights, contoured to the legs to reduce wind drag and eliminate chain snagging, also wick moisture away from the skin and keep the wearer warm even when wet.

Even knowing all that, I first had to overcome some internal resistance to letting myself be seen in a garment that's clearly first cousin to pantyhose, especially since my figure's not ideal for tights. (My girth measures several inches more than my inseam.) Every time I draw on my riding tights, I can't help but think that I look like a Lycra-clad funnel with two downspouts. Still, I've learned to flinch only on the inside when I walk into a small-town diner and find a room full of men in ball caps and bib overalls looking at me. Given the choice between living with the glances and riding with cold legs, I'll live with the glances any day.

Yet even this pragmatic attitude did not prepare me for the comment of my older son. Eric is a Navy diver and works on projects so dangerous that he receives hazard pay. As a diver, he's undergone rigorous training beyond that of regular sailors. His diving class started with 65 recruits and graduated only 13. He's trim, muscular and lean. I mention all of this to explain why I was a bit reluctant for him, as a man among men, to see me in my bike tights.

But a good day for riding occurred during one of his visits home on leave, so I donned my winter riding garb, took a deep breath and bolted for the garage where I store my bike. As fate would have it, I encountered Eric almost immediately. He stopped abruptly, looked me over from head to foot, and then said the words that left me stunned.

"Pretty sexy, Dad. Way to go!"

Chapter 9

SERENDIPITY

"Hey! What *is* this?" I said. "Does every pickup in Idaho come complete with a dog in the back?"

In the first 10 minutes we were in the state, no fewer than four pickup trucks passed us, each with a large canine in the bed, barking a challenge as the vehicle drew abreast. Standing in the truck beds, their chomping mouths were about level with our heads, so each pooch succeeded in startling us. "Don't complain," Scott replied. "We've just entered a new state. They're only barking 'Welcome.'"

Hell's Canyon is the deepest chasm in North America, so we were not surprised that within minutes of crossing the Snake River, we began a 13-mile climb, in direct sunlight and high temperature. I had a hunch that my drained condition resulted from walking the Richland hill in the intense heat the day before. So, weary though I was, I suggested to Scott that we try to ride this hill completely, stopping for rest as needed, but not walking the bikes. Scott, who was feeling okay, readily agreed.

That decision forced us really to learn something about riding steep inclines in the heat. We soon figured out that we could sustain a slow but steady pace reasonably well until our internal temperatures got too high. We began limiting our climb-riding time to 10- to15-minute periods interspersed with seven to eight minutes of rest — in shade when we could find any.

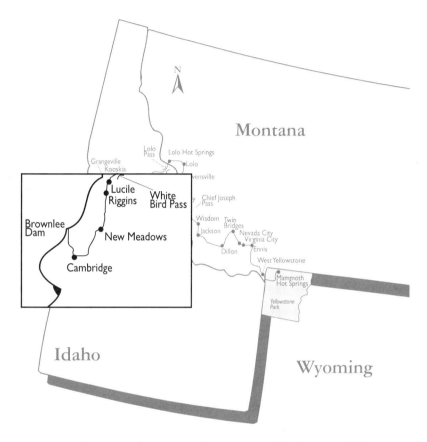

At one such rest stop there was no shade at roadside, so we simply stood, panting, in the sun. We happened to be in front of a house. The rancher — complete with Stetson — came out to get his mail, saw us, and suggested we move to the shade under a large tree in his yard. We did, gratefully. I commented, "Some hill you live on."

"Yeah," he replied. "But you haven't come to the really steep part yet."

Each time our body temperatures returned to normal, we could ride again with a reasonable degree of comfort — for a short time. Sticking to this ride-rest pattern, we completed about a mile during each 15-minute ride segment. This was four to five times as long as it took to cover the same distance on flat ground at a normal touring speed, but the slow pace was okay by us. Thus, in one-mile chunks, we conquered the climb.

But even as we reached the top, my thoughts were on another climb that was yet two days away. In the "mediocre-food" restaurant in Baker City, a retired trucker had asked about our route. After we named the roads we planned to follow as we moved into Idaho, he described the mountain climbs we would encounter. He allowed that we shouldn't have too much trouble with most of them, but when he spoke about White Bird Mountain, he planted seeds of dismay. "You're going to climb White Bird, you say? Ho, ho!"

The map had explained that riders could choose between a new 7-percent-grade highway, which was seven miles long, and an old road, four miles longer, that was even steeper in places and consisted of a series of switchbacks. The only advice the map offered was an enigmatic comment: "The old grade ... is scenic, free of traffic and an unforgettable cycling experience." When we asked the trucker which road he recommended, he only said that they were both terrible.

Ever since that conversation, an uneasy feeling had lurked in the back of my mind. And I was further troubled by the "Route Elevation Profile" on the bike map. The profile showed, in a vertical cross section, the rise and fall of the land our route would cover. On the profile, both the mountain we had just pumped up and White Bird appeared to be of about the same height, a little over 4,100 feet. Both climbs started well below 2,000 feet. Where they differed was in their slopes. The grade out of Hell's Canyon was drawn as about a 55-degree angle. White Bird's, on the other hand, looked almost vertical — a wall with only a slight lean. Our just-completed haul out of Hell's Canyon had been really tough, but although the trucker knew our route included it, he hadn't even commented on it, as though it were too insignificant to bother about. But he had bemoaned White Bird. Recalling our near defeat climbing to McKenzie Pass, and looking back at the ascent we'd just completed, my heart sank. Just how much worse could White Bird be? As if reading my mind, Scott said, "I can't imagine what White Bird must be like."

Finally, putting aside our worrisome musings, we began the descent, riding through superlative beauty. The formidable terrain reminded me of the problem Abraham Lincoln had encountered when the Idaho Territory was first created. The land was so rugged that few political types wanted to move there, even when Lincoln offered them the governorship. And some who did accept the appointment never showed up.

The land remains as wild today, and much of the state is nearly as inaccessible as it was in Lincoln's day. For us, that translated into a ride through long stretches of unfettered wilderness, with little but the highway itself as the mark of human activity.

Despite the spectacular scenery and the success of the climb, however, the malaise I'd awakened with hung on. I did not enjoy cycling that day, and consequently, was relieved when we arrived in Cambridge.

Camping was permitted at the city park, but it offered no electricity, so we investigated a small hotel on the main street. Jack Croly, the innkeeper, quoted a room at a very fair price, which we readily agreed to. He mentioned that he enjoyed hosting riders.

The structure itself, named Hunter's Inn, had been built in 1927 as an "auto park" hotel, café and gas station. It soon became a favorite gathering place for the young men of the Civilian Conservation Corps (CCC) working on nearby projects. After several years of disuse, the building was restored by the Crolys, who added the "Bistro Espresso Coffee Shoppe."

The complex was now a favorite adult hangout for coffee and conversation.

Jack had been a civil servant in Boise but had moved to Cambridge (population 374) in search of a slower-paced life. He seemed to have found it. He turned out to be something of a philosopher, and we spent part of the evening in amiable conversation with him in his combination lobby/living room. Dressed in a golf shirt, shorts and sandals, Jack had a quiet but friendly demeanor. We learned that after he had left Boise, he'd chosen to remain in the state because he loved the mountainous region. He also appreciated the rugged individualism the sparsely settled lands engendered in some people. That night, when I was looking for something to read, Jack loaned me a book about Idaho's hermits. It recounted the lives of several men and not a few women who had survived and thrived in lonesome conditions that most people would find depressing and perhaps frightening.

Inevitably, the conversation turned to our route. Jack labeled several of the mountain climbs ahead as "not too bad," but learning we were to ride over White Bird, he shook his head and said, "That will be tough." He was unsure whether the old grade was any easier, but he knew for certain that the new grade was a "killer."

Before bed, Scott and I returned to the café next door where we had eaten supper. Now we ordered large hot-fudge sundaes. Normally we both have to watch what we eat because we gain poundage easily. But so far while riding, we'd been able to consume all we wanted, and judging by the loosening fit of our clothes, we were still losing weight. Every day, we gobbled nearly double our usual caloric intake. I'd read that riders who average 50 miles a day or less often actually gain weight, probably because the exercise pumps up their appetites and the work is not sufficient to burn off all of the extra calories. But those who ride higher daily mileage have trouble getting enough calories. We found that after some hard rides, our appetites did-n't last long enough to even finish the meals we ordered.

———•◦•———

Although I felt both physically and mentally restored the next morning, White Bird Mountain, still a day's journey ahead, loomed in my imagination with a sense of foreboding. Scott mentioned similar thoughts. But at least the joy of riding had returned.

Because of Idaho's mountainous terrain, there are no direct east-west routes across the state. We'd had to turn southeast after crossing the border. Now, at Cambridge, we swung north-east, paralleling the Weiser River.

In a highway store beyond Cambridge, I noticed a box of used books. I'd brought a murder mystery — a genre I usually enjoy — along on the trip for reading in the tent at night, but after a few pages, I had grown impatient with it and cast it aside. Somehow, the book didn't fit with the life on the road I was now living. The stimulation of the journey needed to be complemented with more thoughtful reading, something that not only filled tent time but also fed my soul. It suddenly struck me as incongruous that I'd spent two years planning this trip, a year training for it, a month preparing my bike, and not more than five minutes choosing a volume for reading on the way.

Since giving up on the book I brought, I had been seeking another, but bookstores were nowhere to be found in most of the tiny communities along the way. That's why this box of used books caught my attention. Looking through it, I found a serious novel, and though not exactly what I was looking for, I carried it to the cashier. She looked surprised, explaining that the books really weren't for sale; someone had given them to her. She told me to keep the one I'd selected and refused pay-ment for it.

"I'm hungry for a peanut butter and jelly sandwich," Scott said, as we entered the community of Council a while later. It was close enough to lunch time, so we headed for a grocery store and purchased supplies. Then we dined at a picnic table in the town square. When we'd finished eating, half of the loaf of bread remained. Since we had no way to carry it on the bikes without crushing it, I suggested we offer it to the family at the next table. With their car and trailer parked nearby, they were obviously travelers, too. Scott approached them with the remaining slices in the plastic bag, and explaining that we couldn't take it with us, held it out. All five family members looked at the loaf as if it were bomb, and the teenagers quickly turned back to their meal. Finally the father took the loaf, and with a mumbled thanks that sounded insincere, tossed it into their car.

On a later occasion, I once more offered half a loaf of bread to some tourists. They quickly said "no" and hurried away. Upon reflection, I wasn't surprised. With America's record of poisoned Halloween candy and letter bombs, people are understandably nervous about accepting seemingly innocent gifts from strangers. Although I understood, I was saddened by the need to be suspicious of our fellow human beings. As I dropped the perfectly good bread into a trash can, I decided that food can't be shared until at least the beginning of a relationship has been established, such as happened easily when we met other bicyclists on the road. Being involved in similar endeavors almost always provided a basis for camaraderie and trust for bicyclists. Neither of the groups to whom we'd offered bread had been riders.

Meeting Lou, another touring cyclist, at New Meadows, was typical of our encounters with riders. We spotted him loading supplies onto his bike outside a grocery store, asked where he was headed, and soon found ourselves in enjoyable conversation. He was an experienced cyclist who had ridden across the nation some years earlier. His panniers were faded and worn, no doubt from a lot of time in the open. Now westbound from

Glacier Park, Lou was heading for his home on the West Coast. He was about my age, but was at least 80 pounds overweight. He had squeezed into spandex riding shorts, but instead of a biker's jersey, he wore an old dress shirt with the tails hanging out. In fact, I doubted jerseys came in as large a size as Lou would need. He must have been self-conscious about his size, for although we did not remark on it, he sheepishly patted his stomach and said, "I'm a bit over my 'training weight.' I'm counting on this ride to jump-start my weight-loss program."

"Well, the climbs ahead of you will surely contribute to that goal," Scott said.

Lou's extra mass probably explained the problems with broken spokes he was having. But like us, he carried extra spokes and knew how to fix his wheels when necessary. Sooner or later, all long-distance cyclists learn to perform emergency repairs on their bikes. When you break down miles from the nearest bike shop, a self-fix job means you can eventually pedal on. And compared to automobiles, which are becoming more and more complex, bikes are easy to service; all the parts are right out in the open and work by simple mechanical principles. With the few basic tools plus the two or three specialized bicycle implements Scott and I carried, we could, if necessary, completely disassemble our bikes.

We asked Lou about White Bird. Since we were traveling in opposite directions, he'd come up what was the "easy side" of the mountain and ridden down the new grade, which he described as "a very steep decline." "It will be a tough ride up White Bird, but you guys will have a great ride getting from here to there," Lou said. "For me, the ride to here has been uphill and into the wind all day. That means you'll have a downgrade and a tailwind."

Our route out of New Meadows ran almost due north. A short distance beyond town, we spotted a road sign that stated we were at the 45th parallel, halfway between the equator and the North Pole. We stopped and each took a photo of the other standing by his bike in front of the sign.

Lou was right about the gradual downslope and tailwind, but the ride was great for another reason as well: It was one of the most scenic sections of our entire journey. We followed the vigorous, churning Little Salmon River as it ran north through narrow valleys and gorges.

The scenery, if anything, grew even more beautiful as we continued downstream. Far from "little," the Little Salmon boiled wildly through stunningly picturesque, rocky chasms as it raced along.

South of Riggins, we noticed a woman standing, staring into the river. She had one hand clasped over her mouth, so that her whole pose signaled anxiety. A police car, rooftop lights flashing, stood nearby. The officer leaned into the vehicle, speaking into his transmitter. Even as we began slowing to offer assistance, the officer waved on a driver who'd apparently had the same idea, so we did not stop. Within minutes, a rescue squad rushed by us heading in the direction from which we'd just come. Looking again at the fuming river, I shuddered to think of anyone caught in it.

Riding into Riggins, I looked at the magnificent landscape — a tumbling river winding in front of a dark-green mountain that was framed by a brilliant sky — and I felt as if I were pedaling into a picture postcard. I wondered what it would be like to live in the midst of such beauty day in and day out. Would I grow to take its splendor for granted? I doubted it.

At Riggins, the Little Salmon emptied into the turbulent Salmon itself, a river that provided a major source of income for the community; many townsfolk made their livings running white-water rafting trips.

In the little store where we stopped for supplies, we mentioned the riverside drama we'd seen. The clerk had heard the rescue squad leave earlier but had no further information. But she said, "Every so often someone goes off the road into the river. They don't always make it out alive." Then, changing the subject, she volunteered that if we were going over White Bird, we'd better be in good shape. Which grade should we take? we asked. The new one, she said. The old one, she added with obvious distaste, has "all those switchbacks."

Continuing northward, Scott pointed to what was obviously a mine entrance snicked into the hillside just beyond the shoulder of the road. The mouth of the mine was sealed with a heavy metal door fastened shut with a substantial padlock. We'd read that there'd been a gold strike in the area in 1860 and wondered if this mine was from that era.

Just as light began to fade, we camped at tiny Lucile, on a bend of the Salmon with mountains all around, pitching our tents so they faced the river. We had ridden our longest day — 95 miles — and still felt good. That accomplishment added to the delight we took in this remarkable day.

Lucile is 20 miles from the base of White Bird. The campground manager, a rugged-looking man of about 60, told us to ride White Bird's old grade because it was better for bikes. His was the first encouraging word we'd heard about the "hill."

We asked him about the mine we had seen. To our surprise, he was its current owner. Yes, it was an old mine, he said, but there was still some gold to be eked out of it. He spent his spare hours picking away at it. But since he also offered to set us up for one of the raft trips run out of the campground, we figured most of his gold came from tourists.

But according to local stories, there was still gold to be found in the nearby hills. Near Lucile, sometime during the peak of the gold-mining era (1871-1873), thieves attacked a pack train loaded with $75,000 in gold ore. Pursued by the law, the bandits were all killed, but not before apparently hiding the gold in the rocks somewhere near a trail paralleling the Salmon. It's never been found.

Given the work of cycling, fluids were as precious as gold to us. Before heading for our tents that night, Scott and I split the half-gallon of milk we'd bought in Riggins. I knew we'd been pouring in lots of liquids, so I'd kept track for that day. Since Cambridge, I'd had a gallon and a half of water, a pint of orange juice, three cups of tea, a pint of fruit drink, a medium Coke and a quart of milk. Apparently my body used it all, because I experienced no increase in either frequency or volume of urination.

After we settled into our tents, I heard the soft whoosh of Scott's CPAP begin, but soon I was more aware of the virile chirping of the water as it raced over the rocks of the stream bed. It was ironic that the same river that had meant disaster to some luckless driver earlier in the day now sang me a beautiful lullaby as I gradually faded off to sleep.

At dawn, many of our fellow campers lined up for the white-water raft runs on the Salmon. We watched as the river guides distributed divers' wet suits to their clients — even though it was July.

The main highway gains elevation even before it bypasses the tiny community of White Bird, which slumbers at the base of the old road — a road that had been the only north-south passage through the area until the new highway was constructed in 1975. We'd made up our minds to use the old route, but first, we had to descend into the town to join it. If we needed any confirmation that we'd made the right route choice, the clerk in the town's small grocery provided it. "Take the old road," she said. "Most bicyclists do."

As it turned out, the old grade was a serendipity. For all the disheartening warnings, White Bird was the mountain where we moved from just "getting up the hill" to "enjoying the climb." The climbing skills we'd learned, the conditioning we'd gained, and especially the wisdom we'd discovered about resting before we got overheated, made the climb, while very hard work, also fun. Periodically, we dismounted and rested, but we were never tempted to walk the bikes.

The views were breathtaking. As we gained altitude, we were able to look *down* on surrounding peaks, look back into the valley we'd ridden through, and look ahead at the series of switchbacks still to ride. And at the higher levels, we benefited from a cooling breeze that enabled us to ride longer stretches without overheating.

We had a continuous view of the new grade. Its constant climb looked as if a giant had laid it out by snapping a chalkline from bottom to top and then notching the highway out of the hips of the mountain. As we watched the stream of traffic lumbering up that highway, we were glad to be on the old road, where we encountered only one vehicle every hour or so.

The old road empties onto the new one just before the summit, and they top the pass as one. We left the older way reluctantly, for it had carried us skyward with a sense of accomplishment and pleasure. We were feeling good.

White Bird Canyon had been the site of an 1877 battle between the Nez Perce and the U.S. Army. As whites began settling on the ancestral lands of the tribe in the Oregon-Idaho-Montana area, seven million acres had been reserved for the Nez Perce by an 1855 treaty. But the discovery of gold on tribal lands sparked friction between the Nez Perce, for whom private land ownership was unthinkable, and whites in pursuit of the yellow rock. Rather than enforce the treaty, the government proposed a new one that reduced the tribe's territory to less than 800,000 acres.

Naturally, the Nez Perce, who had earlier befriended Lewis and Clark, felt shabbily used. But in the face of the growing pressure from settlers and the government, some tribe members signed the new treaty. Although the government maintained that the signers represented the entire Nez Perce nation, the nonsigners compared the action to a neighbor selling someone else's horse. But in 1877, the Army issued an ultimatum, and the "nontreaty" groups reluctantly begin packing to relocate to the treaty lands.

In the midst of these preparations, a trio of hotheaded warriors from Chief Joseph's band slipped away and murdered four whites. The three were soon joined by other tribe members who killed more settlers. Fearing retaliation from the Army, Chief Joseph now felt he had no choice but to lead his followers on a trek to Canada. What followed was a brave but ultimately tragic five-month flight with the Army in pursuit.

The first skirmish took place in White Bird Canyon, where, on June 17, 1877, a force of more than 100 soldiers and volunteers descended on Chief Joseph's group. The tribe, still hoping to avoid bloodshed, sent out a truce party under a white flag, but it was fired upon by the volunteers. The Nez Perce then took the offensive. Although poorly armed and having only about 70 warriors, the band soon routed the whites, who left 34 men dead on the slopes. Some Nez Perce were wounded, but none died in this battle. So well did Chief Joseph's men fight that an early report to the Army's division headquarters estimated the number of warriors at 1,000-1,500!

Although the Nez Perce won other skirmishes, the costs were great. Finally, facing overwhelming odds, Chief Joseph's band surrendered on October 5, in northern Montana, just 40 miles from the Canadian border.

Much of the rest of our trip, as far as Yellowstone Park, would follow the route of the Nez Perce flight.

When we came off the mountain, we found that White Bird was a barrier between abruptly different environments. The mountainous lands south of White Bird gave way to a high plateau of farm and pasture land, with the community of Grangeville sitting in its center.

White Bird was a turning point of another sort for Scott

and me. We never walked another mountain for the rest of the time we rode together.

Shortly after leaving Lucile that morning, we encountered a long-haired hitchhiker, who stepped off the shoulder of the highway to make way for us, nodding a greeting as we passed. That evening, in a café in Grangeville, we saw the same man. In his own way, he, too, had gotten over White Bird.

I hoped he enjoyed it as much as we did.

Chapter 10

HILLS

Cyclists talk funny. Take the word "good," for example. Veteran riders apply this adjective indiscriminately to hills of all sizes. To know what they mean, you've got to be into the spirit of the conversation. Here are some samples:

"Don't worry. It's a good hill." (Translation: "It's just a little hump in the road. You won't have any trouble handling it.")

"There's a good approach to the hill." ("You launch yourself onto the hill from a downgrade. Therefore you'll have enough impetus to carry you part-way up the hill.")

"You have three good hills before you get there." ("Plan on taking twice as long to reach your destination as you thought.")

"This hill is a good test of your climbing ability." ("Enjoy the downhill portion; you'll have earned it.")

"You'll feel good when you reach the top." ("Yeah. Like pounding your head against the wall feels good when you stop.")

"You've got a goooood hill coming up." ("The grade is so steep that the blacktop keeps sliding off. You're gonna die.")

Of course, the word "hill" is itself bicycle jargon for anything from a slight rise in the road to a daylong climb over the Continental Divide.

Surprisingly though, cyclists seldom miscommunicate with one another about hills. The speaker's hand motions, body language and the presence or absence of a diabolical smile usually fill any gap in the vocabulary itself.

Because "good" covers so many conditions, bikers pay close attention when a fellow rider talks about a hill without using "good," for that likely means that there was something about the incline that the rider truly didn't like.

Consider my personal nemesis: a hill within my usual riding territory so nasty that I tackle it only when I want a measure of my hill-climbing conditioning. In fact, it took me three seasons of attempts before I could reach the top without dismounting and walking the bike the last few hundred yards.

This particular hill is deceptive, because the first sight of it comes while wheeling down a spectacular decline that allows a substantial speed buildup. But, like an armed camp surrounded with land mines to deplete any force moving against it, this hill guards itself with speed-sapping topography.

First, the entrance downgrade concludes with a tight "S" curve that forces me to slow down so as not to careen off the edge of the road. Then the road ascends a short but steep foothill; I'm standing on the pedals by the time I top that.

But the real killer — the final approach to the hill proper — *looks like* a gentle downgrade. Actually, that's an optical illusion that led me, when meeting it for the first time, to relax and try coasting. Not only does this stretch not drop at all; it actually climbs. If I stop pedaling, I lose ground. I've yet to figure out how such a significant incline can look like a downslope, but the result is that when I finally reach the real hill, I've lost absolutely all momentum.

It's in that tired, near standstill state that I tackle the final grade, a struggle of downshifting, grunting and copious perspiration.

Since my first losing attack on the hill, I've gotten in better physical shape and added lower gears and a "granny" chainring to my bike. Now, I can attain the top, usually grinding almost to a stop before finally rolling over the crest.

It's a good hill.

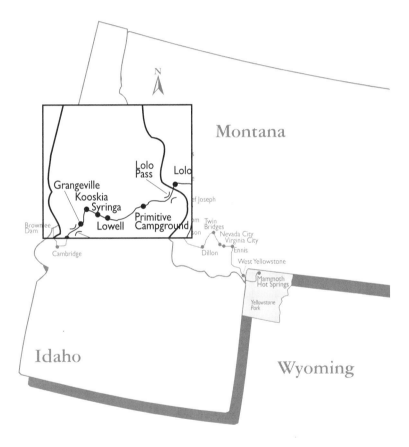

Chapter 11

FOOD

Grangeville is the county seat of Idaho County, an area as large as the entire state of Massachusetts, but much more thinly populated. Grangeville itself, a town built around the meeting hall of Idaho's first grange (a farmer-stockman organization), has only 3,200 citizens. Grangeville is also the home of the only bicycle shop we passed during our entire sojourn in Idaho. Fortunately, we didn't need its services.

We did need a place to camp. At the town's RV park, we found all the sites with electric taken, so the manager couple invited us to set up our tents on their yard, where Scott could plug into an outlet on their mobile home.

I found this couple fascinating. Although they both hobbled from excess weight and moved with apparent pain, the pair nonetheless carried every detail of the large campground in their heads and seemed to find joy and purpose in keeping the place humming smoothly. In their late 60s or early 70s, they functioned with a kind of synergetic alacrity, with one stating a thought and the other completing it — a symbiosis no doubt necessary because both did their thinking out loud. Thus, standing there with them, Scott and I were privy to their reasoning process:

She: We could put them in Site 37B, but ...

He: ... there's no electricity at that site for his sleep

machine. 78A's available, but the ...

She: ... ground there is too stony for tents. Why don't we ask ...

He: ... Thelma if we can put them next to her site and plug into her outlet. No, that won't work because ...

She: ... she's not here right now. I think we should ...

He: ... let them use our yard.

After we set up, the husband, who was heading into town anyway, drove us in his truck the few blocks to the city center, where he recommended a restaurant. Inside, Scott and I both ordered a casserole made with spaghetti noodles, sauce and cheese. It tasted good and was filling, but as we'd observed elsewhere in the Northwest, nobody seemed to know how to make the Italian-style spaghetti that is readily found in mid-America. Don, my father-in-law, had even alerted us not to expect it.

I have no idea what accounts for this anomaly, especially since so many other dishes are universally available across the nation. For example, the omnipresent hamburger, the staple of every Western café we visited, was actually invented by two brothers from an Ohio community near my own. In the late 1800s, Frank and Charles Menches, from Canton, sold food at fairs and festivals, including their specialty, fried pork-sausage sandwiches. While at New York's Erie County fair at Hamburg in 1875, they were unable to purchase pork, so they bought chopped beef instead.

After frying a sample patty, they weren't sure about the taste, so they doctored it up with salt, coffee and brown sugar. When they sold the first one, the purchaser asked what they called the sandwich. On the spot, the brothers came up with "the hamburger" since they were in Hamburg, New York. The beef industry owes a lot to those two Ohio boys.

———

Leaving Grangeville in the morning, both of us noticed

that we felt exceptionally vigorous, as if we had at last completed a conditioning period and were now fully tuned for riding — and indeed, for the rest of our ride together, our cycling was stronger.

Our route now turned northeast, descending from the farmland plateau to the Nez Perce reservation along the South Fork of the Clearwater River. The descent, through country fully as beautiful as we'd seen anywhere, disappointed us as a ride. In the process of being resurfaced, the highway offered seven miles of fresh tar, loosely covered with pea-sized stones — a treacherous veneer for our skinny tires to grip. We coasted down slowly, braking all the way. Forced to pay intense attention to the skittish pavement, we could only glance at the surrounding hills.

At the bottom, Highway 14, not our route, headed off due east. The road had caught my attention earlier while studying a map of Idaho. Why, I wondered, did the artery slither out into the middle of the state and then deadend at Elk City? If it had continued its easterly run, it would have eventually intersected Highway 93 in Montana, where the TransAmerica Trail is routed. As it was, however, we had to proceed northeast to join 93 at Lolo, miles north of the imaginary 14/93 intersection. The Grangeville campground husband had explained that the intervening country was simply too rough to warrant building a highway (and it would have to cross the Bitterroot Mountains, too). There was, he said, a Forest Service dirt road to the border, but it was passable just about three months of the year, and then only in a four-wheel drive vehicle.

At Kooskia, I spotted a post office and ducked in to purchase stamps for some postcards I'd bought in Grangeville. Being Saturday, and nearly noon, the window was already closed, but the woman behind the counter spotted me in the lobby, opened the door, and cheerfully sold me the stamps.

Exiting Kooskia, we joined U.S. 12 and began the ride

toward Lolo Pass over the Bitterroots, which mark the boundary between Idaho and Montana. U.S. 12 rides the northern bank of Middle Fork of the Clearwater River to Lowell, and then shadows the Lochsa River almost to Lolo Pass, so we had flowing water constantly on our right. Although well-paved, U.S. 12 winds along shoulderless, snaking through an area so rugged that the road was not completed until 1960. Our map warned us to beware of the heavy truck traffic on the highway, but as we traveled it on a weekend, we dodged more RVs than semis.

Quite a few motorcyclists traveled U.S. 12 while we were on it. Where automobile riders usually just passed without acknowledging us, these leather-garbed motorbikers usually waved or gave us a "thumbs-up" sign. Indeed, though we used a different form of propulsion, we did feel a bit of kinship with these riders on two wheels who journeyed as we did, exposed to the elements.

During lunch in Syringa (where we enjoyed the soup recommended by motorcyclists exiting the café), I wrote postcards to family members, but the cashier explained that the mail from this Lilliputian community had already been picked up, and no more would leave until Monday. She lived in Kooskia, she said, and offered to mail our cards from there on her way home. Appreciatively, I handed them over.

Lowell, seven miles farther on, was the last community before a 66-mile stretch that offered no services other than National Forest campgrounds, and not all of those even had water. We planned to purchase groceries at Lowell's general (and only) store. To our dismay, we found it shut tight. A storm on Lolo Pass had taken down power lines, and Lowell had been without electricity for two days. The storekeeper apparently decided to close for the duration. Reluctant to backtrack several miles to Syringa, we crossed the river at Lowell's bridge and found that the commercial campground on the opposite shore, though also without power, had an odd mix of canned goods and some stale bread for sale. We bought the bread, a can of mixed fruit and some cherry pie filling — enough for supper and breakfast.

As we headed on, Scott said, "You know, we'd be smart to carry a bit more food with us for emergencies. If we hadn't already had the peanut butter and jelly left from the other day, we'd be facing a couple of meals without much nourishment."

He was right. Our so-called "emergency supplies" consisted of a bag of dried fruit and nuts plus some granola bars. Those items were effective pick-me-ups between meals, but not sufficient for meals themselves. Some cyclists carry high-tech energy bars, but those are seldom available outside of sports specialty shops, which almost never exist in towns of the size we rode through. I guess these bars pack a special mix of nutrients for those engaged in strenuous activity, but those I've tried tasted like sawdust and tar. Not many nutrients get in if you can't stomach the bar to start with.

Wes, our Baker City host, had mentioned that in his capacity as an engineer with the Forest Service, he'd designed three foot bridges to span the Lochsa River, opening rugged sections of the forest to backpackers. Now, passing those bridges, we saw that they were indeed well-designed and blended with the landscape.

We stopped that night at a primitive campground in the middle of the no-services stretch. Scott had to make do without electric. Eating both supper that evening and breakfast the next morning from the strange mix of groceries we'd been able to buy gave us a new appreciation for hot café food, however unimaginative the menus. We resolved that in the future, we would carry a small stove of some sort even though we didn't plan to cook. The cold food would be a lot more palatable if we could wash it down with a cup of hot tea or coffee.

I was slightly ahead of Scott as we pedaled out of the

campground the next morning, riding without much attention to what I was doing. So I failed to notice that as Scott drew up on my right, my bike was meandering into his path of travel. In a split second we collided. I managed to stay upright, but Scott's bike flopped over. He flew over the handlebars and somersaulted into the bushes. For a terrible instant, the thought, "I've killed my brother" grabbed my mind. After a few seconds, however, Scott got to his feet, dusted himself off, and said calmly, "I could have done without that." A sense of relief washed over me, followed quickly by annoyance at my carelessness.

"I'm really sorry, Scott."

Scott examined his bike, and then said, "Well, it looks like both I and the bike are okay. No harm done."

"I'm glad for that." Then noticing some scrapes on Scott's helmet, I added, "A fall like that makes these helmets we're wearing worth their weight in gold." Scott agreed.

A couple of days earlier, when riding into picturesque Riggins, I had doubted that I would ever take stunning scenery for granted. But our ride this morning proved me wrong. Even exquisite scenery, when it continues without dramatic change, can become boring. Riding upstream, we climbed gradually toward Lolo all day. The Lochsa, a river whose name means "rough water," took on a monotonous similarity mile after mile. We'd eaten most of what we'd purchased the day before, so when lunch time came, we paused only long enough to munch a couple of handfuls of dry fruit and nuts. As we rode on, we passed the time by discussing what good meals we planned to order when we finally found a café.

By midafternoon, we reached the mountains, and at their base sat Lochsa Lodge, the only restaurant in the 90-mile stretch between Syringa and Lolo Hot Springs. An old hunting lodge of log construction, the interior walls sprouted deer and elk heads and other trophies of bygone hunts. A bear skin, with head attached, garnished the wall near our table.

Famished, we ordered full meals. The food was tasty, but after we each ate about half a plateful, we were filled up. The long, tiring ride following the insufficient breakfast had actually dampened our appetites.

Afterward, we rode over Lolo Pass in the rain and camped under cloudy skies at Lolo Hot Springs on the Montana side of the Bitterroots.

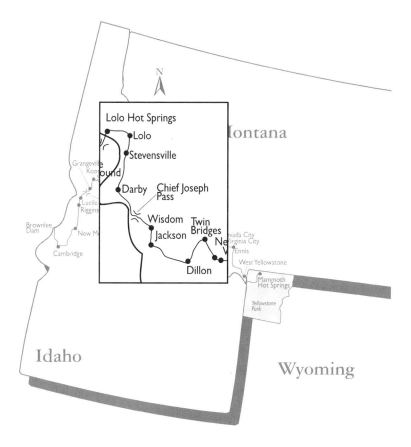

Chapter 12

VALLEYS

When we crossed the Idaho/Montana line, we left the Pacific Time zone and entered Mountain Time. In the same hour, we crossed another sort of time boundary: the inner one that makes the end of the trip loom nearer in the traveler's imagination than the beginning of it does in his memory. In reality, we *were* nearer our terminus than our starting point. Scott and I entered Montana on the 16th day of our 23-day trip. But the amiable melancholy I felt had less to do with the actual number of days remaining than with the realization that re-entry into my usual life loomed near. It was the emotion of the traveler on the last leg of a good trek — as ours surely was — when the meaning of the journey is in the trip itself rather than in the destination.

Day 17 dawned rainy and cool, so we hung around, eating a leisurely breakfast in the Hot Springs café. Pancakes, available at every café we'd haunted, made excellent cycling fuel, but I'd eaten so many of them by now that I decided to order the hot oatmeal, even though I don't really care for it. That was a mistake, because I'd forgotten how much I dislike it. I forced down several spoonfuls, but finally gave up, resolving to return to pancakes the next day.

By 10, the sky cleared and we hit the road, only to find ourselves in rain within a few minutes. This precipitation fell, however, while the sun continued to shine. "Gee," Scott said, "we say Ohio has changeable weather. Here, different weather comes without bothering to change!" As we would discover, unsettled weather would characterize most of our time in Montana.

Before reaching Lolo, we saw the site of what came to be called Fort Fizzle. As the Nez Perce continued their flight after routing the Army at White Bird, other soldiers and volunteers threw up a hastily constructed bulwark on this thoroughfare to the Bitterroot Valley, thinking to stop the Indians. From this fort, the white forces watched in frustration as the Nez Perce, within sight but out of gunshot range, simply bypassed the main trail and continued their journey.

By the time we turned south down the Bitterroot Valley on Highway 93 at Lolo, the rain had stopped and the day warmed. The valley, spanned between the ragged Bitterroot Range to the west and the smoother Sapphire Range to the east, consisted of farmland and residential clusters, and put us in mind of Oregon's Willamette Valley from the early part of our trip.

We were no longer surprised that the bike route followed busy highways. In Ohio, bike routes are usually directed to low-traffic back roads, but there, even most secondary roads are paved. In mountainous Idaho and Montana, road building is an expensive and backbreaking undertaking. Thus in many areas, the main road is the only road. Most of the side roads — and there weren't many — were surfaced only with gravel.

In a few instances, however, we were routed to paved roads paralleling 93. While on one of these, just north of Stevensville, a police officer directed traffic back to the main highway. There'd been an accident down the road, he explained. "But you guys can go ahead. On bikes you'll have no trouble getting through." A couple of miles later, we came to the crash site. A fire truck, a rescue vehicle, two police cars and a television news van blocked the road. Firemen, some using the "Jaws of Life," swarmed over the wrecked car, which was wedged deeply into a roadside ditch. As the occupants were being extracted, two rescuers unfurled a tarp, which they then used as a screen to keep the TV cameras from filming the victims.

"It looks pretty bad," Scott said.

As we wended our way around the emergency vehicles, I thought about how quickly a pleasant journey can become a tragedy, and I empathized with the people in the car. Even if perchance they were not badly hurt, their lives had at a minimum been interrupted in some negative way. Remembering how, only the day before, I had blundered into Scott, causing him to catapult into the bushes, I was even more grateful that our mishap had ended without injury to Scott and without terminating our journey.

As we continued on, we passed another police car pulled into a driveway. Next to it stood the officer, writing something on a clipboard, and a young man in handcuffs. We assumed the latter had caused the accident.

A short time later, we stopped for a cold drink at a small store and mentioned the accident, stating our guess that the victims had lost their lives. "No," said the storekeeper. "We just heard it on the scanner. Those people are okay."

"That's good to hear," I said.

"Yes. But after they routed all the traffic to the main road, another crash occurred over there. The people from *that* accident had to be life-flighted."

Riding on the valley floor all day, we covered a lot of ground despite our late start. By Darby, our overnight stop, we'd made just over 87 miles. Ironically, now that I no longer pushed for 80-mile days, we had, without fanfare, had several days with significant mileage. The ride from Ochoco Reservoir to Dayville had been an 80-miler. Prairie City to Baker City was just over 71 miles and included three mountain passes. And we had stopped then only because I needed a repair. The next day, which included the strength-sapping crawl over the Richland butte, we still covered nearly 75 miles. We'd had a short day from Oxbow Dam to Cambridge — 41.5 miles — but the next day had been our 95-mile trek. And so it continued — occasional short rides but several high-mile days.

I'd been expecting too much too soon. By now we were at the top of our biking form and an 80-plus mile day, while still exceptional, wasn't surprising now. Later on we would learn that many cross-nation riders, including those considerably younger than we are, considered 65 miles a good day's journey.

The map showed a bicyclists' hostel a few miles before Darby, so we stopped there first to check it out. It was a small building (locked tight) behind a private residence (nobody home). Finding no other cyclists there either, and needing to be in town to get a hot meal anyway, we continued to Darby, where we found camping available behind a motel. The camping charge was actually lower than the stated fee of the hostel.

Although we camped in our tents behind the motel, our modest fee included access to showers in a guest cabin and use of the coin-operated washer and dryer.

———◆———

At morning, the air was cool, and rain appeared imminent, but we set off anyway. For the first time since the coast, we needed to keep our tights and long-sleeve jerseys on all day, and added our jackets whenever we stopped for more than a few minutes.

Highway 93 is the main artery through the valley, offering a wide, well-paved roadway. South of tiny Conner, however, the road narrows and begins climbing. We passed several businesses where logs were being smoothed and rounded on giant outdoor lathes, making them uniform for log-home construction, a major industry in the area.

As we proceeded, the region took on an impoverished look. That, coupled with the wooded hills gradually closing in around us, reminded us both of some of the low-income areas of Appalachia.

Highway 93 ascended toward Lost Trail Pass (so named because the Lewis and Clark expedition had some difficulties finding their way over it). We ate lunch in a lodge situated where the serious climbing began. The printed menu included some history of the pass. One of the first cars actually to complete the climb was an early Ford. It took two days and considerable help from a block and tackle to reach the other side, a distance of about 14 miles.

Although the sky looked threatening all day, rain still had not fallen. But as we worked our way up toward the pass, we could hear thunder rumbling in the distance. Taking a rest break at about 6,500 feet, we spied a heavy storm on a neighboring peak. Suddenly Scott exclaimed, "That's coming this way fast!" We started to pull on our jackets and caps, but quickly realized the storm would be upon us in seconds. As the temperature dropped abruptly, we rode rapidly to a copse of trees about an eighth of a mile farther on. Even as we arrived, we were pelted simultaneously by golf-ball hail and a chilling downpour. Yanking ponchos over our already-wet clothes, we hunkered down under the meager limbs to wait out the storm. The hail beat our heads so painfully that I ran back to our hastily deserted bicycles and retrieved our helmets. Moments later, we were forced to abandon the trees as the gully they stood in became a stream. Hearing lightning crash nearby, uneasiness swept through me, giving me a truly fearful moment. The hail and rain continued, but there was nothing to do but stand there and take it.

During one of the darkest moments of the storm, a car, which was already crawling along due to the suddenly slick pavement, slowed even more. The woman behind the wheel cranked down the window and shouted, "Do you need help?" Scott and I exchanged quick glances. Did we need help? This mountain tempest was a new experience for us, and we weren't sure what fate to expect from it. But then, agreeing quickly, we decided to take our chances.

"No, we'll be okay," I called back, no doubt sounding more confident than I actually felt. "But thanks for asking." As her car disappeared around the bend, I wondered if we had made a mistake.

But then, as suddenly as the storm had begun, it was over. Within minutes the sun shone, the air warmed, and the road dried off. By the time we completed the final mile to the top, the sky looked as if rain and hail had never been on the day's menu. But a little evidence remained: The clear-plastic map pocket on the top of my handlebar bag had been shredded to splinters by the hail.

A route change — east again — took us yet farther upward from Lost Trail Pass to Chief Joseph Pass (7,241 feet), where we paused for the obligatory photos next to the Continental Divide marker.

Coming off the mountain, we entered Montana's Big Hole Valley, a high mountain basin approximately 59 miles long and 39 miles wide. With an average elevation of 6,245 feet, it's more than a mile above sea level and nearly twice as high as the average elevation of the state. Before reaching the first town, we came to the Big Hole Battlefield National Monument, an interpretive center for another U.S. Army/Nez Perce battle in 1877. The Army attacked Chief Joseph's people in a surprise move that left a number of the Nez Perce women and children dead. The warriors regrouped and pinned the soldiers down for a few days while the tribe buried and mourned its dead and then slipped away. Losses on both sides were heavy. The video in the center told the story of the fight and flight, filling in the events that had taken place on ground Scott and I had covered in recent days.

In tiny Wisdom (population 120) that evening, we

bypassed the town park for a motel. We were still pretty wet from the storm and welcomed the opportunity to dry out.

At the café, one at last with a fuller menu, I asked the waitress how the town had been named. Saying I was the first person ever to ask her, she excused herself and returned with a handwritten note from the kitchen. Reading from it, she explained that when Lewis and Clark traversed the region in 1805, they named the spot Wisdom because of Thomas Jefferson's sagacity in acquiring the Louisiana Purchase for the fledgling United States.

Actually, she wasn't exactly right. I learned later that the town wasn't founded until after 1875, but Clark did name the nearby river Wisdom to honor Jefferson's decision. Today the river is called the Big Hole River.

When we entered the town, we noticed a white church steeple on a building a few blocks behind the main street. In a practice unlike our familiar Midwest, where churches inhabit most main streets, the Northwestern towns we'd passed through seem to treat church buildings as latecomers who'd arrived after the main street lots were taken. Frequently, churches were relegated to back streets.

Although both Catholic and Protestant missionaries had introduced Christianity into the Northwest and the Rocky Mountain areas beginning in the 1830s, their endeavors did not meet with as much success as in the Northeast and the South. Many of the East-Coast settlers had come to America because of their Christianity, seeking a place where they could practice their brand of religion unhampered by governmental interference and persecution. But in the Northwest and the Rockies, those whites who came early were motivated by the fur trade and later by gold. The native population, as well, did not embrace Christianity as strongly as did the tribes in some other regions. And the expanse of the land itself also made establishing religion tough. Some of the 19th-century pioneers boasted that "the Sabbath shall never cross the Missouri." Of course, it did, but even in the late 20th century, the Pacific Northwest was still acknowledged as the "least churched region" in America.

Strolling around after supper, I walked past this white church on the back street. It boasted no denominational designation and bore only the name, "The Church of the Big Hole."

The community's only other house of religion, a Catholic church, was tucked into our motel complex, squarely between the strip of rooms themselves and the residence of the proprietors. It appeared to have been constructed to match the motel. I asked the innkeeper about the churches. She didn't know of any denominational tie of the white church. It was simply the Protestant church, she explained, where "everybody goes to get married and buried."

"Do you mean the Protestants go there and the Catholics come here?" I asked. No, she said, *everybody* used the Protestant church for weddings and funerals. Mass was held periodically for Catholics in the adjacent building by a visiting priest. (A brochure about the Big Hole communities I found later listed the white church as Presbyterian.)

A cluster of very old log buildings occupied a full block near the white church, and a couple of them appeared to be occupied. These were remnants of the town's early housing. A few still barracked Forest Service personnel, we were told.

Returning to the same café for breakfast, we met Dick and Eli Krahenbuhl, a father and his 11-year-old son, on a 400-mile-circle bicycle journey. Dick had been a rider on the original TransAmerica bicycle trip in 1976 and had met his wife, a fellow rider, on that trip. Learning we were from Ohio, he mentioned a friend in that state, in a "really tiny community" we'd "probably never heard of," Red Haw. Actually, Scott and I had cycled through Red Haw the previous autumn, and Scott knew the town's United Methodist pastor.

Big Hole Valley is in Beaverhead County, an area as large as Connecticut and Rhode Island together, but with a population of only 8,000. Riding out of Wisdom, we passed huge pastures and immense hayfields. The pastures each contained hundreds of cattle. (In fact, in Montana, cattle outnumber people by 12 to one.) Here and there, the hayfields sprouted large devices perhaps 20 feet high that looked like catapults abandoned after a siege. These were haying devices, called "beaverslides." They were invented in the Big Hole Valley in 1910 to create the giant haystacks needed to feed the area's cattle through the long winters. Many are still in use. The Big Hole bears the nickname "The Valley of 10,000 Haystacks."

Periodically, we'd spot a ranch compound, always hundreds of yards from the road, with a backdrop of snow-capped mountains. Invariably, the entrances to these compounds were framed by two upright poles supporting a crossmember on which the name of the ranch was carved or otherwise inscribed.

Riding on through the quiet openness of this land, we eventually came to Jackson. Although it's a community of only 50 souls, it boasts a hot spring, around which a private owner has built a fence and attached a motel. According to the motel owner in Wisdom, the hot spring enabled the Jackson innkeeper to hoist his prices. Fortunately, there was no fence in 1806 when the members of the Lewis and Clark expedition stumbled onto the spring. They enjoyed its hospitality without cost, heating meat and soaking their aching bodies in its 104-degree water.

Lunching in Rose's Cantina across the street, we told Rose, who was operating the grill, about our hailstorm experience the previous day. "Yeah," she said, "We haven't had a hailstorm for about two weeks." In Ohio, it's not uncommon to go for years between significant hailstorms in the same location.

East of town, we came upon a lone woman rider halted on

the roadside. Thinking she might need assistance, we stopped, but found she had merely paused to snap a photo. Beth, trim and brown from the sun, had only her gray hair to betray that she was a senior citizen. She cheerfully acknowledged being 66. Although unaccompanied at the moment, Beth traveled as part of a nine-member tour organized by Adventure Cycling Association, the makers of our bike map. Westbound, they'd started in Virginia. Although the tour members camped together each night and took turns cooking, by day they strung themselves out on the road according to their own riding speeds. "How do you like climbing the mountains out here?" Scott asked.

"Actually, I found the Eastern mountains to be a lot tougher. They're not nearly as high above sea level, but they go up and down so much that we hardly got any rest in between. After those, the mountains out here are a piece of cake."

After we were underway again, Scott said, "Well, that certainly took me down a few notches."

"Yeah, it was kind of deflating. We're finally managing to climb these hills without exhausting ourselves, and a 66-year-old woman calls them 'a piece of cake.' Sheeesh!"

As we proceeded, we met most of the other riders from Beth's group, including a couple on a tandem. We had an enjoyable conversation with them, mostly swapping route information.

The map showed two mountain passes between Jackson and Dillon, the first of which, Big Hole Pass, at 7,360 feet, is one of the highest maintained roads in Montana. However, since the valley itself is already so elevated, our climb to the top was over before we felt the need for our first rest stop. Remembering our hailstorm welcome to this valley, I said, "Well, it seems like our visit to the Big Hole started with a bang and ended with a whimper."

On the summit, we stopped and snacked with the last two Adventure Cycling Tour members. One of these, a man from the Netherlands, moved with a limp and appeared to have the use of only one arm, which should make riding difficult. But since he'd ridden there from Virginia, he apparently managed quite well.

Actually, I wasn't that surprised. Because the bike carries the rider's weight, people with an assortment of disabilities often can navigate competently on a bicycle. Some victims of multiple sclerosis who are unable to walk can nonetheless ride. And somewhere, I'd read about a man who'd lost the use of one leg to a stroke. He taped the foot of that leg to his bike pedal and forced it around by pumping with his good leg. Although his doctor had said he'd probably never be able to use that leg again, the biking became the therapy that proved the doctor wrong. Eventually, the man regained almost full use of the leg.

Even in my local bike club, there were two men who rode well despite joint problems. One needed a knee replacement and the other had a deteriorated hip. Both hobbled badly on foot, but on their bikes, they sped over the miles.

Unlike running, for example, cycling is not a high-impact activity and does not put side-to-side stress on tendons and joints.

Riding the long valley between the two peaks, we labored against a buffeting crosswind so strong that it threatened to blow us over. The wind, coupled with a darkening sky, finally caused us to abandon plans to take a side trip to Bannack, the ghost-town remains of Montana's first territorial capital, four miles off our route.

Many noncyclists don't realize how even a light wind affects riders. Both headwinds, which slow forward progress, and crosswinds, which force cyclists to expend extra energy to stay on course, tire riders quickly — but both are facts of life for those who bike. In rugged terrain, winds often follow the twists and turns of valleys and gorges, just as forced air from a furnace moves through the bends of heat ducts. Thus, breezes can continue to bang riders biking in valleys from the same relative angle even though the highway snakes around. Personally, I prefer steep hills to a stiff headwind any day; I eventually reach the top of a hill, but winds frequently continue all day.

The fact that we were so close to Bannack but could not see it reminded me of a comment by George Meegan, a man who walked from the southernmost tip of South America to the northernmost shores of Alaska. He referred to what he could not see while traversing any given area — that which lay beyond his sight horizon — as the "tragedy of travel." While his observation, that the "thin line of one's trail" narrows the traveler's experience, is valid in one sense, it seems pessimistic to me. I welcome the part I *can* see as a broadening of my experience. The very fact that I encounter an area slowly from the seat of a bicycle, rather than rapidly from a moving car, means that there is time for the sights, sounds, smells and feel of a landscape to establish themselves in my memory.

Continuing to work into the wind, we eventually arrived at Dillon, the seat of Beaverhead County. There, we were turned away from the first campground we tried, with the clear impression that the manager didn't want cyclists in his park. We found instead a KOA at the edge of town, where the woman in charge let us have a site with full hookups for only $1 over the usual tent fee.

The first drops of rain sent us to our tents a bit earlier than we'd planned, and soon a full-fledged thunderstorm, complete with strong winds and pounding rain, beat on our tents for more than 90 minutes. The tents we were using, gifts from our respective wives just for this trip, were the most expensive ones we'd ever slept in. The storm provided their first real test. When both tents kept us and our gear completely dry, we praised Jeanine and Noreen for not skimping on them. (On a previous tour, using my older, cheap tent, I'd gotten soaked in a night rain and spent the miserable hours till daylight cursing the so-called shelter.)

Chapter 13

RELIEF

One hardship for cycle tourists is the lack of suitable arrangements for the relief of bladder and bowel. This circumstance is especially distressing because the available portable equipment is too cumbersome to lug along on a bicycle rack.

Nonriders will perhaps comprehend the scope of the problem when I point out that bike touring usually entails traveling on country roads where other traffic is light and where, consequently, public toilets are almost nonexistent. There is *occasional* other traffic, however, and this is precisely the rub. Even if you've had the road to yourself for the entire last hour, you can be certain that someone will drive past, gaping, 20 seconds after you lower your shorts.

Why, you ask, not first seek the privacy of shrub or sycamore? The answer is that, in many parts of the nation, the expression "open country" is an understatement of monstrous proportions. Trees are often rooted only in somebody's yard or in woodlots well back from the road or in copses made impenetrable by briars, poison ivy and heaped rock cleared from fields.

There is, of course, the occasional country store, but some claim to have "No Restrooms." At least that's what the clerks say. You leave in disgust (and perhaps agony), knowing darn well that there must be *some* arrangement for the clerks' convenience. They just won't share it. They will, however, graciously tell you about a public facility just eight miles out of your way.

A cyclist with whom I rode for a few days in Kansas employed a useful technique for relieving himself. He had no kickstand on his bike, so rather than lay his bike down every time he had to urinate, he simply stood straddling it, taking care of his needs with no concern about passing traffic. Standing over the bike, his pose was so unlike the usual posture that most motorists were likely unaware of what he was doing.

Bike touring is one activity where potty parity is already in effect. The limited supply of stations and lack of cover hits men and women the same.

For riders in farm country, a solution for both sexes appears by about the end of July, when, if there's been enough rain, the corn is at last high enough to keep one's modesty intact.

There are days when cycling is almost a spiritual experience, when the mix of temperature, sunshine, smooth highways, striking scenery and a well-fitted bike make the heart sing. On such days, we may even be able to rise above the ache of muscle and the drench of sweat. But sooner or later, the reality of this basic function always brings us back to earth. In the most fundamental sense, cycling is a physical activity. However much riding lifts the spirit, the necessity for field relief will not allow us to long forget the flesh.

Perhaps that's as it should be. We are never all spirit, any more than we are ever fully defined by our bodies. This humble corporeal function that none of us can ignore, and which we share with the rest of the animal and plant kingdoms, reminds us that we are created beings and beneficiaries of the gift of life.

Chapter 14

TOWNS

The turns of our continuing route formed a rough capital "M" on the map, with Dillon as the foot of the first leg. Twin Bridges was the top of the first upright, Ennis the top of the second, and Adler the point of the dip in between. We wouldn't reach the M's second foot, Cameron, until the next day.

A few days earlier, I'd noticed that my rear tire looked smooth, but still had some life in it. I decided to simply keep an eye on it, a vow I then stupidly forgot. Eleven miles beyond Dillon, one of the few communities we visited that even had a bike shop, my tire went flat. An examination revealed that it was worn through in spots to the threads. I carried three extra tubes and a patch kit, but no spare tire.

Scott offered to pedal back to Dillon for a tire, but I didn't want to add 22 miles to his riding day. We decided that he would stay with the bikes while I hitchhiked to Dillon. I hadn't hitched in 25 years, but somehow I didn't feel any apprehension about it now. Wheel in hand, I crossed the road, stuck out my thumb, and promptly caught a ride with the first vehicle to pass, a pickup towing a horse trailer. It was driven by a rancher with his young grandson along. I explained my plight as the man set the truck in motion. Since my bike uses standard 27-inch tires, I mentioned that in a pinch, I can usually find the tire I need in Wal-mart or Kmart. The rancher said

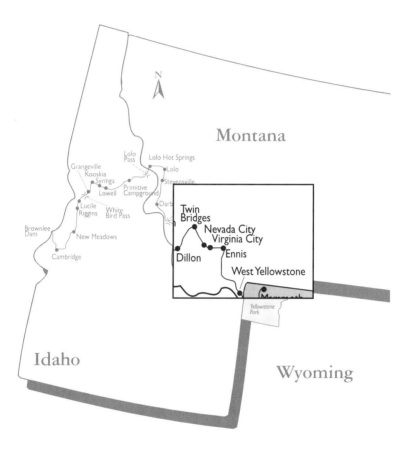

that Dillon, even though it was the county seat, wasn't big enough for stores like that.

Learning that he raised horses, I told him about my daughter's volunteer job. He seemed quite impressed and agreed that riding could be therapeutic for physically disabled people. "You'd have to pick your horses pretty carefully, of course," he added.

Despite pulling the trailer, he insisted on driving down a side street to deliver me right to the door of the bike shop and mentioned that if I was still in town when he left three hours later, he'd take me back to my bike.

In the store, I quickly found what I needed and then had another stroke of good fortune. An employee happened to be ready to head out of town and gave me a ride in his car to where Scott waited. This gave me an opportunity to inquire about a practice Scott and I had noticed when we pedaled out of Dillon earlier. Despite the heavy rain during the night, the irrigation systems in the fields beyond the town pumped at full throttle. "I wonder why," I had said.

"I don't know," Scott replied, "but there must be a sermon illustration in it somewhere." I laughed, remembering that when I was a parish pastor and responsible for delivering sermons week after week, I was always considering how things I noticed or read could be used to illustrate the themes of my homilies.

In the car now, the driver explained that irrigation is even more effective when the ground is already wet; less moisture is lost to evaporation. After he had driven me back to my bike, I told Scott of this explanation. I wasn't too surprised when, after our trip was over, Scott described the irrigation-after-the-rain practice in the pastor's column of his church newsletter. He used the illustration to observe that people are more likely to "soak up" spiritual nourishment when they have already "watered" the ground of their souls with prayer and Scripture reading.

With my new tire installed, we were soon back on the road. Within minutes, we came upon a prominent rocky bluff on the left side of the road. Because of its resemblance to the head of a beaver, it gained the moniker "Beaverhead Rock." On August 8, 1805, Sacagawea, the Shoshoni woman who helped guide the Lewis and Clark party through the area, recognized this landmark and informed the explorers that they had entered the land of her people.

Twin Bridges, where we dined yet again on hamburgers and fries, was near the confluence of three tributaries of the river Lewis and Clark had named the Jefferson. They dubbed the tributaries Philosophy, Wisdom (from which the town of Wisdom got its name) and Philanthropy, all supposedly presidential virtues of Thomas Jefferson. Evidently, later residents didn't think much of these appellations, and renamed the streams Willow Creek, Big Hole River and Ruby River. The town name, of course, came from spans that had been constructed over two of these watercourses.

In Laurin, 21 miles farther on, a few houses huddle around a Catholic church. If there is any more to the community than that, we couldn't see it. So small that the main road bypasses it, Laurin hasn't even a store. We could see the church from the highway and noticed that it was constructed of reddish stone, a building material we'd seen nowhere else in the area. We detoured onto the short main street to investigate. Unlocked, the church offered a well-kept and quiet interior, beautifully appointed. We spent a few minutes soaking up the atmosphere.

By late afternoon, as we neared Nevada City, we began to notice heaps of rocks littering the landscape for miles. Gold had been discovered in Montana in 1862, and these were tailings from the area's mines. Some of this rock bore the same reddish color of the Laurin church, leading us to speculate that the congregation had used mining waste to construct their building.

Nevada City, a restored ghost town remaining from the gold-rush heydays, operates as a tourist attraction/museum today. Apparently no one actually lives in the town anymore. The place has been the backdrop for a number of westerns, including Little Big Man. One unique structure is a two-story outhouse that can be entered from either of the two floors of the old hotel. Small as the town was, it once had a distinct Chinatown district.

Nearby Virginia City, dating from the same era, also has the Old West look but is a living town of 200 that survives on tourism. During the peak of the gold rush, 35,000 people inhabited the area, and highway bandits made a handsome living robbing prospectors on the roads leading to the village. Eventually the townsfolk figured out that their sheriff belonged to the thieving gang. They relieved him of his responsibilities by slipping a noose around his neck and then kicking the box he was standing on out from under him. In a six-week period, these vigilantes hanged 22 road agents, bringing a new level of safety to the area.

After a soup and pie supper in Virginia City, we cycled three miles up to the peak beyond the town. We'd now been riding for 20 days without a day off, and while we felt good overall, we both noticed that our knees stiffened up every time we stopped for more than a few seconds. When we resumed, the first few strokes of our legs were torture. But as we continued pumping, the feeling passed and we felt okay while moving. Both of us were now taking pain relievers morning and evening, and that seemed to reduce the aches and pains somewhat. (Some time later, when a store clerk asked how we managed to ride so many miles, Scott answered instantly, "Ibuprofen!")

Our labor to achieve the summit was made especially worthwhile by a spectacular 10-mile glide down the other side. Surrounded by stunning vistas of the Rocky Mountains, we flew downward in ecstasy, at times hitting 42 miles an hour. I often wonder what a blowout would do at that speed; I hope never to find out from firsthand experience.

A mile more brought us to Ennis. In the campground there, we met Jim, a solitary cyclist who had set out on a three-month journey from Oklahoma to Canada without previous cycling experience. In his first week, he told us, the crankset on his new bicycle broke, forcing him to hitchhike with the bike back 100 miles to the nearest shop. Now, in midjourney, he was an experienced bike tourist.

We invited Jim to join us as we walked downtown for a snack. At midlife, between careers and divorced, he'd embarked on his journey in search of something he had yet to define, but, we suspected, it was a where-to-with-my-life-next quest. As he told us his story, his voice seemed to convey sadness and a quality of wounded gentleness.

Jim, who had lived a hippie lifestyle as a young adult, and then the responsible existence of a family man, was now not sure where he fit. Learning that Scott was a pastor, Jim mentioned that he'd thought recently about entering the ministry, an idea he was still considering. He asked Scott whether he enjoyed being a parish pastor, and Scott said that he did.

We ate our snacks at a table in a convenience store. At the next table, an older man sat alone drinking coffee. After Jim, Scott and I were seated and had begun talking, the man suddenly interrupted and asked, "Are you in town to fish?" We said, no, we were biking through. "Biking, heh? That must be some ride."

"It is," I replied, and then quickly returned my attention to Jim and Scott. I felt a little awkward. Normally I enjoy talking to local people. This man was by himself and obviously wanted to join our conversation. But at the moment, Jim was talking about his search for meaning; to let someone else join us who didn't share the ride experience would have changed the complexion of the conversation and feel like an intrusion. Scott and Jim seemed to sense this as well, for when the man made a couple more attempts to insert himself into our discussion, we answered him politely but briefly and asked no questions in return. After a few moments, he swallowed his remaining coffee and left.

When we returned to our tents, Scott and I told Jim that he was welcome to join us for breakfast in the morning. "Thanks," Jim said, "I might do that."

When we arose, we found Jim dressed and waiting for us. We strolled together to a café. Over our meal, Jim told us about another lone cyclist, George, whom he'd encountered and ridden with for a few days. George had ridden eastward from Texas along the nation's southern boundary and was now returning westward on the TransAmerica route, eventually to complete a loop back to Texas. Jim had appreciated George's company for a while, but in time tired of his forceful opinions on just about every topic. So when George decided to spend a few days in Yellowstone, Jim headed out alone. Still, Jim said, if we happened to see George, say "Hello" for him.

Jim's ride would begin with a climb up the long hill we'd sailed down the previous evening. Ours trailed out the opposite direction over reasonably level terrain toward Cameron, the second foot of the "M." That town had a listed population of 10, and counting the workmen erecting a building next to the town's store, we probably saw them all. As we rode by the work site, one worker said loudly, "Hey, Joe. Did you hear about that mountain lion the other day that jumped out and ate two bicyclists?" They all laughed while glancing to see if we'd heard. The laughter sounded good-natured.

The rest of the day's route offered no towns at all, and I found the ride less interesting for their absence. As a young man, I'd backpacked quite a bit and thoroughly enjoyed days on end of wilderness existence. But in recent years, I've found myself drawn more to the small communities that dot our land. Large cities have never been able to capture my imagination, but something about little towns feels right to me. In any case, road cycling and small towns go well together.

These days, a lot of America's small towns lead precarious existences. Although some owe their birth to mining or industry, most are sustained to a large degree by agriculture. As advances in mechanization enable fewer farmers to produce more and more bounty, greater numbers of farmers and ranchers sell out. Their acreage becomes parts of larger operations, sometimes consolidations owned by corporations. When the farm families leave, the towns that flourished on the farm trade begin to wither.

Other forces depress small-town economies as well, chief among them the shopping malls and the proliferating discount stores. Most hometown stores simply cannot compete.

So great is the threat to small communities that my denomination has fashioned a statement about it that's included in the "Social Principles," one of the guiding documents of the church. It says:

> We support the right of persons and families to live and prosper as farmers, farm workers, merchants, professionals and others outside of the cities and metropolitan centers. We believe our culture is impoverished and our people deprived of a meaningful way of life when rural and small town living becomes difficult or impossible.

Ironically, one reason shopping malls have such appeal is that they have canned some of the best features of small-town America. Small-town downtowns were once both business districts and places to meet friends and hang out. Now, in many places, malls have taken over these functions. They provide comfortable space for people to congregate. According to one study I read, 40 percent of the people who flock to malls do not intend to purchase anything. They come just for the connection with other people and for "something to do." Americans spend more time in malls than anywhere else except at home and at work, the study said.

Part of the reason for the phenomenal success of malls — and there are more than 3,000 of them in North America — is because they provide well-ordered centers around which suburbs and housing developments can cluster. Small towns were once that kind of center; in sparsely populated places like western Kansas, they still are.

Fortunately, the news about small towns is not all gloomy. Some rural communities are reviving and even thriving as industries take new interest in little-known places. The work ethic of residents of these locales is often far superior to that of urban denizens, and salary expectations range lower. In addition, urbanites seeking less harried communities and retirees yearning for quiet places to homestead in their final years also boost rural populations. And most recently, the work-from-anywhere communications networks have increased the likelihood of small-town survival.

Although our continuing ride now took us away from towns, we did see lots of men — and not a few women — fly fishing in the Madison River, which the highway paralleled faithfully. Clearly, fishing was a big draw to the area.

Two events marked the day. In midmorning, a brief storm showered us with marble-sized hail and a light rain. We kept riding through this storm. And in late afternoon, we saw where half a mountain had slid away in a 1959 earthquake, blocking the Madison, forming Earthquake Lake, and drowning or burying 28 people. The Army Corps of Engineers eventually cleared a channel for the river, but the gash left on the mountain still looks fresh, like a decayed tooth with one face broken off.

Between the storm and the slide, there was only one place to buy food, a restaurant lodge. I ate a meal there, but Scott, who wasn't feeling very hungry yet, downed only a bowl of soup. The map showed three cafés beyond the earthquake area, and he figured he would eat more at one of those.

His plan was ruined, however, when two of these were closed and the third we could never find. Scott munched on some dried fruit and granola bars we had with us, but by the time we finally reached West Yellowstone at day's end, Scott was famished.

The maps we used are great for cyclists. They mark the locations of restaurants, grocery stores, motels, campgrounds, post offices and gas stations. But with over 4,000 miles of route, it is impossible to keep the information up-to-date, let alone give hours of operation. Each set of maps arrives with some postcards addressed to Adventure Cycling so that riders who discover changes can notify the Association. Annually, Adventure Cycling issues a one-page update addendum for each map in the set, but some changes never get reported, or change again by the time the addendum comes out.

By the time we got to West Yellowstone, I was pretty hungry, too. In this town, we had a large selection of places at which to eat. Its permanent population is just over 900, but as a gateway town to Yellowstone Park, the community overflowed with tourists and so offered an abundance of motels, restaurants and gift shops. The main street was a neon arcade. Despite my appreciation for small towns, this one didn't suit me. Still, it would have to do for the night, even if the tiny spot allotted to us in the campground, cheek by jowl with other campers, was the most expensive of our trip. At least the staff was friendly and loaned us the necessary extension cord.

Yellowstone Park begins where the town line ends. In the morning, three miles into the park, we entered Wyoming.

Chapter 15

WONDERS

It was time to pick our end point. Since abandoning my scheme to get to Pueblo, we had no precise idea where we'd finish. Actually, even before leaving home, we had agreed that if for any reason we didn't reach Pueblo, we would simply take a bus or rent a car from wherever we ran out of time, so we now reverted to that plan.

Not so easily done, it turned out. The cost of one-way car rentals was prohibitive, and buses did not run from just anywhere, we discovered. Indeed, they ran from nowhere we could reach in the riding days we had remaining, except from West Yellowstone itself. I should have checked out bus routes before the trip, but I had naively assumed bus service was far more widespread than it actually is.

What a bummer! So mundane a thing as a bus schedule had put a major crimp in our plans. But Scott, who had previously spent time in Yellowstone, viewed the circumstances as an opportunity to revisit some places in the park that he had especially enjoyed. He proposed that we cycle to Mammoth Hot Springs, which was located in the northwest corner of the park, and then return to West Yellowstone and the bus. Our original itinerary would have missed the Mammoth area. Though I remained disappointed by the turn of events, Scott's suggestion made sense, and I agreed.

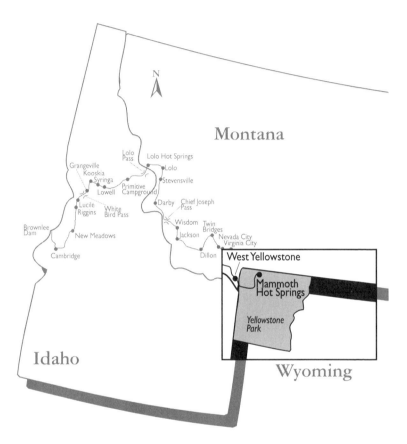

Actually, my mood wasn't all because we'd been stymied by the bus. Over the last couple of days, I had become aware of mixed emotions. On the one hand, I missed my wife and kids and looked forward to seeing them again soon. On the other, I wanted to continue the trek all the way to the East Coast.

We rode to Mammoth over the worst road of our entire journey. A park brochure explained that because of the long winters and the repeated freezing and thawing, fully 80 percent of the park's roads are substandard. Certainly the one we traveled was. Also, the warm season was so short that road repair could not keep up with the weather damage the pavements sustained. Having no shoulder and being so broken and pot-holed that we could barely lift our eyes from the highway immediately in front of our tires, the road also exposed us to a near-constant stream of traffic that sped around us without waiting for such niceties as "assured clear distance."

Although the region was impressive, it bore the aftermath of massive fires that had raged through hundreds of thousands of park acres in 1988. We passed hillside after hillside of still-standing fire-killed trees, looking like barren sticks. New ground cover was beginning the healing process, but it would be years before the area returned to its former beauty.

Viewing fires as a natural part of a woodland's life cycle led to the Forest Service's natural-burn policy in Yellowstone. For 16 years, the policy, which meant letting fires burn themselves out, had worked well. But in 1988, the forests were too dry. As the fires began to get out of hand, Yellowstone's chief ranger canceled the natural-burn plan and instituted full-fledged countermeasures. But by then, the several separate fires were too big, and in the end more than a third of the park's 2.2 million acres were consumed.

In some of these burn areas, scattered growths of small shaggy-barked evergreens appeared. None of these appeared very old. I assumed they were "dog-hair" lodgepole pines. I'd learned about them from a park naturalist's lecture while on a family vacation in Glacier National Park a few years earlier. She described the life cycle of a forest, beginning with fires. Such conflagrations are not necessarily bad things, she said. Fires play an important role in the clearance and regeneration of forests. Fires open the canopy of leaves and needles so that sunlight can reach the ground, thus permitting species of trees that would never survive in the darkness of a mature forest to germinate and grow. This is especially important in coniferous woodlands, for conifers effectively block the sun. Also, she said, the ash from burnt wood helps reduce the acidity of the soil, giving new growth a better start.

One of the first trees to grow after a fire is the dog-hair lodgepole pine. The cones of lodgepoles have a special characteristic. The seeds of these trees can remain locked in their cones for years — 50 or 60 years is normal and 150 years is not unheard of — until a forest fire heats the cones enough to cause the release of the seeds. This type of cone is called "serotinous." Several other conifers, including California's giant redwoods, have serotinous cones as well. Trees with this sort of cone owe their birth to fire.

After a fire, tiny lodgepole seedlings begin to take root, as many as 300,000 per acre. Not all survive, but enough do to hold the soil together and provide shelter until other species can re-establish themselves.

I find it hopeful that even a raging fire can make new growth possible in the magnificent forests, just as human trials and difficulties can stimulate growth and new possibilities in our personal lives.

Come to think of it, I know a few people who must have serotinous cores. They've gone through personal trials that burned away some of the outward structure of their lives and left them emotionally scorched. Yet out of their tragedies they have rebuilt their lives and even reached out to others in pain.

Despite the fire damage around us, Scott and I still spotted clusters of wildlife, including herds of elk and deer. Then we came to a spot where cars and RVs littered both sides of the road in haphazard fashion, reducing the passage area to a single lane. People hustled from the vehicles with cameras at the ready and someone called to us, "It's a moose!" As we slowed to dismount, I somehow failed to get my right foot disengaged from the pedal's toe-clip, and flopped over in front of several dozen people. I was unhurt, but coupled with the lousy pavement, the necessity of dodging vehicles all day and the rain that dribbled off and on, the fall seemed the final indignity. I arose, out of sorts, annoyed at the whole situation. The fall must have looked worse than it was, because Scott was immediately concerned and let the opportunity pass to kid me about my clumsiness.

Most serious cyclists, whether racers or tourists, use a type of pedal that in some fashion attaches the rider's shoe to the pedal. (The shoe is a special, inflexible-sole affair that causes the wearer to walk funny.) The main purpose for the attachment system is to keep bikers' feet from slipping off the pedals, a situation that occurs easily when revolving the crank rapidly. Bike racers also like the attached-foot arrangement because they can not only push on the downstroke, but also pull on the upstroke. That's very tiring, but in a race it can gain a cyclist a few seconds' advantage.

When the foot slips off, generally one of three things happens. If the foot slides off the back of the pedal, the rider's shin plunges downward and bangs on the pedal. (I once received a nasty gash in my leg this way before I switched to toe-clips.) If the foot slips off the front of the pedal, the crank continues its revolution and slams the calf of the rider's leg. (I've had bruises to demonstrate that.) Or, when the foot loses grip, the rider is thrown off balance and falls. (Yup, I've done that, too.)

Toe-clips like mine are a stirrup affair with a cage on the front of the pedal into which I slide my foot. They are clumsy to get into because the weight of the cage encourages the pedals to dangle cage-side down whenever one's feet are not actually in them. To enter them, I first have to pump a stroke or two on the bottoms of the pedals until I gain enough momentum to kick the pedals upright and slip quickly into them before they droop back over — a neat trick when heading uphill. Once in them, however, they work great, but one has to remember to draw one's feet backward out of them when dismounting.

The other system for connecting one's shoes to the pedal is called "clipless." With that system, a cleat on the bottom of the cyclist's shoe snaps into a pair of gripping jaws on the pedal, similar to the way ski boots attach to skis. Most clipless pedals have identical jaws on both surfaces so that it doesn't matter which side is up when mounting them. To disengage, the rider simply pivots his heel sideways.

Clipless systems are relatively expensive, but as I dusted myself off, I decided to consider them for future riding.

We followed the crowds and at least did get a glimpse of the moose, who was nonchalantly munching greens not far from the roadside.

The best part of the highway itself came as we neared Mammoth Hot Springs. At midafternoon, we came to a section of road that curved around the horizontal face of a mountain. But here, rather than blasting mountain away to create roadbed, the highway had been attached to the mountainside at a 90-degree angle and supported on the outside edge by concrete pylons rising up from the mountain's sloping thighs below. This passage began a long, scenic downgrade that ended at the hot springs, aptly named "Mammoth."

This wonder of nature made the ride worthwhile. It also somewhat alleviated my disappointment at not being able to continue farther on the TransAmerica Trail. The boiling springs formed a sizable hill, the face of which was composed of grayish-white mineral deposits. From the network of board-walks elevated a few feet above the fragile surface, we inspected the area close-up.

Mammoth village itself included facilities not at all like the rustic buildings we'd seen elsewhere in the park. Substantial permanent edifices of gray cut stone, including a formal-looking dining building, a hotel, a post office, a museum and other structures brought to mind a college campus or the luxury spas of the early 20th century. The village was nearly lost in the fires of '88. Fortunately, rain began to fall shortly after the area was evacuated.

Housing arrangements for park visitors include both the hotel and cabins, and we inquired about vacancies, hoping to find electricity for Scott's CPAP. Everything was booked up, so we spent the night in the Mammoth Hot Springs campground, making do without electric. Although this campground, like the others we passed in Yellowstone, bore a notice saying it was full, we knew that didn't apply to backpackers and cyclists. Since we don't require level, graveled sites, there's virtually always space where campers in small tents can set up. Without the protection of hard-sided RVs against the park's grizzly bears, however, we carefully obeyed the campground rule that we take no food or even toothpaste into the tents with us. Instead, we parked that stuff in the bearproof steel cabinets provided for tent campers.

In the morning, we retraced the previous day's route. When lunch time came, we stopped in a picnic area to make sandwiches, our last meal on the road. The finality of this hit me when, after eating all we wanted, Scott held up the peanut-butter jar. "I guess there's no reason to keep this any longer. It's not empty, but we won't need the rest." He threw it in the trash can.

"I might as well get rid of this, too," I said, pitching in one of my water bottles that had started leaking a couple of days earlier. Somehow what we were doing felt like a burial.

Scott said, "I'm not ready for this trip to be over."

"Me neither," I answered. I'd been feeling kind of glum all morning, and now I understood that I was grieving the end of the journey with Scott.

Back in West Yellowstone, we spent another night at the high-priced campground. In the morning, we left our bikes chained to the campground fence and our equipment in the tents while we wandered the shops looking for gifts for our wives and children. The bus would leave at 5 p.m., so after lunch, we began preparing for our departure. From one of the town's bike shops, we obtained two boxes. Then, outside the chamber of commerce, where the bus stops, we disassembled the bikes and packed them for the bus ride home.

Previously we had inquired inside if we could leave our gear for a few hours while we explored the town, but had received a nasty retort from the woman at the desk. She spared no scorn while informing us that the chamber was neither a bus station nor a storage facility. Her tone angered me and added to the distaste I'd already developed for this community.

Was her attitude because we were to be bus passengers? Scott and I, dressed in now-worn biking clothes and displaying the leathery, sun-toughened skin typical of people who live on the road, didn't look like tourists, so perhaps she felt free to be offensive. I could hardly imagine a less likely candidate for a job with an agency whose mission it was to make a town appealing.

We rode the bus for three days and nights, all the way back to Ohio. I expected that to be an ordeal, but aside from the wearisome sitting and the discomfort of sleeping on a bus seat, I actually found the ride an adventure in its own right. Both Scott and I interacted with fellow passengers more than we ever would have on an airplane flight, and we enjoyed hearing the stories of their journeys.

It was just as well that the trip back took so long. The tedious hours and the enforced inactivity gave me time to sort out my feelings and prepare to re-enter my everyday life. I doubt many people can conclude something that is both as satisfying and as enticing as our trip and then return to their previous existence as though nothing significant had happened — as though merely completing a task on a list: "Well, that's that. Now to pick up my dry cleaning." At least I could not. As the bus moved eastward, I began to appreciate the time it gave me to "decompress."

One of the issues I needed to wrestle with was the sense that although my journey with Scott was over, my ride across the nation was not, and I was not ready to accept the portion we'd finished as fulfillment of the entire goal. I'd want to complete it sometime, but at the moment, I had no idea how or when. I hoped, however, that this year's segment would buy me at least a few years of contentment.

There was another benefit from the bus ride. While Scott and I have always been brotherly close, the shared experience of the bicycle trip deepened our friendship. But now we were returning to separate lives, and I doubted that the intensity of companionship we achieved would be sustainable apart from life on the road. The bus provided time for a little space to insert itself between us.

This occurred even physically, for we soon discovered that when the bus was not full, the opportunity to each occupy a double seat rather than share one was more comfortable. Then, as the bus filled, boarding passengers sometimes seated themselves next to Scott or me, and we would eventually fall into conversation with them rather than interacting only with each other.

The first night, however, we did sit together. Long after darkness fell, the bus stopped somewhere in eastern Montana. A teenage boy, boarding at the last minute, took the seat behind Scott and me and promptly fell asleep. At dawn, we noticed him studying us. Finally he said "You two rode your bikes through Jackson, Montana, a few days ago, didn't you?" Yes, we said. "I saw you in the store there," he explained, and went on to describe what we'd been wearing. Yes, that was us, we acknowledged.

"Neat," he said. "Someday, I like to do that, too."

In Cleveland, Ohio, we finally left the bus. Noreen had come to pick up Scott, and I was going to catch a local shuttle to where Jeanine would meet me. Neither Scott nor I are very demonstrative; we customarily say goodbye by shaking hands. But now when the time came to go our separate ways, we looked at each other and suddenly knew that a handshake wasn't going to do it.

Simultaneously, we each reached for the other and embraced for joy.

Part 2

Chapter 16

DAUGHTER

Naturally, my trip with Scott was a major topic of conversation during my first few days back home. I regaled my long-suffering wife and not-so-patient children with story after story from the adventure. Finally Jeanine said, "I'm glad you had a good time. Did the trip satisfy your goal? Is it out of your system now?"

"Er ... Well, sort of. For the time being anyway."

A look of dismay flashed across Jeanine's face, but all she said was "I see."

Still, within days, our lives returned to normal, and I resumed my previous schedule. I felt good about what I had accomplished and reasonably content to delay the completion of the journey until some unspecified date in the future.

Then, unexpectedly, I received a sizable cash bonus at work. When I told Jeanine the news, she said, "Look, you're not going to be satisfied until you complete your ride. This money would make it possible for you to do that and for the rest of us to do something we like, too." And soon we had a plan. During my daughter's spring break from high school, she and I would ride the eastern end of the route, the portion across Virginia. Then, when summer came, Jeanine and all three of our offspring would vacation in Disney World while I pedaled the middle section of the nation.

Except for not being together, it was, to my mind, a nearly perfect arrangement. My wife and kids enjoy theme parks much more than I do. So while they reveled in the Magic Kingdom, I would find my enchantment in the realm of the wanderer. And I was profoundly grateful to have been excused from trudging through Walt's empire.

I especially looked forward to riding with my 15-year-old daughter Becky. At various times in the past, both of my sons and my daughter have ridden excursions with me, but neither of the boys ever caught my passion for biking. Becky had, however, and she became my most frequent cycling partner — first in a baby seat mounted over my back wheel, and then on a succession of gradually larger bikes.

While I was eager to have Becky along for the company, I had another hope for the time together. Thus far, Becky's teenage years had had their share of tense moments, and I thought the freedom of the road might bring some relaxation.

Becky had been a cheerful, bright child, with an easy, outgoing nature. As often happens with fathers and daughters, she and I got along especially well. On car trips, for example, Becky and I sang together, played word games, and held conversations where Becky displayed what seemed to me surprisingly mature understandings for her age. She'd been fun to be with.

Adolescence, however, had not been as sunny. Some of it was the usual moodiness and shortsighted life-view that characterize teen years for many youths. In Becky's case, though, this sometimes put her at odds with Jeanine and me, because while she needed to begin plotting her own course, she had not yet gained the skills to assert herself without turning discussions into contests of wills.

Then, too, there were some tough blows from which we were not able to shelter Becky. In eighth grade, she was the victim of a serious personal trauma, and while trying to deal with her feelings about it, a group of kids who'd been her friends from grade school on, and to whom she'd confided her hurt, made her an object of ridicule. She was further stung when the resulting depression led to her being dropped from a church youth team created to represent America at a Russian peace camp. This was especially rancorous because Becky had earned her place on the team by preparing an essay and other materials and successfully negotiating a screening process. We'd been dealing for a year with the aftermath of all this. Becky was now wiser, but also sadder.

It hadn't all been gloomy, of course, and we still saw signs of the "old Becky." We had no illusions that she could go back to the innocent optimism of childhood, but we wanted the joy of life to return in strength to her. I found it hopeful that she was still interested in bicycling with her dad.

Physically, this portion of the cross-nation trek would be as challenging as the West. The TransAmerica Trail in Virginia presents 31,790 vertical feet of climbing, more than in any other state along the route. Colorado boasts its 11,542-foot-high Hoosier Pass, while the highest peak we would encounter in Virginia barely measures 3,000 feet. But the total vertical feet of climbing in Colorado is only 16,070.

We decided to ride a tandem bike. Though we'd ridden shorter trips together on separate bicycles, for this journey with its high-mileage days, Becky was concerned that her energy might give out before mine or that the push might trigger problems with her asthma, which was generally controlled but flared occasionally. (Becky had planned to join me for my bicycle jaunt across Ohio a couple of years earlier, but had been forced to withdraw a week beforehand because of asthma problems.) So we decided that a "bicycle built for two," where, we assumed, she could simply stop working hard if she needed to, but where we still stayed together, was the solution.

Good tandems, built strong enough for the stresses of fully loaded touring, cost $2,000 and up when new, more than I could invest. After no success finding a used tandem through ads in our local paper and the bicycle club newsletter, I went online in CompuServe, where, in the Bicycling Forum, I described what I was looking for. Within a few days, e-mail from a tandem rider suggested I contact a couple in Dayton, Ohio, who were planning to purchase a larger-frame tandem and were selling their Burley (one of the leading tandem brands). On a bitterly cold day in December, Becky and I drove the 500-mile round trip to Dayton and purchased the five-year-old Burley for $500.

Although the tandem appeared in good condition, I remembered the difficulties I'd had with my single bike that had necessitated the replacement of several parts in Baker City, Oregon. So as the unusually cold winter rolled on, I went over the tandem thoroughly, checking every part. I was later to find, however, that not every mechanical problem can be anticipated.

In the process of working on the long bike, I discovered that it was geared for racing, something that would handicap us when climbing mountains with loaded panniers. I replaced the rear-wheel gear cluster with one offering a wider spread of gears and changed the middle and "granny" chainrings to smaller sizes, making lower gears available. In the end, the tandem was geared similarly to my single bike.

I also reinstalled the rear drum brake that the previous owner had removed. For normal riding without the weight of camping equipment and supplies, standard rim brakes, similar to those on single bikes, are sufficient. But loaded touring tandems, with twice the weight but only about the same wind resistance as a single bike, roll downhill so rapidly that rim brakes alone soon overheat. Tests by one tandem designer showed that rim temperatures can hit 300 degrees, damaging not only the rim, but also the tire and tube. The solution is a third brake, attached to the hub of the rear wheel. This drum brake, which is similar to the rear brakes on automobiles, provides the necessary slowing and stopping power.

Having my daughter along presented one concern I'd not had on previous portions of my journey. Becky is a pretty girl, with attractive red hair and a figure that's obviously feminine. I knew we'd be traveling through some sparsely populated areas where there'd be no immediate help if she caught the attention of unscrupulous men in passing vehicles. I assumed that being with me would discourage most unwanted attention, but I'd be basically powerless against a group or an armed individual.

In all my travels, I seldom worried about my own safety, or felt the need to. But I remembered reading in one of Peter Jenkins' books about his walk with his wife across America, where, on a lonely stretch, the couple fled the highway and hid in the woods because of a carload of men who'd driven slowly past them one time too many. The pair watched from the bushes fearfully as the men came back, apparently searching for them.

But I also read several accounts of women who bicycled lengthy journeys completely alone with no safety problems at all. Also, in all the riding Becky and I had already done together, there had not been a single untoward incident. Statistically, cyclists face far more risk from careless drivers and holes in the blacktop than from rascals. But to assure myself that I wasn't placing Becky at excessive risk, I posted an inquiry in the Cycling Forum of CompuServe. I heard back from several tandemists who all said they'd had no problems while riding with wives or girlfriends. A couple of two-fer riders said they carry cellular phones when riding but have never had to make a distress call.

One rider added, "We refrain from making obscene gestures and retorts to the local high-schoolies, who love to tell you to get off the road." That was good advice I'd been following for a long time anyway.

Satisfied that the risk was no more than we faced walking down a quiet street together, I resolved to stay alert, but to not deny Becky the opportunity of the trip.

The cold and snow hung on longer than usual through the winter, forcing us to delay most training/conditioning rides until barely three weeks before our April departure. On the one earlier ride we managed during a brief February thaw, Becky, who is a confident rider on her own bike, found herself uneasy on the tandem because of its tendency to lurch to the right as we pushed down on the left pedals and vice versa. In the front "captain" position, I wasn't bothered much by the swaying, but Becky, in the "stoker" seat, reported that she constantly felt as if we were going to fall. And with neither steering nor braking control from the back seat, Becky had no options for controlling the oscillation. As we rode 20 miles that day without capsizing, she began to trust that I would keep the bike upright, but the uncomfortable we're-about-to-crash sensation continued.

As the winter reclamped its icy hand, I began reading about tandems. I learned that the side-to-side movement is a common problem on these long wheelbase vehicles. It results from the added power of two riders pumping with the pedals "in phase" — the way most tandem cranksets are set up. In other words, when the captain's right pedal is at 12 o'clock and his left pedal at 6 o'clock, the stoker's pedals are in identical positions. The suggested remedy is to set the two cranksets out of phase, with the captain's leading the stoker's by up to 90 degrees. Many tandemists, especially those who race, don't like this arrangement because it makes standing up on the pedals more difficult, and some other riders avoid it because it "looks odd." Nonetheless, I determined to try it.

We did, when the weather finally broke. Not only did the out-of-phase setup eliminate the yawing, delighting Becky, but we found that we had more power when climbing. We had, in effect, converted the stretched vehicle from "two-stroke" to "four-stroke" power.

But although the ride was more in-line now, Becky soon let me know that riding on the rear seat was a quite different experience from piloting her single bike. She couldn't see straight ahead, making it hard to anticipate bumps and turns. Wheeling down a steep hill with a right turn at the bottom, Becky yelled, "Slow down, Dad."

"Why? I've got the bike under control."

"That may be what it feels like to you, but from back here, I'm just along for the ride. It makes me uneasy having no control. I'm a person who likes to be in charge."

And after I made the turn as sharply as I would have on my single bike, she added, "Hey, don't forget that this long thing can't turn as tightly as a regular bike! I almost went into the curb!"

Fortunately, she was patient while I learned to think as a tandem captain, telling her before I made turns and warning her of pavement irregularities. I got better at it, but still occasionally surprised her.

Because the winter hung on so long, we began our journey with precious little conditioning time. Becky possessed the natural flexibility of youth, but my fitness, achieved through my ride with Scott, had slipped woefully as I watched weekend after weekend go by with weather not fit to ride. The roads remained icy for weeks, with shoulders plugged by piled snow. And cold so deep that it was actually dangerous to ride blasted the region. I understood a comment by a fellow bike club member: "Why does it take nine months and 5,000 miles of cycling to get into shape and only two weeks to turn back into a slug?"

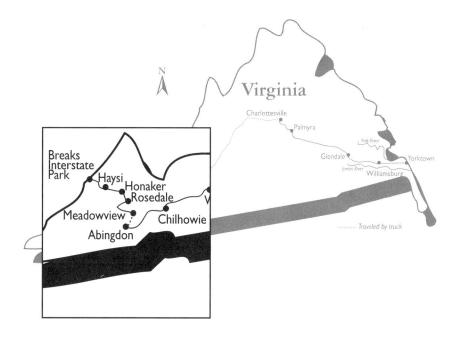

Chapter 17

SNOW

We began our ride across Virginia on a Friday in early April. We gambled that the weather that far south would be at least three weeks further into spring than our home state of Ohio.

We gambled and lost. The gray day barely hit 40 degrees, almost identical to Ohio's early spring chill. A waitress where we ate breakfast commented that the previous day had been sunny and 71, but that a week of cold touched with damp snow now dominated the forecast.

My parents drove us to the starting point: the Breaks Interstate Park, a scenic hump in the southwestern toe of Virginia where it bumped up against Kentucky. The starting-out photo they snapped of Becky and me standing behind our loaded tandem shows two riders bundled to the neck against the cold.

Becky seemed slightly apprehensive as we began pedaling, but after we rocketed down the first slope and successfully pumped up the grade that followed, she appeared to relax and began showing interest in our surroundings. She had just completed a school unit on geology and was able to fill me in on the terrain we were traversing. "This area was probably formed by an 'upheaval,'" she said, and went on to explain the differences between that sort of geological event and others formed by "convolution," "subduction" and "folding."

Eventually we came to a short but extremely steep upgrade. Becky was still pedaling gamely upward when I found it necessary to dismount and complete the hill on foot. It's not a good sign when the experienced cyclist is the first to flag. That hill also taught us the fallacy of our assumption that Becky would be able to stop pedaling and just go along for the ride. Powering the big bike required both captain and stoker to pump — and vigorously, especially when going uphill. I was grateful that Becky had no interest in being merely a passenger.

The tiny community of Haysi sits near the bottom of a steep downgrade. Rolling into the community, we saw a store and decided to stop for a hot drink. Because of the downslope, however, we must have been rolling faster than I thought. When I applied the brakes, I had the sensation that we not only were not going to stop but were going to career out of control and fall over at high speed. At the last second, the extra stopping power of the drum brake took hold, and we jolted to a standstill. I stood over the bike with my heart pounding and adrenaline racing. Becky had a wide-eyed expression as she said, "Let's not do *that* again."

After warming up in the store, we returned to the bike, only to discover the front tire flat (the result of our crunching stop?). I replaced the tube with a new one and inflated it with the frame pump. Two miles later, it, too, went flat. When I examined the tubes closely later, I found a small tear in the first, but I never could find a flaw or hole in the second one. Replacing the tube with yet another, we proceeded gingerly.

Given the teenage gloom that had dogged Becky in recent months, I worried that the two flats occurring so early and so close together in our journey might spell discouragement for her. Instead, I was glad to find her cheering *me* up, telling me not to let the tire problems worry me.

Further on, a large, unfettered dog raced out, barking a challenge as we cycled past his domain. I used my usual tactic, shouting loudly, "Go home!" But Becky, who loves animals, said, "Don't yell at him, Dad," and then began a conversation with the dog: "Hi, Boy. How ya doing? Don't like people riding past your home, do you? You better go back now so you don't get hit on the road."

And darn if the mutt didn't obey!

In midafternoon, we stopped at a small roadside grocery in tiny Council. Inside, the clerk and three older men who apparently were just hanging out in the store took an interest in our trip, and soon Becky was telling them all about it. Becky has always had the ability to converse well with adults. Once, when she was 3, I had her with me in a crowded airport as we waited for Jeanine to arrive on a flight. The entire time we waited, Becky worked the crowd, striking up conversations with one stranger after another. I had to keep a sharp eye on her to make sure she didn't wander too far away in her pursuit of people to talk with. As a teenager, a bit more reticence had set in, but given an opening, she still easily engaged grownups in conversation.

The men filled us in on the road ahead and mentioned that we had a huge climb directly in front of us.

Back on the highway, the grade started almost immediately. When I shifted into our lowest gear, the chain jumped off the small chainring. The sudden release of tension caused the pedal to plummet downward. My whole body lunged forward; I slipped off the seat and banged my crotch painfully on the top tube of the frame. The movement looked comic, however, and Becky laughed.

Smarting from the bump and irritated at the bike, I dismounted and placed the chain back on the teeth of the small ring. Everything looked okay, but when we got back on and tried to crank, the chain again jumped free.

Thinking dark thoughts now, I once again reset the chain. When it malfunctioned yet a third time, Becky said, cheerfully,

"Don't let it get you down. Try the middle ring." We did, and the chain stayed seated, although starting on an upgrade in the midrange ring required more effort. Once we were rolling, I shifted down to the small ring and the chain engaged properly.

The climb, over a mountain called "Big A," took us to about 2,500 feet by way of a steep five-mile ascent consisting of numerous switchbacks. We quickly discovered that a tandem loses momentum much more rapidly on upslopes than does a single bike. Even with both of us pumping at full power, we were forced to our lowest gear combination almost immediately, while our speed dropped to a meager 3.6 miles per hour. At that laggardly rate, we had barely enough forward impetus to keep the bike upright, and we wobbled so much that passing traffic veered left to allow us extra room. Still, we managed to pump up most of the incline, walking only for two brief stretches where highway construction reduced the road surface to gravel.

If tandems demand extra effort climbing, they pay it back descending, and we flew down the other side. But when the terrain then changed to rolling hills, we found we had very little energy left. We were both suffering from the lack of conditioning rides before the trip.

As light began to fade from the gray day, we limped into Honaker. With a population of 1,500, it was the largest community we passed through all day.

Because it was so cold, we decided to stay in a motel, but soon learned that Honaker offered neither motel nor campground. The waiter at our supper stop mentioned a motel five miles further on in Rosedale, but I was concerned about riding on the narrow highway in the dark. A few moments later, the restaurant owner came to our table and offered to drive us in his pickup truck to Rosedale. We gladly accepted.

En route, he explained why he liked the area — mostly because it was "home." At the motel, I tried to press some cash on him, but he waved my offer off and said he was glad to help us out.

The motel, we found, while clean, was badly in need of repairs and remodeling. When we got to our assigned room, we first had to slip in sideways and push the two beds together so the door could swing farther open. Even with that, we still had to completely unload the tandem before we could maneuver it into the small space. After that effort and unpacking, we determined that the heater wasn't working in the room anyway.

What did impress me though, was the clerk's attitude when I reported the no-heat problem. He seemed genuinely distressed that we'd been inconvenienced. He immediately came to the room, and when he, too, failed to elicit cooperation from the heater, he helped us haul our belongings to another room. Finally settled, I was too tired even to patch the inner tubes from our earlier flats, and left them for morning.

Getting ready to shower, I found my inner layer of clothing damp with perspiration. But thanks to the specialized "wick-away" fabric of my bike shirt, I hadn't chilled as badly as I usually did when we stopped throughout the day. Regular cotton or cotton-blend T-shirts, though okay as long as I continue to generate body heat from exertion, keep the moisture against my skin and rapidly turn cold during rest breaks. The more expensive bike-shirt material proved worth its added cost by moving the sweat to the outer layers of clothing.

The new day awoke as overcast as the previous one and offered an added feature: a light layer of snow that clung to rooftops and vehicles. Fortunately it melted on contact with the highway, leaving us a wet but passable rolling surface.

Breakfasting at the restaurant adjacent to the motel, we found it just as bleak as our room. I ordered hot tea, which dismayed the proprietor, since he had no tea bags. He solved this, after a fashion, by microwaving some ice tea. It was ... well, okay. When his wife brought my pancakes, she placed a bottle of corn syrup beside my plate with the explanation, "We have maple syrup in the back I can get if you want it, but I thought I should use this up." I suddenly understood why Becky and I were the only customers in the place.

Still, like the man who'd arranged the second room for us the night before, our host and hostess were unfailingly polite and friendly — almost as if to say, "We may not be able to accommodate you properly, but our manners shall not fail us."

The snow changed to a drizzle as we pedaled into the day. Within 10 miles, we found ourselves wending upward toward another peak — Clinch Mountain — easily as severe a climb as the one to Big A the day before. This time, though, the road was little traveled. Thus, when we wobbled at a slow speed, our concern was less that we would bump into traffic and more that we'd veer over the hillside that fell away rapidly from the right shoulder of the road. We became more steady as we climbed, however. We took a couple of rest breaks, and when we resumed riding, the chain popped off the small ring in a repeat of the previous day's performance. The drizzle had stopped, but at the higher altitudes, snow lay in a damp powder on the ground. The activity of climbing kept us plenty warm, but each time we paused, we began to chill within a couple of minutes — special-fabric clothes notwithstanding.

Coming around a bend in the road, we were challenged suddenly by a Dalmatian dog who rushed toward us, barking fiercely. This time, neither my shouting nor Becky's kindly patter had the slightest effect. My concern skyrocketed when I noticed foam around his mouth. We were high on the mountain, surrounded by forest, and far from any habitation. Where had this animal come from? Spying neither collar nor master, I feared that he might be a wild dog and possibly diseased. But as we continued pedaling, we noticed that he behaved more as if he were protecting an area and warning us off than seeking to attack.

And indeed, once we rounded the next bend, he did not follow.

At the top, we discovered that our drive chain would no longer shift onto the big ring, depriving us of the high range of gears we wanted for the descent. Puzzled, I lifted the chain onto the big ring by hand, and began the downward plunge. I found it necessary to brake frequently, not only because of the wet pavement and S curves, but because the wind from the higher speed was bone-chilling. The drum brake proved invaluable as the tandem hurtled downward for approximately five miles.

Even at the controlled speed, however, the wind chill took its toll. We'd planned to warm ourselves in a grocery indicated by the bike map, but we found it out of business. In Hayters Gap, a one-church, no-store community, we inquired for any sort of establishment where we would find food, but the man pointed down the road and said the closest place was five more miles, near Meadowview. He'd been bringing an object out of a building — a tree branch mounted on a stand with a small, carved house ensconced in the smaller branches at the top. Becky asked the man if he was a woodcarver. He said the item was indeed carved, but he had purchased several of them from an artisan in Tennessee and resold them in Virginia. Still, he seemed as proud of the works as if they were his own creations and brought several of them out for us to admire. Each one was unique, and I could see that someone had put a lot of work into them.

We continued, using only the middle ring until we came to a mile-long climb. Hoping against hope, I shifted to the lower ring, and the chain immediately jumped free. When I tried to reseat the chain this time, it refused even to settle completely around the chainring, causing me to look more closely. To my surprise, I noticed that several teeth were bent about 20 degrees inward, toward the bike frame. Having no way to straighten the teeth and little hope that a repair would last anyway, I knew we needed a bike shop. As we pushed the bike up the rest of the hill, the cheerfulness that had buoyed Becky until now finally failed her. She looked tired as she asked, "What will we do?"

"We'll make it to the next town," I said, "and we'll get a ride somehow from there to a bike shop. Then we'll go on."

"But we're not going to cover enough miles to get across the whole state before our time runs out. I want to complete the ride."

Hearing Becky say that, I knew that I'd once again fallen into the miles-to-cover trap, and this time I'd dragged Becky in with me. With Scott, I'd finally let go of the 80-miles-per-day goal, but then we had comfortably averaged 70. So when planning the ride with Becky, I'd taken 70 for our daily goal. What I'd failed to take seriously enough was the significantly less pretrip conditioning Becky and I began with as well as the three fewer hours of daylight riding time April offered. Once again, my optimistic goal setting was creating stress.

Well, this time I would make use of what I'd learned with Scott. "We're not going to worry about distance," I said, trying to sound reassuring. "Miles alone are not the purpose of our trip. We'll figure something out." Although not certain at that moment what that "something" would be, I resolved to take whatever steps necessary to keep the journey from turning into an ordeal for my daughter, who had so willingly accompanied me on this adventure.

We aimed for Meadowview, the next town, and gratefully, we found the terrain on the way rolling rather than mountainous. Our middle chainring, the only one still functioning, allowed us to use the six midrange gears and wheel the remaining distance to a country store on the outskirts of the town. I felt as weary as Becky looked, and when we staggered into the store, we were desperate for food. At the lunch counter, we placed an order for hot sandwiches but were so hungry that while those cooked, we devoured cookies and fruit from the grocery section. We were so depleted that for a time we both trembled involuntarily.

After resting for nearly an hour and consuming about twice what we normally ate for lunch, we climbed back on the bike and cycled the last mile to town, where, in the local diner, I offered to hire someone to drive us to a bike shop. The owner of the establishment, a man in his 30s, agreed to help us.

While we waited for the owner to finish his lunch, a wrecker driver asked about our situation. Hearing that we had had what he called "transmission problems" in the mountains, he immediately recommended a route change. The TransAmerica Trail, in the interest of scenic vistas, continued southeast, traversing the Blue Ridge range and dipping into the mountains of the Mount Rogers National Recreation Area before swinging back northeast to follow the valley beside the Blue Ridge Mountains. "Assuming the mountains are what caused your transmission problems," he said, "you'd be wise to skirt that area. The climbs are every bit as tough as the two you've already come over. Besides, if you get into more bike problems down there, you're sunk. There's not very much even open in that area at this time of year."

His advice made sense for another reason as well. Turning northeast through the Blue Ridge region would save about 30 miles and help to put us back on schedule. I told Becky I thought we should follow his suggestion, and she agreed, but wondered aloud how she felt about altering our plans so early in our trip.

The nearest bike shop was about 10 miles away in Abingdon and slightly off route. Riding there in the restaurant owner's pickup, I commented to him about the beauty of the area. "Yes," he said, "that's part of what drew me back here after I'd moved to Florida. But it's tough to make a living here. I own that restaurant plus work two other jobs."

When he mentioned that he also raised horses, Becky

immediately got interested and told him about her volunteer work with disabled riders. "There's a place like that here, too," our driver said. He and Becky continued talking about horses for the remainder of our jaunt.

At the destination, our good Samaritan ascertained that the shop had the parts we needed before leaving. And then, like the man who'd shuttled us to the motel the night before, he refused my offer of payment.

The store was in the midst of a bike sale, and very busy, so I purchased a new chainring and, on the sidewalk outside, installed it myself. Looking at the shift cable to the front derailler, I noticed that it had too much slack. I'd put new cables on the bike before the trip, and new cables do have a tendency to stretch, especially from hard use. The slackness now prevented the derailler from lifting the chain to the big ring. We waited until the store's mechanic was available, and he used a special cable puller to restore the full range of gear-shifting capability.

Following our new route out of town, we resumed the ride. Route 11, also known as Lee Highway after General Robert E. Lee, parallels Interstate 81 and the mountains of the Blue Ridge range. Following the valley floor, it offered us a rippled terrain with occasional gradual upgrades, but nothing as steep as the roads we had ridden before Meadowview. But after about an hour on this road with pastoral scenery that seemed to change little mile after mile, Becky commented that, while easier to ride, this highway was boring.

Having to devote less energy actually to covering the distance, however, left more for conversation. Becky suddenly volunteered, "School's not much fun anymore. It's all serious all the time." A high-school freshman, Becky was a good student — straight A's — whom we've never had to prod to do her homework. But she clearly had less enthusiasm for her schoolwork since the previous year, when some key friendships with classmates went sour.

"Yes," I said, "the work does get harder as you advance through school."

"No, it's not just that it's harder. I can handle that. It's almost like somebody just decided that there can't be any happiness in learning anymore. In grade school we learned, but there were Valentine parties and recesses and milk breaks. It wasn't so stressful. Learning itself was often made into a game, like spelling bees. If we finished a test and there was time remaining, we'd play a game. Now, if we finish anything early, we have to 'sit quietly until the bell rings.'" She spoke this last phrase in a deepened voice, mimicking an oh-so-serious teacher. "It hardly ever lets up," she added. "I'm a person who needs some downtime. But now it seems like all I do is get up, go to school, come home, do my homework, and by then I'm tired and ready to go to bed, only to start all over the next day."

"That's kind of what it's like for grownups, too, when we go to work," I offered.

"But at least you get to choose your work. I have no choice. You can choose a job you enjoy."

"That's true, but most careers, no matter how much we like them, have some aspects that aren't enjoyable. I like my job overall, but there are still some times when I'd rather be elsewhere."

Becky sighed. "It's no wonder they say kids are growing up too fast today. They start forcing us to be grownups as soon as we leave sixth grade."

By the time we reached Chilhowie, our usual supper hour had passed, and despite the relatively easier route, we were again frantic for food. We selected a restaurant and hurried in. A waitress in her 20s, who saw us ride in, brought cold drinks immediately and then began asking about our journey. She seemed genuinely interested, so we told her where we'd been and where we were headed. She practically gushed over us in her admiration for our endeavor. I understood her enthusiasm when she said, "I wish my dad had done something like this with me when I was a kid."

After eating, we estimated that we had enough daylight remaining to cycle to the next community. With the time-consuming climb over Clinch that morning, the forced walking of subsequent hills, and then about three more hours lost to bike repairs, we'd achieved just over 40 miles since breakfast. But now Becky and I exchanged glances, each recognizing exhaustion in the other, and said almost simultaneously, "Nah." We headed instead for the motel next door.

Chapter 18

FRIEND

Earlier in the day, I had noticed two figures on bicycles heading toward us on the opposite side of the road. While they were yet too far away to see clearly, I said to Becky, "I wonder if those are cycle-tourists like us." Becky scanned down the highway with her younger eyes and then said, "No, they're not cyclists; they're just a couple of kids on bikes."

As they drew nearer, I saw Becky was right. The boys looked about 14. But seeing them suddenly brought back a memory of Jonathan, one of my earliest cycling companions. He was a classmate in junior high school in Saratoga Springs, New York. We were drawn together initially, I think, because neither of us cared to be involved in school sports and because both of us were fairly good students. Neither of these were qualities much appreciated in junior-high social circles.

An only child, Jonathan lived with his parents in a homey old farmhouse near Kaydeross Lake, a few miles outside Saratoga. His mom, a warm, friendly housewife, made me feel welcome in their home. Soon Jonathan and I were spending many Saturdays together at his place.

His father worked for the local newspaper, whose office occupied the corner just across the side street from my home. On Saturdays, Jonathan rode into town with his father in their car, bringing his bicycle in the trunk. Then Jonathan and I cycled back to his house. We spent the day together. After a supper of beans, franks and brown bread, the family's traditional Saturday evening meal, Jonathan's dad drove me and my bicycle home.

I loved Jonathan's room. It had probably once been either the formal parlor or the dining room, and as such had no door. It connected to the living room at a large, open arch, giving the whole room an airy feel. National Geographic maps studded the walls, and a telescope dominated a windowed corner. On Jonathan's desk was a map he'd drawn of an invented country that existed only in his imagination. It never occurred to us to talk about how Jonathan felt about his domain, but it was a perfect room for a wanderluster like me.

The road in front of Jonathan's front door bounded pasture land that extended to Kaydeross Creek, a smallish stream in dry periods but a minor torrent that overflowed its banks each spring when engorged by melting snows.

On an early spring Saturday when the creek was in full flow, Jonathan and I decided we should explore it by raft. Some round beams from an old barn that had been torn down were stored in an outbuilding on his family's land. We dragged these, one at a time, to the water's edge, a distance of perhaps a quarter-mile. There, we joined them together by nailing some boards across them at right angles, forming a platform of sorts.

Because the beams were small, the five we had hauled barely provided enough buoyancy to carry our combined weight. They actually floated slightly below the water's surface when we both stepped on to our raft, but we were wearing rubber boots that kept our feet dry.

With water swirling around our booted ankles, we pushed off, poling ourselves downstream with long saplings. In the rushing current, we moved along rapidly through forest and farmland. After perhaps an hour, we began to tire, so with much effort, we reversed direction and poled our way back upstream to our starting point.

By then it was nearing supper time, and I walked with Jonathan back to his house, already savoring the baked beans in my mind.

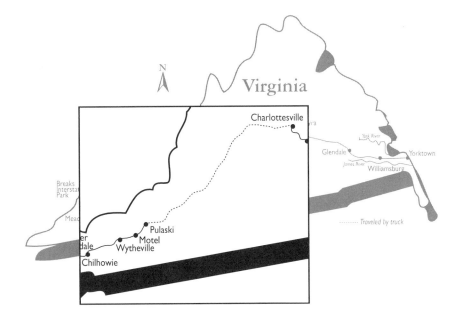

Chapter 19

ASSISTANCE

The next day was Easter, and also the first day of Daylight-Saving Time. We adjusted the clock in the bike cyclometer accordingly. Stepping out of the motel into the chilly morning, the first of our trip to offer a blue sky, I thought of those attending Easter sunrise services outdoors. I imagined they'd be grateful for a brief liturgy.

This was the first Easter I could recall when I had not been in church for at least the main service of the morning — a situation also true for Becky — and I was not altogether comfortable with my decision now not to attend. I'd planned to seek out a church on this day, but then decided that taking time to attend a service would further cut into our mileage. For although I'd vowed not to let white-line fever drive us, we both still wanted to make our best attempt. In my mind, this day would yield a make-or-break decision about whether to truncate our trip. Becky, who had already said she wouldn't feel right going to church in jersey and tights, gave me no argument. But later I decided my choice sent the wrong message to my daughter, and I told her so.

"Don't worry," she responded. "I know what Easter means. We talk about the Resurrection all year long in church. Easter's a special day, but its message is with us all the time."

The road ahead continued through countryside that rose

and fell in a series of swells. It would not be overly difficult pedaling. And, although this day was as cold as the preceding two, the sunshine at least gave this one a more optimistic cast.

As we proceeded, Becky observed geographic features she'd learned about in school, and pointed them out to me. "There's a meander," she said, indicating the path of a creek in the distance. "It's well on its way to becoming an oxbow lake."

That was a term unfamiliar to me, and I was proud that my daughter paid good attention to her studies. In the driver's seat, I wasn't able to take a lengthy look at the feature she referred to, so I asked her to explain. She launched into a description that included differing speeds of water flow on the inside and outside of the meander, the wearing away of banks and the deposit of water-borne soil on the opposite side. When I didn't quite get it, she suggested I wait until she could diagram the process for me. (She later did so, expertly, on a napkin during our lunch stop.)

Near Rural Retreat, the TransAmerica Trail joined Highway 11. We were back on route.

In midafternoon, we climbed a long but not especially steep grade into Wytheville, where Becky requested we stop for a rest. Once off the bike, I noticed that Becky did not look well. When I suggested getting some food, she mentioned that her stomach was upset. I knew what she meant; I'd had a few minutes of nausea myself earlier in the day. I parked her on a bench in front of a supermarket and told her to rest. Clearly, the push of the last three days had caught up to Becky. We needed to give her a good rest in someplace warm. The longer we sat on the bench, the colder we got.

Eventually, Becky said the nausea had passed, and we headed for a nearby restaurant where we were able to get hot chocolate and warm food. Seated inside, Becky looked distraught and said, "I'm sorry to have stopped us. I feel bad holding you back. I don't want to ruin the trip for you."

Although Scott and I posed in front of the Columbia River Maritime Museum at the start of our trip, we didn't go inside. The road was calling, and we were eager to get underway.

These rocky "sea stacks" on Oregon's coast had once been part of the mainland itself.

The grade and the heat forced us to walk part of the long climb out of Mitchell, Oregon, but we were rewarded with a beautiful view.

Scott, atop the second of the three mountain passes between Prairie City and Baker City, Oregon.

Sixty-five and going strong, Brendon Ryan, from Dublin, Ireland, was in his 10th week of a solitary coast-to-coast ride.

More than 150 years later, the ruts made on the plains by prairie schooners are clearly visible from the parking lot of the Oregon Trail Interpretive Center.

Finally into Idaho, Scott looks back into beautiful Hell's Canyon.

Although the majority of riders we met were young adults, some were senior citizens. At 66, Beth called the western mountains "a piece of cake" compared to the eastern slopes she'd already encountered.

A chillingly cold day marked the beginning of my ride with Becky on our "bicycle built for two."

Becky at the Breaks Interstate Park on the boundary of Kentucky and Virginia.

David Stanley, the stranger-turned-friend who drove us from Pulaski to Charlottesville, Virginia, stands with Becky in Charlottesville.

The Yorktown Victory Monument, which commemorates America's triumph over the British in the Revolutionary War, was the end point of our father-daughter ride across Virginia.

Although I look happy here, I was feeling very sick. I did not yet know that I was suffering from acute dehydration.

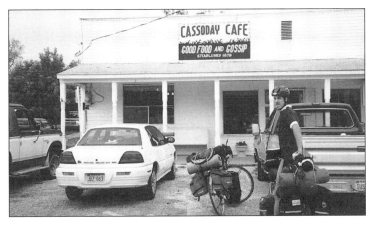

Dave Barnas, whom I met by chance in Kansas, outside the Cassoday Café, where we enjoyed an outstanding buffet. Dave and I rode together for five days.

"Yodeling" Katy Lopeman sang to us and gave us camping space and breakfast. She is one of several people who offer hospitality to cycle tourists on the TransAmerica Trail.

Ferrying across the Ohio River from Illinois to Kentucky.

"You're not. The purpose here is not just to cover miles; it's to be together."

"But you can't be having a good time. Think of the problems with the bike and the unexpected cold and now me not feeling good."

"A good time is a relative thing, Becky. After all, the most important thing is going very well: You and I are getting along just fine, and I'm enjoying your company." I wasn't just trying to make her feel better; it really was pleasurable to be with Becky on this bike adventure. "You know, you could be in Disney World with great weather, but if you weren't getting along well with your companions, it could be an unhappy trip. This one is going fine for me."

After food and rest, Becky said she felt well enough to continue. As we rode on, Becky did seem stronger and her cheerfulness returned.

Animals had continued to draw Becky's attention throughout our ride. She frequently commented on the cattle and horses she observed in the surrounding pastures, often describing the horses by their coloring — roan, bay, pinto, etc. She had learned the correct nomenclature during her volunteer work the previous summer. The plight of animals plucked her heartstrings too. Coming across a cat recently killed on the highway, she said, "Aw, Daddy, look." Since becoming a teen, Becky usually referred to me as "Dad," but, I'd noticed, she tended to revert to "Daddy" when her most tender feelings were touched.

Further on, the road began climbing sharply, but Becky pedaled okay. At the top of one hill, she suddenly cried "Stop!" Three horses stood in a fenced enclosure near the road, and Becky wanted to get personally acquainted with all three. One by one they came to the fence where Becky petted them and spoke to them in a friendly chatter.

Later, alongside the highway beyond the little one-store

community of Max Meadows, Becky spied a 20-year-old Virginia license plate. She added it to our load as a memento of the trip.

We were carrying a tent and sleeping bags but had yet to use them. As evening approached, I considered whether we should camp out and again decided the night would be too cold for our three-season sleeping bags. It was important that Becky not catch a cold as that was often a prelude to asthma trouble for her. We would stay in a motel again, I decided.

A few miles beyond Max Meadows sat a cluster of gas stations, restaurants, motels and convenience stores — a quick-stop area that had grown up along the interstate to service long-distance travelers. We still had some daylight remaining, however, and debated about continuing another five miles to the next motel area. "I don't mind going on," Becky said, "as long as it is not all uphill. Why don't we ask someone what the road is like?"

"We can do that, but don't count on the information being accurate. Noncyclists don't think about roads the same way that cyclists do."

But Becky wanted to try, so we asked a store clerk. "That road is nice and flat," he said authoritatively. "There are no hills at all."

Though I remained skeptical, his assurance was enough for Becky, so we set out. As soon as we rounded the first curve, the road began a steep and lengthy ascent. "How could that guy think this was flat?" Becky asked indignantly as we puffed up the grade.

"Because when you're in a car, hills don't make much difference. Traveling at 60, you can cover 10 miles in 10 minutes, regardless of terrain. You just don't notice a few hills." Indeed, route-condition reports, distance estimates and information about the existence of services are notoriously unreliable when given by nonriders, even if they've lived in the area for years.

I was accustomed to using their information as only the roughest of guides.

After topping the long grade, we pedaled a series of rollers over the remaining miles of this "nice and flat" road, eventually arriving at a motel where we stopped for the night.

It was time for a decision. In spite of Becky's temporary illness in Wytheville, we had still covered 52 miles. It was a decent ride, but not the 70 miles we needed to average daily to make Yorktown, the end point of the TransAmerica Trail, in the five days remaining. Assuming that we could continue to ride 50-mile days, I took our map and measured off four 50-mile segments — 200 miles — from Yorktown backward. That placed us at Charlottesville. We needed to use tomorrow to find a way to get to Charlottesville — though I wasn't sure how we would accomplish that. When I told Becky of the plan, she voiced some disappointment at not being able to achieve our original goal. "Getting a car ride sort of seems like cheating," she said. But she agreed that we had little other choice. Within minutes, she was sound asleep.

We breakfasted at a truck stop a few miles beyond the motel, and it occurred to me that we might be able to hitch a ride on an 18-wheeler. There were a number of semis idling in the lot, but very few drivers to be seen. I assumed several were still bedded down in their sleeper cabs. Feeling a bit like a beggar, I approached a couple of fellow diners — men sitting alone — and inquired if they were truckers. Neither was. Next we checked the adjoining repair shop, where we did find a few drivers. They listened politely to our request but then explained that they were all towing sealed trailers; there'd be no way to load our bike. Finally, we made the rounds of the parked trucks, and spoke to the two drivers we found with their rigs. Neither was heading toward Charlottesville.

Plan B: We'd ride the 10 miles to the next town, Pulaski,

and see what help we could recruit there. (Unfortunately the bus was not a viable option because of the requirement that we disassemble and box the bike.) As we cycled toward that town, a black pickup truck passed us. The sign on the vehicle's door announced that the occupant was a farrier. Despite Becky's experience with horses, she didn't know the term. I explained it was a person who shoes horses. Moments later, we spied the same truck stopped on the shoulder with the driver, a husky young man, looking under the hood. As we passed, he called out, "Where are you headed?"

We stopped to talk. His truck had blown a head gasket, he explained, and a tow truck had already been called. We told him about our trip and about our immediate dilemma. He said he'd like to be doing what we were, but then pointed at a large mountain in the distance. "You don't want to go to Pulaski on this road," he said. "Pulaski's on the other side of that mountain, and the next five miles are a really rough climb. My truck has trouble on that grade — even when it's running right," he added with chuckle. He suggested we backtrack a short distance to a side road. "That one runs around the base of the mountain and will get you to Pulaski quicker." He then offered an idea that eventually solved our finding-a-ride problem. "There's a Senior Citizens' Center in town. They might know somebody who could help you."

Wishing him good luck with his truck, we followed his directions and soon arrived in Pulaski, a town of 10,000, about 45 minutes later. We found the Senior Center in the downtown area.

Inside, two women staffers listened to our plight. I explained that I'd pay $50 plus gas to anyone who could transport us. While neither knew of a retired person with a truck or van, they both made a few phone calls. None of those calls yielded the desired result immediately, but one of the men they contacted thought he might be able to work something out and suggested we linger at the Senior Center until he called back.

The staffers said we were welcome to stay as long as we liked.

We sat in the comfortable reading area amid display racks offering "Living With Osteoporosis" pamphlets and information sheets about Social Security. The older of the staff members, a kindly woman with natural hosting instincts, soon brought Becky a mug of hot chocolate and me cup of tea. At lunch time, as she prepared to leave for the local burger joint, she offered to bring back food for us. When I accepted and handed her cash, she produced a newspaper coupon entitling us to one meal free.

The younger woman, Tina, was 40-ish, attractive, and possessed a loud, friendly laugh. As seniors came to the center for the day's activities, we heard several ask Tina how her packing was going. She explained to us that this was her last week at the center. She'd been accepted as a flight attendant by a major airline and was leaving the next week to attend the training program in St. Louis. A while later, a man of about Tina's age came in and the two entered her office. A few moments later, Becky nodded toward Tina's office window, through which we could see Tina in tears. While we waited to learn if we had a ride, a private drama played itself out in that office. Shortly thereafter, the man exited, looking serious, and then Tina came out, no longer weeping. We hoped she been able to conclude whatever had needed to happen.

The day before, Becky, who is an advanced piano student and normally practices every day, mentioned that her "fingers were itching" to play. Now, spotting an old upright piano in the center's back room, Becky asked if she could play it. Soon she filled the rooms with the sound of classical pieces she'd learned for various recitals. And later, Becky sat chatting with the elderly ladies who arrived for the Monday craft class.

More than three hours had now passed since we'd arrived at the center. We began to feel comfortable with the two staffers and apparently, they with us. Eventually I said to Tina,

"It must be hard moving away from this friendly town."

"Oh, it is," she responded. "I grew up here and my parents are still in this town. I've really never been away from here for long before. I've wanted to be a flight attendant for 12 years now, but I could never get my husband to move with me. So I gave up the dream 'cause I thought it was important to hold the marriage together." She laughed sardonically. "But that didn't work anyway. The marriage still fell apart. Here I could have become a flight attendant 12 years ago and not lost anything I wasn't going to lose anyway! But now I'm going!" This time her laugh sounded joyful, and I was glad for her.

Eventually, the someone the staffers had phoned called somebody who called somebody who called somebody, and the message was finally phoned back to us to contact a certain David Stanley in Dublin, a nearby community. When I phoned him, he explained that he was glad to help us, but because of another obligation, he couldn't leave until morning. However, then he'd pick us up at 6 a.m. and have us to our drop-off point in time for a full day of riding. I quickly accepted, and he suggested a motel where Becky and I could stay. He'd meet us there in the morning.

Thanking the two women for their generous help, and wishing Tina success in her new life, we set off for the motel, a 10-mile ride. On the way, we stopped at a laundromat to wash our clothes. It had been so cold that we'd each been wearing our only cold weather outfit every day since we began. The prospect of clean clothes, even if they wouldn't stay that way long, was welcome.

That evening, in the restaurant adjacent to the motel, Becky asked our waitress if the ice cream on the menu was "hard or soft."

The question seemed to stump our server. Finally, she replied, "Let's just say it's mediocre!" Becky smirked at me, hardly able to contain herself while I explained to the woman that my daughter was inquiring whether the ice cream was of the scoopable or soft-serve variety. "Oh, it's hard," the waitress said.

"But is it *okay?*" Becky asked with a devilish gleam in her eye.

"Oh, yes. It's fine." The waitress took Becky's order for a scoop of the "mediocre" stuff and left, apparently unaware of the less-than-rousing endorsement she had given the dessert.

In our room, Becky immediately snapped on the TV. One of the things I like about camping is the absence of this cyclops, but Becky, raised around television, regarded the motel TVs as a bonus for the trip. I didn't complain, especially since she fell asleep each night shortly after we got to our room anyway. This night, before I flipped the set off, I heard a local weatherman refer to the "latest cold and snow on record in Virginia, at least for years and years."

Mr. Stanley was a trim man in his 60s I guessed. As he drove us toward Charlottesville, with the bike strapped on the back of his car, we learned that he was a retired veterinarian who still handled some duties for area animal hospitals. In fact, he needed to start our drive so early because he had a surgery scheduled for later in the day.

He and Becky immediately connected over the subject of animals. We found several other connecting points as well. David was an active layman in the United Methodist Church, the denomination in which I am ordained, and he had two children in the ministry as well. He had participated in overseas short-term mission trips, as had my wife. He had a son and daughter-in-law who were graduates of MIT, a school that had recently expressed an interest in Becky because of her science grades. David was able to give Becky somewhat of an insider's view of that institution, secondhand of course.

But more to the point, David was a bicycle-tourist. He and I had pedaled in many of the same parts of the country. We compared notes on cycling in Montana, the location of his most recent tour. And every Sunday morning, he and a group of friends pedaled over the mountain outside of Pulaski. the one the farrier had advised us to detour around. David agreed that loaded as we were, we'd received good advice from the horseshoer.

One added point of congruence. Although David had five grown children, the one who cycled with him most frequently was his daughter.

Chapter 20

TEAM

At just about 9 a.m., David pulled into the parking lot of the Thomas Jefferson Museum on the southeastern edge of Charlottesville. The TransAmerica Trail ran on the road immediately in front of the museum. When I tried to hand David the money, he refused it all, including the portion for gasoline. "But I agreed to pay this," I protested.

"But I didn't agree to accept it," David replied with a smile. He gave a friendly wave and headed his car back the way we'd come.

During the last mile of our ride to the motel the previous evening, we'd noticed that, once again, the front shifter wouldn't lift the chain onto the big ring. I'd assumed the problem was simply more cable stretch, so I had planned to adjust the cable before riding in the morning. I attempted that soon after David departed. To my annoyance, however, I found that the housing around the cable was deteriorating and preventing the cable from moving freely. We needed a bike shop again. The map showed only tiny communities until Richmond, so I knew we'd better find a shop before leaving Charlottesville.

Following directions provided by an employee of the museum, we rode the two miles into town to the bicycle shop. Even though the mechanic/manager of the shop immediately set other work aside to assist us, the repair, including three test

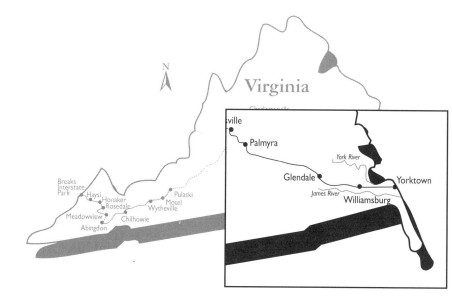

rides between adjustments, ended up consuming a couple of hours. Becky wandered the shop. All at once she came to me with excitement on her face. "They've got a Terry!" she exclaimed, and pulled me over to look at the special bike.

Georgena Terry is a designer and manufacturer of bicycles for women. Prior to her entry into the field, most bike builders simply modified men's bikes for women, with the result that female riders had difficulty finding comfortable bicycles. But Terry created a line of bikes expressly for women's dimensions. To fit smaller women — a category to which Becky, to her displeasure, belongs — Terry developed a frame that uses a standard-size rear wheel (700C — about 27 inches) and a smaller, 24-inch front wheel. The back wheel provides the normal range of gear ratios and rolls the bike forward over the full circumference of a standard wheel, but the smaller front wheel enables the handlebars to be closer to the rider, thus accommodating women's smaller upper bodies.

Becky had wanted a Terry ever since she heard about them, but at its usual price of $1600, the bike was beyond her budget. However, the bike now bringing the shine to my daughter's eyes was a used model being sold by the store on consignment for a college student. The price was $330. Becky soon had it out for a test ride, and when she returned, she said, "Dad! It actually fit! I don't have to stretch to ride it. My shoulders didn't hurt." I guessed accurately what she'd say next: "You know, I could sell my other bike, use my babysitting money, and go onto half-allowance ...." Before long, Becky had negotiated a loan from me. I wrote a check and arranged to pick up the bike on our car trip home from journey's end.

With the tandem again working properly, we retraced our route back to the museum and then climbed a pretty good upgrade on the road toward Monticello, Jefferson's hilltop estate, and past Ash Lawn, the home of the fifth president, James Monroe. We had visited Monticello previously on a family vacation and hadn't planned to stop this time. And now that we were finally on the road again, neither of us wished to lose any more of the time David had helped us gain.

David had driven us out of the mountainous region of the state. The terrain ahead had its share of ups and downs, but from Charlottesville to the coast, it gradually descended to sea level. Our route now ran mostly east and slightly south, and we began our run toward the sea.

The day, while still chilly, was perhaps 10 degrees warmer than any day of our trip thus far, and generally sunny. For the first time, I removed my wool scarf. In midday, my windbreaker came off as well, but the air remained cold enough that I was never tempted to remove my wool sweater or long-sleeve jersey. And by evening, I was wearing the jacket again.

We ate supper in Palmyra, population 200. With the bike-repair delay, we'd covered only 25 miles; we planned to log another 15 before sunset, but as we followed the TransAmerica Trail out of town, we were greeted by a sign announcing a detour ahead. Viewing the indicated alternate route on my map, I saw that the detour would take us at least 10 miles out of our way. It would be nearly dark before we rejoined the route, and we would still have miles to go to find accommodations for the night. "I'll ask about the road ahead at a house," I told Becky. "Sometimes bikes can get through a construction area where cars can't pass." I selected a house at random and headed for the door.

"No," said the man who answered my knock, "there's no way through. There are two bridges completely out." And he knew of no alternative to the marked detour. "I'm the local United Methodist minister," he said. "I've sometimes put cyclists up at the church. You're welcome to stay there tonight."

I was pleasantly surprised to have stumbled onto the parsonage, and quickly identified myself as a United Methodist minister also. After consulting with Becky, we accepted his offer of housing. The pastor and I talked briefly about the connection we shared. He then directed us to the church, and drove there himself to unlock the door and show us where to unroll our sleeping bags — in a heated classroom.

Before leaving the building, he invited us to view the sanctuary and told a little about the friendliness of the congregation and his pleasure at being appointed to serve this church.

As darkness descended outside, Becky mentioned that she didn't much like the idea of sleeping in a church. Since Becky's no stranger to church life, her comment surprised me until she explained that she found the creaking sounds of the old building unsettling. Nonetheless, we were both soon asleep.

By morning, I had figured out a new route to spare us the detour. The Virginia map showed a scenic highway, State Route 6, which followed the James River all the way to

Richmond, and the main highway through Palmyra intersected with Route 6 a few miles from town. This route would allow us eventually to rejoin the TransAmerica Trail on the far side of Richmond. The only drawback I could see was that we would have to pedal through Richmond itself, and large cities often are not bike-friendly. Still, the new course seemed the best option.

Becky had not slept well and had little energy for the ride. Eventually we realized why. The classroom we'd slept in was on the church's basement level. Very likely, dust or mold had triggered her allergy, causing her sinuses to drain all night with the accompanying discomfort. And for a while, the day seemed to go no better for Becky. Her saddle caused her discomfort, so I angled it downward slightly. That seemed to relieve her bottom, but the new angle threw more of her weight forward on her hands, causing them to ache. Soon she asked me to return the seat to its original position. She clearly was not having a good day, and at one of these seat-adjustment stops, she walked smack into a highway sign while heading back to the bike. Luckily, she was wearing her helmet so she wasn't seriously hurt, but now she had a headache to add to her woes.

Still, we pedaled along well, passing through the little communities of Fork Union, Columbia and Georges Tavern, and Becky began to feel better. At noon in Goochland, we found a restaurant offering Chinese cuisine — Becky's very favorite — and the infusion of won ton soup and a chicken-and-broccoli entree seemed to complete her recovery. And soon after lunch, Becky solved her saddle problem. She'd been using a gel-filled seat cover, counting on the cushioning for added comfort. But now she removed the cover and noticed immediate relief.

Riding through a forested area in midafternoon, Becky commented, "It might be interesting to be a forest ranger."

"That was my ambition at one time," I said.

"Why didn't you follow that up?"

"Well, I would have, but before I finished high school, I

felt I was 'called' into the ministry. Still, sometimes I think I might have really enjoyed forestry. At the time, though, I was so heavily involved with the church that it kind of blinded me to considering other careers very seriously. I was a committed Christian, but perhaps overly so."

"That's not all bad," Becky said.

"Of course not. But the narrow interpretation of 'Christian lifestyle' taught by the denomination I grew up in also caused me to reject some perfectly normal and healthy teenage activities. I ended up as kind of a self-exiled outsider. On the other hand, though, my faith kept me from making some of the bad choices some of my peers made."

Becky was quiet for a while, then said, "You know, I believe in God, but even if someone could prove that God didn't exist, I still think I'd want to live as a Christian. It's a good way to live."

"That's good thinking, Becky."

Nearing Richmond, we followed a road that led through beautiful neighborhoods of impressive homes and churches that resembled college campuses. In Richmond itself, this road became a narrow but heavily traveled thoroughfare, with neither shoulder nor sidewalk, so narrow, really, that we dismounted and walked the bike, hugging the edge of the road. Eventually a resident standing in his front yard directed us to a side street on which we were able to ride across the city without unreasonable competition from traffic.

We ate supper in Richmond, but decided to push on. According to the TransAmerica Trail map, a hostel existed near Glendale, the point where we'd rejoin the Trail, and we hoped to stay there that night. The hostel sat behind a church, and the map provided the phone number of the parsonage to call ahead to arrange for the hostel to be opened. When we phoned from Richmond, the pastor's answering machine picked up the call. Hoping she was simply out for a few hours, we continued toward Glendale.

Twice more we phoned, but with no success. By the second time, we were near the church and daylight was fading fast, so I left a message saying we were coming and hoped for the best. We arrived at the small country church, completing a 75-mile day, to find no one around and the hostel, a hut-type building behind the main edifice, locked. The adjacent parsonage was dark as well.

With little choice remaining, we pitched our tent on the church grounds and scurried in for the night. A good deal of the church's land contained a cemetery, which was unfenced and continuous with the lawn. The only spot offering much privacy and that was not actually in the cemetery itself was still a mere 10 feet from a headstone. I asked Becky if she'd be bothered by the proximity, but she said no. She did wonder if camping adjacent to a burial ground was disrespectful of the dead, but agreed we were out of options. I was interested that Becky had been uneasy about the sounds in the Palmyra church the night before but expressed no concern at all about sleeping near the dead.

The day had been warm enough that we'd again been able to peel off one layer of our cold-weather outfits, but as dusk turned to dark, the temperature fell rapidly. We donned all of our layers again, including even our scarves, added stocking hats, and burrowed into our mummy bags. Despite all that, we both became chilled during the night and slept fitfully.

———◦•◦———

We were awakened at daylight by the sound of aluminum ladders being dragged out of the church. A man had come to paint the trim on the building. The pastor, a middle-aged woman, stood nearby. She said "Good morning" only after I said it first. When I inquired if she'd heard my message on her machine (in which I'd mentioned that I was a UM minister), she acknowledged that she had, but then expressed neither interest in our presence there nor apology that the hostel had been unavailable. She was not unfriendly, but neither was she welcoming. Her manner was simply that of a busy person who didn't want to get sidetracked.

So why did it bother me? I wondered. No doubt because we had become accustomed to attracting friendly curiosity and attention at most of our stops. Waitresses and fellow diners where we ate, motel clerks where we stayed, storekeepers where we shopped, and strangers along the way all asked where we were going, where we started, how long we'd been on the road, and similar questions. The attention, I now realized, was addicting, so when our journey failed to provoke even mild marvel from this pastor, I felt as though I'd missed a "fix."

As we packed up, the sun shone brightly and the day began to warm appreciably.

We backtracked a couple of miles to catch breakfast at a grocery we'd noticed the night before. As I paid for our microwaved sandwiches, the clerk, a woman of about my age, glanced out the window at our two-seater and then back at us. "Grandfather-granddaughter team?" she inquired.

Becky giggled.

"No, this is my daughter," I said. The lady looked embarrassed and started to apologize, but I said, "It's the beard. It makes me look older. It's a common mistake."

Outside, Becky said, "Don't let it bother you, Dad. I don't think of you as old." The woman's question amused more than bothered me, but I appreciated Becky's concern that my feelings might have been hurt.

Pedaling past the church once more and on down the road, we observed several historical markers. Two Civil War battles, one in 1862 and another in 1864, had been fought in the area. Within minutes we passed a national cemetery and moments later, stopped at a National Battlefield Park, where the battle of Malvern Hill had taken place. At this location, a Union Army under General George B. McClellan, retreating from a failed attempt to capture Richmond, commanded the high ground. From this vantage point, the troops held off the attacking Confederates commanded by General Robert E. Lee, and inflicted massive casualties on the Southern forces.

Despite the now-stilled cannons parked in the tidy field, the peacefulness of the morning and the sparkling blue sky made it hard to imagine the site as a field of carnage. While we read the description of the battle on the display board, two friendly dogs showed up, and Becky spent several minutes trying to snap their photo with the weaponry in the background.

Back on the road, we at last found ourselves too warm in our tights, jerseys and sweaters, and thankfully stripped to shorts and T-shirts. We were again paralleling the James River, and now the highway offered us a flatland ride. Several old plantation houses, open to the public, made this highway that led to the restored 18th-century town of Williamsburg a popular byway for tourists. The historical attractions and wooded riverlands also accounted for the numerous bed-and-breakfast establishments along the road.

We paid with aches and soreness for the long miles on the bike the day before, and we stopped often to stretch and give rest to our saddle-weary bottoms, aching hands and, in my case, a stiff shoulder from too many hours hunched over the handlebars. Despite the frequent breaks, we arrived in modern Williamsburg by midafternoon, having logged 50 miles. The day was still warm, but needing showers and fearing the return of cold after sunset, we bypassed a campground for a motel on the edge of town.

The final morning: We had only the length of the Colonial Parkway between us and our end point. Since breakfast, we'd ridden the few miles to the re-created early settlement of Jamestown. The parkway, in an elongated "S," snakes across the peninsula between the James and York rivers, connecting Jamestown with Yorktown and tunneling beneath old Williamsburg on the way. On an earlier family vacation, we had explored all three locations, so we felt no compulsion to visit them now. The journey itself remained our objective. We set out with the rapidly widening James on our right. It would continue its course until it found freedom in the Chesapeake Bay.

Becky was pensive. On the motel television, we'd seen a 2-year-old girl, deemed newsworthy because she was the youngest person ever admitted to Mensa, the organization for people with genius-level IQs. "I kind of feel sorry for her," Becky now said. "She'll be 'different' her whole life, and that interferes with a lot of friendships." Referring to our former community, Becky added, "In Bellevue, I was marked as 'the smart one.' In a way I liked that, but it does tend to make other kids treat you as an outsider." The subject was especially poignant to Becky at the moment. The previous year, Becky's primary social group, a bunch of "brainy" kids, had suddenly spurned her following a painful incident over which she'd had no control. Their behavior was of the stupid, junior-high sort, but it had hurt Becky deeply.

In the year since, she'd been warily building a few new friendships with other teens, not part of the whiz-kid group, and she spoke of them now with appreciation.

I asked Becky her feelings about the incident itself. Speaking without the layer of emotion that had interfered with some earlier attempts to discuss it, Becky talked of what she had learned about herself and of the perspective she was slowly gaining about the situation. Clearly, the incident was a broken thread in the fabric of Becky's childhood, but I was cheered to hear how she was stitching around it so that the garment of her life remained intact.

Bikes are not permitted in the parkway tunnel. Instead, the TransAmerica Trail proceeds directly through Colonial Williamsburg. We parked the tandem behind the tent of a street vendor dressed in 18th-century garb and walked the streets for about an hour, revisiting locations recalled from our family holiday — though, not having purchased admission tickets, the only buildings open to us now were the stores. Becky pointed out the incongruity that with all the artisans practicing their crafts using methods from the colonial era, a garden on the main street was being readied for planting by a man in modern dress pushing a gasoline-powered tiller.

As we reclaimed the bike, a young woman approached us, asking the usual questions. She added, "I'm planning to start bike touring myself. I can hardly wait." We assured her that it was a great way to see the country — and at a pace that permitted a kind of intimacy with the landscape that car travel precludes.

The final stretch now: Continuing on the Colonial Parkway, we crossed to the other side of the peninsula and found the York River on our left. Though not as wide as the James, the York was at this point nearer to the bay than where we'd left the James, and the scent of the ocean floated on the air. In the distance, we could make out the outlines of the lengthy highway bridge that spanned the mouth of the York from Gloucester Point to Yorktown on our side of the river.

We rode the final mile and were soon on the lawn of the Victory monument that commemorated the surrender of British troops at Yorktown, bringing America's War for Independence to a close. We dozed, waiting for my sons to arrive to transport us home.

"How far have you come?" a voice asked. Stirred from my slumber, I looked up at the speaker, a Park Ranger (the Yorktown Battlefield is administered by the National Park Service). A long way, in terms of geography, but also a long way on the inner journey. I supplied the geographic answer at first, but when the ranger remained interested, I told him about turning 50 and realizing it was time to salve the ache to go and see.

"I can understand that," he replied. "I'm four years older than you are. I've always wanted to hike down the Grand Canyon, but I've got a touch of arthritis now. I may have waited too long. But there are still more things I want to do and more places I want to see."

"I hope you'll get to see them," I said. "Sometimes you have to just start."

"You're right about that."

As we continued to wait, I realized again what a wonderful touring companion Becky had been. Yet, since Williamsburg, I'd noticed that a tone of irritability began coloring Becky's responses. The trip together, I suspected, had been a temporary respite from the pressures of growing up. Now that we were about to re-enter the "real" world, the teenager struggling to demark the boundaries between herself and her parents re-emerged. But now I was comforted. The "other" Becky, the optimistic one with a keen interest in life, was still there, part of the mix of the young woman she was fast becoming. I had new hope that after the erratic course of adolescence, my beautiful daughter would be guided by the head and heart of the gentle but astute companion who'd pushed the pedals with me across this second leg of my ride across America.

Part 3

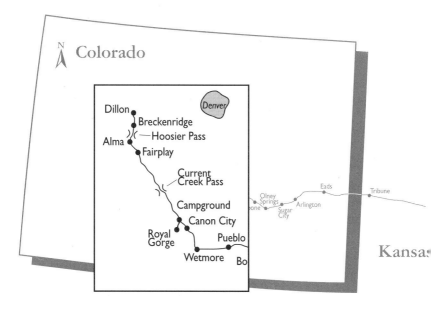

Chapter 21

ALTITUDE

On a journey that's as much inward as outward, a gap of 500 miles is beside the point — or so it would seem. But my decision to resume my trek in Colorado instead of returning to Wyoming felt like a betrayal of my original intent. In terms of available time, though, it made sense. I had just three weeks to cycle what I could of the TransAmerica Trail as it stretched across Colorado, Kansas, Missouri, Illinois and Kentucky. If I went back to Yellowstone, I'd likely get no farther than the Mississippi River before time ran out.

While I didn't like skipping a chunk of the transcontinental route, especially one promising Wyoming's beauty, I wasn't sorry to miss the midsummer congestion around Yellowstone — and the terrible roads in the park itself. But I wasn't ready to move out of the mountains yet, so in late July, I flew to Denver, where a friend drove me 50 miles west to Frisco, back on the bike route.

I arrived unsure of whether I was clever or foolhardy to relaunch there. Frisco perches at 9,000 feet, and I'd been back home long enough that I was no longer acclimatized to high altitudes. (My hometown rests at about 1,000 feet.) The bike map warned of possible headaches, insomnia and shortness of breath. But Frisco's elevation placed me well up the slope toward the Hoosier Pass crossing of the Continental Divide.

At 11,542 feet, Hoosier soars higher than any other point on the entire TransAmerica Trail. The bike map characterized this climb as "moderately difficult."

My decision was, as it turned out, foolhardy.

The ride began easily enough. Though the highway ascending to Breckenridge teemed with traffic, the well-paved bike path that paralleled it let me pump unimpeded all the way to the popular resort town. I shared the wide path with several recreational riders, most of whom sailed by heading downhill. Though the thin air seemed not quite sufficient when I pedaled rapidly, I did not find the climb difficult when I moderated my pace.

Breckenridge sprung into existence in 1860 when gold was discovered in the area, but today the gold it mines comes from the wallets of skiers and tourists. Its permanent population is less than 1,500, but I spotted numerous bike shops, bars, restaurants, outdoor stores, craft boutiques and other businesses aimed at tourists.

The town and the immediate area around it, known as Middle Park, were accidentally not included within the mapped boundaries as our nation, in its run toward "Manifest Destiny," staked its official claims in the West. The Louisiana Purchase included northwestern Colorado, but when the territory was divvied up into counties, the Breckenridge area was somehow overlooked. Nor was it addressed by the Adams-Onís Transcontinental Treaty with Spain, which established the boundary between Spanish territory the United States across the Rocky Mountains all the way to the Pacific Ocean.

In reality, of course, Americans had settled the area and long thought themselves part of the nation. But when the citizens of Breckenridge learned that their home ground might not officially belong, they looked into the matter. Miles of red tape later, in 1936, Colorado's governor held a ceremony in Breckenridge and proclaimed Middle Park a part of Colorado.

I pedaled through the village just a week shy of the 60-year anniversary of this event.

The word "park" is used differently in the West than in the rest of America. Here, it means a basin or open, level area surrounded by mountains, generally with enough good land to make grazing or farming possible. Because of the gap in my route, I'd missed Colorado's North Park, but after Hoosier Pass, I would wheel through South Park.

The path ended in Breckenridge, but so did most of the traffic, so pedaling on the highway beyond the community was less risky. I had recently switched to clipless pedals, so resuming the uphill journey after each rest stop now went smoother. I didn't have to fool with trying to get my feet into pedal cages that preferred to hang upside down. Ten miles still separated me from the summit, and the initial four of these passed under my wheels slowly as I labored upward.

Then my chain broke.

In itself, this was no catastrophe; I carried spare links and the necessary tool to repair the chain. But the break occurred because of a mistake I made in shifting, evidence that my thinking process was muddled. Each step of the repair seemed to require a separate unit of thought, and I felt as if I were standing outside my body, watching as I went through the necessary steps. I stood, still straddling my bike, looking back at the chain lying on the pavement. Slowly a thought formed: "Oh, I should pick up the chain." That done, it eventually registered that I should move the bike off the road. Likewise, each successive part of the repair process first had to be phrased in my mind before I could carry it out. And even after I replaced the damaged link, I threaded the chain back through the rear derailler incorrectly, an error I've never made before. Unquestionably, the reduced oxygen in the atmosphere was addling my brain.

When I returned home, I read a magazine article about

several climbers who had perished on a climb of Mount Everest earlier in the year. Although I was nowhere near the altitude at which they died (above 27,000 feet), I was able to identify with some of what the article said about thin air. It pointed out that the brain requires 20 percent of the body's normal oxygen intake, so that when there is less oxygen in the atmosphere, thinking can become confused. A test of climbers at 26,100 feet showed that they took half-again as long to understand a sentence as a 6-year-old would.

The crawl upward soon degenerated from challenging to agonizing. Rest stops, despite increased frequency and length, became successively less beneficial. Of greater concern was my growing sensation of nausea. A mile from the top, I surrendered all pretense of riding and began walking the bike, leaning on its handlebars for support. For the first time in my riding experience, I seriously entertained the notion of flagging down a car and asking for a ride, but I settled for resting every few yards. When I finally grimaced my way to the top, I felt as though I had the flu or had ingested some bad water.

Nonetheless, after a long rest that at least restored my breathing to normal, I asked a motorist stopped at the top to snap my photo next to the summit sign. For the shot, I forced a smile despite the dismaying swish of my gut and the sensation that my head was about to snap its tether and soar skyward.

Getting to a lower altitude now overwhelmed all other goals, so I mounted my bike for the six-mile lightning glide to Alma, the first town on the down route.

Initially I'd thought to aim for Fairplay, a slightly bigger and somewhat lower community only six miles beyond Alma, but when a gentle upgrade entering Alma forced me to begin cranking the pedals, powerful cramps seized my inner thigh muscles, making pedaling impossible. I limped into Alma where a citizen told me that I could camp anywhere beyond the last house on the town's single side street.

It was still early afternoon, and I'd covered only 25 miles. I hoped an extended rest might enable me to recover and proceed, so I dropped to the ground in the first available side-street clearing, unrolling only my sleeping bag and mattress pad.

In better health, I'd have never settled for the site. Almost next to the road, the uneven ground bulged with thorny weeds and dog droppings, and I'd no sooner stretched out than gnats swarmed on me. These forced me to pitch the screened portion of my tent and crawl inside for self-preservation. I dozed erratically until, after about three hours, I stuck my head out and vomited. This was not altogether unwelcome, for afterward, I began to feel better.

The leg cramps, however, continued, so severe that I could not even curl up fetal-like in my sleeping bag. I resigned myself to remaining in Alma till morning.

Picking my way gingerly to the town's general store, I purchased a beverage and sat on the bench in front sipping it. A local man of about 50 anchored the bench's other end. In quick succession he told me that Alma, at 10,363 feet, was America's highest community, that it had been built on mining, that Pullman of the Pullman railroad car fame had gotten his start mining here, that the town had dwindled after the gold petered out but was now growing again as a vacation-home area. When I mentioned my illness coming over the pass, he pointed out that at the town's altitude, the air contains one-third less oxygen than at sea level.

By evening, although my stomach still rebelled at the thought of a full meal, I was able to down a small pastry and a glass of milk at the local bakery/café.

I then installed the rain fly over the tent and slept, more or less, until daylight.

Before 7 a.m., I planted myself on a bench in front of the bakery, waiting for it to open. From my main-street vantage point, I noticed that almost without exception, each establishment had its front door right at the sidewalk. Those like the bakery that featured a front porch were forced to build it right over the walk. The total effect shouted "Old West."

An Alma resident joined me in waiting to get breakfast. Living so high had its challenges, he explained. "The snow gets pretty deep in the woods, but not too bad in town because the fierce wind blows it off the streets." What about working at this altitude? I asked. Do you get used to it? "Somewhat," he said, "but you get winded pretty quick. Like if you are digging a fence-post hole — pretty soon you'll have to stop and rest. You'll be all out of breath."

Once the bakery opened, the smell of frying potatoes enticed me in, but when I actually sat down to eat, another pastry was all that I could stomach. Still, I felt reasonably well.

The ride to South Park's Fairplay was mostly downhill, but contained just enough rises that I knew it would have been impossible to navigate them the previous day with my legs still cramping.

Fairplay, another mining town, earned its name from the idea that every miner should have the same right to stake a claim and protect his property. As boom went bust, the town bid for tourism by declaring itself the burro capital of the world, after the hardy little beasts of burden the miners had used. With some success, this questionable claim to fame gave the town a focus and did lure visitors. As it happened, I rolled into town in the midst of the "Burro Days" festival.

I stopped for hot tea in a café, and a man at the counter started telling me about the town. This husky, middle-aged chap sported long hair bound into a ponytail, a wild beard and a mustache with the tips waxed into an upward curve. He wore boots, jeans, a buckskin vest over a long underwear top and a derby hat. A single earring completed the ensemble. His job that day was to weigh in the burros for the race to the top of a 14,000-foot peak, a much feted event of the festival.

The race, beginning in Fairplay (America's third highest town, this community advocate told me), required each entrant to run alongside a burro for 15 miles up to the top and another 15 back. The race did not necessarily go to the swiftest runner because the burros sometimes refused to cooperate, and each runner had to stay with his burro for the entire course.

He urged me to stay to see the race, and I was tempted, but with only three weeks to ride this leg of my trip, I felt compelled to move on. All long-distance riders, but especially those on limited schedules, have to find their own balance between stopping to smell the roses and keeping faith with mileage goals. On the one hand, seeing the country is the point of the ride. On the other, too many lingerings mean that less country is seen. And balance is needed because the joy of the journey evaporates easily when pushing hard to cover distance for its own sake.

So I left Fairplay with mixed emotions. Another mostly downhill run took me through tiny Hartsel and then up a reasonable incline toward the final pass, Current Creek. Because the day's route gradually exited the mountains, I could not escape the feeling that the most majestic scenery loomed over my shoulder. Several times I stopped my bike, turned around, and drank in the view.

The landscape I traveled through, though mostly high-desert range, was obviously all privately owned. Although I saw no crops, almost no homes and few cattle, four-tiered barbed-wire fences paralleled the highway on both sides and the occasional gates were all chained and festooned with "No trespassing" signs.

Before reaching the last pass, I encountered a husband-wife cycling team riding westbound. John and Mary Sheldon, from New Hampshire, were riding the TransAmerica Trail while between careers. They hoped the trip would help them decide what to do next. We spent about 30 minutes exchanging information about the routes that lay behind us. I would see John's and Mary's names again and again in the bike logs certain merchants maintained along the route.

By late afternoon, I had covered 72 miles. Suddenly nausea returned and minutes later, the wind shifted, buffeting me with a strong headwind for the remaining five miles to the Royal Gorge area. With the returned illness, the struggle against the wind became a demoralizing, strength-sapping battle. As I ped-aled weakly up the last grade, another cycle-tourist pulled along-side. "Are you all right?" he asked. "You were wobbling pretty bad." When I explained that I wasn't feeling well, he suggested we stop and eat together. We pulled into a fast-food restaurant.

I ordered only milk and my new companion, Harrison, ordered coffee. Pulling supplies from his panniers, Harrison assembled and devoured three liverwurst, mustard and cheese sandwiches and one peanut butter and honey sandwich. My stomach did flip-flops as I watched him. Finally, however, I decided food might help me, and I ordered some. After forcing it down, I did feel a little better.

Between bites, Harrison, who appeared to be in his 20s, explained that he'd already ridden a good part of Europe and viewed cycling more as a "way of life" than as a "hobby" or a "sport." Harrison intended to ride farther yet this day, but first planned to detour to see Royal Gorge.

This stunning cleft in the earth is over 1,000 feet deep, with the Arkansas River churning through the bottom. Visitors come to see not only the gorge itself, but also the nearly quarter-mile-long suspension bridge, billed as the highest in the world, that spans the gap. Incredibly, the bridge isn't a link in any highway system. It was built in 1929 with private funds. Today it's the keystone of a tourist attraction that includes cable-car rides and an incline railway, all open to the public for a hefty fee.

Since the bridge really doesn't lead anywhere, to view it, Harrison and I would need to ride an eight-mile round trip into Royal Gorge park and back out. Though we set out together, Harrison immediately forged ahead, so that within minutes, when it became clear to me that I had not the energy to pedal the mostly uphill road to the park, he was nearly out of sight. I turned around and headed for the nearest campground. I did not see Harrison again.

I felt rotten most of the evening, so I did little more than just sit at the picnic table at my campsite and catch up on my log. For a few minutes, I visited with the couple camped next to me. In their 30s, this pair from Texas was vacationing on a motorcycle. Like me, they carried all their gear in saddlebags and tented each evening. The man pointed to my bike and said, "I told my wife to notice your narrow saddle. She complains occasionally about ours being uncomfortable." He indicated the broad double seat on his machine. "I don't see how you can stay on that tiny one."

I explained that for extended cycling, the skinny saddles are actually better than the wide-fanny versions, because they chafe less as the rider's legs pump up and down. Also, the small saddles are not mounted on springs, as some of the wide ones are. Because springs tend to subtract from the thrust of the rider's legs on the downstroke, the absence of springs allows the rider to expend slightly less energy on each revolution of the crank.

Still, he was right about the potential for discomfort with the tiny saddles on today's bicycles. Virtually every long-distance rider I know has been forced to try a few different designs until finding a seat that worked with the rider's particular anatomy. I went through four, each from a different manufacturer, until I finally settled on a leather saddle made in England. Even then, I had to ride on it for a few hundred miles before it became broken-in enough to be comfortable.

Lots of riders consider using a leather saddle retrogressing. The necessary break-in period and tendency to stiffen when wet are drawbacks of leather seats. Most modern saddles feature a foundation of plastic, padding of foam or gel and a covering of nylon, Lycra, suede or very thin leather. No break-in is required because they never change shape. Rather, the rider finds one that more or less conforms to his or her shape and gets used to it. I found one state-of-the-art saddle that worked reasonably well for me, but it was never as comfortable as my leather one. Like the cowboys of old, experienced cyclists might change "horses" from time to time, but they take their saddles with them from mount to mount.

By nightfall, the nausea subsided, and I slept soundly.

In the morning I felt nearly normal and ate a good breakfast. Leaving my gear at the campground, I rode to Royal Gorge on my unloaded bike. Aside from sweating profusely and becoming aware of a powerful thirst, I managed the journey all right. The view of the gorge and river from the free vantage point pierced me with a shudder of awe.

But I remained very thirsty. And neither water from my bottles nor a soda pop from a machine at the park entrance did much to slake it.

The day's continuing journey began with the final significant drop from the mountains. I coasted for nearly five miles on the wide shoulder of Highway 50, right to the edge of Canon City, and when the highway leading out of town snaked upward, I pedaled it easily, so much so that I pronounced myself cured. An unchallenging ride brought me to Florence, where I turned south for the 11-mile run to Wetmore. The directional change set me into the teeth of the wind, making this leg hard work. Still, I rode strongly, further evidence, I thought, that my bout of unwellness had fled.

This new road also led me into new terrain. Though still in sight of mountains, I now rolled through high, wind-blown prairie. A few miles from Florence, a vast, multibuilding prison complex occupied a huge campus, but big as it was, against the even lustier landscape, it seemed insignificant. What terrors, I wondered, did prisoners who'd grown up in cities feel when forced to live in the openness of a hardscrabble panorama broken only by dry arroyos and sagebrush?

A roadside plant caught my eye — a globe-shaped fruit growing on a ground vine. When I spotted the first plant, I assumed it was a melon that had volunteered from a seeded rind tossed by a passing motorist. But then I began seeing them often. Eventually I realized they were a wild gourd of some sort.

I hadn't been quite ready to eat lunch in Florence, which offered several restaurants, but the map indicated cafés in Wetmore, and I was famished by the time I got there. What the map neglected to say was that neither of the cafés nor the single grocery in that small community was open on Mondays. The nearest food, a citizen informed me, was back in Florence or 24 miles to the east in Pueblo. Fortunately, I had a can of beans with me that I heated up on the small emergency stove I'd added to my gear since my ride with Scott.

Or maybe not so fortunately. Not more than 10 minutes after leaving Wetmore, I began to feel sick again. The beans lay in my belly like an anchor, and when I drank water, it would not stay down. As I pushed on, my thoughts progressed from "Maybe I should get this checked out" to "I better see a doctor" to "I don't think I can even make it to Pueblo."

Because I was riding alone, my wife had insisted that I carry a cellular phone. I began to think I might have to use it. The last hill I climbed left me exhausted and desperately sick. But I knew from the mileage on my odometer that I had to be near Pueblo, and since a downgrade now unrolled before me, I decided to coast down, hoping the town sat at the bottom.

As the hill ended, I saw some edge-of-town settlements, but the highway spurted upward again, and I knew I couldn't climb it.

Across the road, some people worked on trucks in a garage. I levered myself off the bike and hobbled over. "Can you direct me to an emergency room?" I asked.

"What's wrong?" asked the older man, immediately concerned.

"I'm not sure. I'm biking through, but I've gotten sick."

With no more explanation from me than that, the man, who I later learned was named Randy Croft, took charge. He said, "Leave your bike here. We live right next door and we'll take care of it. My son will drive you to the hospital. It's still several miles away." His grown son, Aaron, pulled up in a car, and I crawled in. Randy handed me his business card inscribed with his home phone number. "Call me when you're released and we'll come and get you." Aaron floored it and drove me rapidly to the hospital.

The emergency room modeled efficiency. A nurse interviewed me within two minutes of my entry, a doctor checked me over three minutes later, and five minutes after that the first of three liters of intravenous fluid pulsed into my arm. "Chronic dehydration," the doctor diagnosed. "It happens easily at high, dry altitudes. There's not enough air pressure to keep the moisture in your body. You need to drink lots more water than usual when you're working as hard as you were at that height."

Later, after seeing my blood test results, she added, "You're severely dehydrated. Your enzymes and blood sugar are all out of whack, and your muscles were even starting to break down."

Five hours later, after finally squeezing out enough urine to prove that my functions were returning, I was released.

I phoned Randy. "You're not planning to go on tonight, I hope," he said.

"No. I should probably go to a motel."

"No need. You can stay with us as long as you need to. I'll be over to pick you up in a few minutes."

At Randy's home, I met his wife Shelly, who seemed not at all rattled that a stranger would be spending the night in her house. I'd be sleeping in their youngest son's bedroom. Jesse, their 4-year-old, usually ended up in his parents' bed anyway,

Shelly explained. I also met Adam, their teenage son, who had thoughtfully moved my bike inside the house because there had been a possibility of rain. After a hot shower, I dropped gratefully into bed.

———•◦•———

Jesse greeted me first in the morning. Randy, a building contractor, rose early each day for work, and Jesse made a habit of getting up with his dad. The two shared some private time together daily while Shelly slept a little longer. This morning, as I joined them, Jesse, who'd been asleep when I arrived the night before, was full of questions about my bike, so I showed him how I loaded everything up. Then I handed him my tire pump, and he laughed when I demonstrated how to squirt air onto his face. Later, when I was ready to leave, this cute, smart little guy solemnly replaced the pump on my bike. When he discovered that he couldn't quite figure out the Velcro strap that secured it, he told me about it, obviously worried that I'd lose the pump.

A good feeling permeated this household — a strong sense that the people who lived there cared about being a family. Randy told me that Shelly home-schooled their children, "not for religious reasons, but because of the gangs in the public schools."

Later, when I noticed Randy alone in the kitchen, I walked in and laid several bills on the counter. "I'd like you to take this. I really appreciate what you did for me. You may even have saved my life," I said without exaggeration.

"No," he replied. "I don't want it. I appreciate that you offered it, but I believe people have to take care of each other. We were glad to do it."

As the recipient of this generous philosophy, I was profoundly grateful.

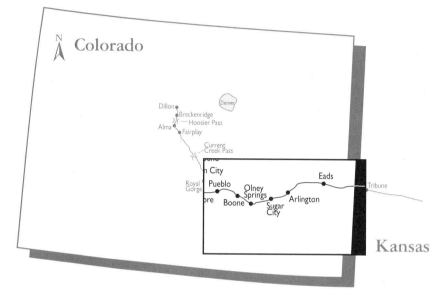

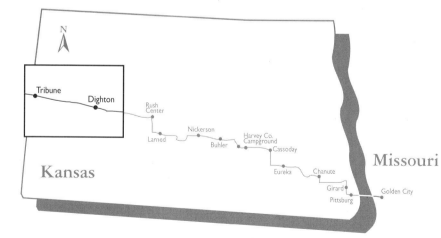

Chapter 22

DISTANCE

My stay with Randy and Shelly imparted a warm feeling about Pueblo, but as I rode east out of town that morning, an occupant of a passing pickup truck screamed in my direction in an attempt to startle me. Usually when people pull this unimaginative stunt, they make a fast getaway. Being still in town, however, the truck was stopped by the next traffic light and I overtook it. Peering into the cab at the young man in the passenger seat, I thought of several clever remarks about his IQ, maturity level and lack of creativity. But realizing that he'd probably take his revenge on the next cyclist he chanced upon, I instead tried an appeal to his rationality. "You know," I said, "one of these days you'll cause an accident that way."

"Maybe," he said. "Hopefully." Then the light changed and the truck pulled away.

I had too much to be thankful for to let him ruin my day, and I continued my journey with a light heart.

Approaching Pueblo the day before, I had gradually left the mountains behind. Now, beyond that city, the transition was complete and I pedaled out into a flat, dry land of grass and sand, greened only where irrigation showered life-giving water. Following Highway 50 and then Route 96, I paralleled the tracks of a railroad.

The terrain was a rail-builder's dream. Although Pueblo

sits just below 5,000 feet and the land basically descends all the way to the Mississippi River, the drop is so gradual as to be virtually meaningless over a distance of a few miles. Notwithstanding that each successive town I passed through across eastern Colorado displayed a slightly lower altitude figure on its highway sign, I felt as though I were on a level plain.

So flat was the land that whenever trains churned by, as they did several times a day, I could see the entire string of cars, even though it usually stretched for more than a mile. So flat was the land that I could sometimes make out the grain elevators of the next town while still within the environs of the one before it.

Still, when actually rolling over the surface, I found it undulating enough to require occasional gear shifting, though only within a limited range.

A few miles east of Pueblo, I stopped and looked back. Already the mountains had dropped below the horizon. I was truly on the Great Plains.

More than 20 miles stretched between Pueblo and Boone, the first town east. When I cruised into the welcome shade and green of Boone's small town park, I realized that in this land that hungered for detail, each community is an oasis, especially when one progresses between villages under one's own "horsepower."

In the brief time I spent in Boone, the community (founded by two of Daniel Boone's grandsons) displayed a few of the attributes that make small-town life appealing. In the park, several children, apparently participating in a vacation Bible school program, listened as an adult in a Bible-period costume told "his" story. Nearby, the proprietor of the town's only store hung a "Back-in-five-minutes" sign on the door while he strolled to the post office. A young girl rode past slowly on a bike, chaperoned only by the dog trailing behind her. A plaque in the park listed the sons of the community who had served in World War II. A gentle peace lingered in the air that not even the rumble of the train shuffling through disturbed. I left town only reluctantly.

Another 20 miles of riding delivered me to Olney Springs, where I bellied up to the lunch counter in Ding's Café, one of the don't-miss-it locations John and Mary Sheldon had recommended. Ding, the ebullient woman at the stove, welcomed me in speech garnished with a Mexican accent. She produced a notebook, her most recent volume of cyclist logs dating back to 1983, and invited me to write a comment. After entering a few words about my hoped-for destination, I scanned the recent entries and quickly found John's and Mary's appreciative remarks. The comment of another eastbound rider caught my attention as well. It said, "A journey of 4,000 miles begins with a stack of pancakes and one turn of the pedals."

My lunch was excellent, made even more memorable by the free slab of pie, a treat Ding extends to every cycle-tourist who stops in.

Olney Springs was the first of four closely spaced towns, each six miles apart, and I rode through them in quick succession. A green belt swathed the fields from Crowley to Ordway, the result of active irrigation, but the watering stopped abruptly before Sugar City, the last of the four. Named for the sugar beet, this final community had once prospered as a cog in the sugar-industry wheel. But the sugar plant was gone now, and the remainder of the village tottered aimlessly toward senility. Its business district consisted of a grain elevator, around which I saw no activity, a post office and a café with shades drawn against the afternoon sun, bearing only the name "Café" on a barely noticeable sign. Not one person was visible on the streets. Camping was permitted in the town's small park, but it offered neither water nor toilets. Food would not be available again until Haswell, 34 miles east, but I found Sugar City too depressing to linger. I settled for a quick lemonade in the café — only 40 cents a glass and free refills — then set off again.

To my dismay, I discovered that what had been a crosswind had shifted while I quaffed my lemonade. I now battled a stiff headwind. This strong and steady breeze from the east cut my average speed nearly in half and sapped my energy. Of necessity, I revised my plans. At this rate, I'd never reach Haswell before dark and would no doubt tire before then anyway. The map showed that Arlington, a settlement of a few houses and a part-time post office, sat on the highway 20 miles away, and I thought I could make it that far. Although the map indicated nothing about camping in Arlington, I figured I'd find something.

First, however, I returned to the Sugar City café and ordered a couple of burgers to go, for supper on the road.

Wind, when it blows strongly enough to impede progress, quickly becomes a major focus. It blustered against me powerfully now. Watching the mileage counter on my cyclometer gradually register higher, I counted each gained mile a victory and constantly refigured how far I had to go, as if that would somehow reduce the intervening distance. Grasshoppers, which all day long had been springing onto the blacktop — and occasionally into me — from the roadside grass, now became even more active, impelled by the gale.

When I had finally conquered half of the miles to Arlington, I sat on a bridge railing above a dry creek bed and ate my supper. Except for an occasional semi or a farm truck now and then, and a ranch house every 10 miles or so, I had the whole panorama — even if it was starved for variety — to myself.

Minutes later, alarm empowered my legs to push the pedals harder as the sky grew angrily dark. Able to see to the horizon in all directions, I suddenly felt extremely vulnerable. The wind was blowing a storm my way, and the monstrous thunderhead brooding to my left seemed to drop closer and closer to the ground. Was that a tornado developing beneath it or simply the imprint of a heavy shower? I couldn't be sure, but I labored against the wind with renewed commitment if not vigor.

Still, what harbor was I sailing for? I had no reason to expect shelter even if I reached Arlington. Traffic was so infrequent that I could count on no help from a motorist. What would come would come. If it was a tornado, I'd dive for the ditch beside the road. For anything else, I'd have to see ....

Suddenly, heavy drops pelted me. I dismounted hurriedly, jerked on my jacket and hunkered over my bike. Two minutes of dousing rain hurtled down on me followed by one minute of small hailstones, and then ... an abrupt clearing of the skies and a stunning rainbow spanning the road ahead. The storm moved rapidly away.

The wind remained, but after the terror of the preceding hour, it had lost its ability to command my attention. I slogged through it and reached Arlington at dusk, suddenly finding loneliness a greater adversary than breeze. Given that mood, I was glad the day was far gone. I'd soon be asleep, so there'd be little time to brood.

A minuscule colony of houses perched on the south side of the highway, but I saw no one at all. Even the houses showed little light. The train track unrolled on the north side of the road, but directly across from the houses, on the strip of land between pavement and rail, bloomed a small grove of trees. A pile of broken telephone poles had been jumbled into a clearing among the trees, bathing the air in "essence de creosote," but I found a spot beside the poles and erected my tent in the dwindling light.

If Arlington actually has any human population, you couldn't prove it by me, but within seconds of my taking up residence in the grove, a large, brown dog slithered out from under a fence across the highway and introduced herself by slobbering on my hand. She then settled down a few feet from my tent, apparently ready to share my squatter's rights.

My saddle had gotten wet while the storm dumped on me, so I took the can of mink oil I carried in my pannier and rubbed some into the leather. Then, as usual, I placed a plastic bag over the seat to keep it dry during the night. Riders on plastic-based seats are spared this latter precaution, but I never found it burdensome.

Exhaustion drove me into my sleeping bag minutes later, and though I awoke several times during the night when trains thundered by on one side of my tent and tractor-trailers whined by on the other, I quickly fell back to sleep. Toward morning, my canine companion, who'd apparently remained on guard outside my tent all night, cut loose with a high-volume bellow as she bounded into the brush to drive off some hapless intruder, probably a raccoon or a rabbit.

At daybreak, I crawled out of the tent and looked at the houses across the road. Although no one had been visible the previous evening, I assumed morning would bring people outside if only to drive off somewhere for work, but I still spied not one person. The settlement did not look abandoned, and the dog appeared fed and well cared for. Where were the people?

Finally, after I ate a meager breakfast from my emergency supplies, a work truck trundled in from out of town and pulled into the clearing. A logo on the cab's door identified the truck as a vehicle of the Union Pacific Railroad. The driver rolled down the window but remained in the cab, drinking coffee from a thermos. I decided to ask him a question about the railroad that had me puzzled. Walking to the truck, I said good morning. He responded in a friendly manner, so I launched my query.

"I've been wondering who owns this rail line," I said. "My map identifies it as a Missouri Pacific line, but the locomotives I've seen all say Southern Pacific. And your truck says Union Pacific. Which is it?"

"It's Southern Pacific-Union Pacific. They just merged. It hasn't been the Missouri Pacific for quite a while." He went on to observe that the move toward consolidation is rapidly reducing the number of railroads in America. He wasn't sure that mergers were a good idea.

Moments later, still having seen no residents in Arlington, I pedaled into the misty morning. The breeze blew from the south, giving me a manageable crosswind. Though visibility was not severely reduced in the gray light, distant objects lacked distinct outlines and vivid colors. I had little concern about traffic not seeing me; only two or three vehicles passed in the hour it took me to reach Haswell. Several trains rumbled by in that time, however, and the engineers invariably waved. Ever since Pueblo, the rail line had consisted of a single set of tracks, with only occasional sidings. Since rail traffic passed me in both directions, a command center somewhere had to be skillfully orchestrating train movement, shunting eastbound traffic onto sidings to permit westbound freights passage and vice versa.

The single source of food in Haswell was the gas station, which maintained a supply of microwaveable sandwiches. I wolfed two of them, washing them down with orange juice. The station was the only place with food of any kind in the 50-mile stretch from Sugar City to Eads, so most cyclists stopped there, as the station's well-worn bike log testified. "Did you have any bad weather back there yesterday?" the attendant asked. I told him about the dark sky and storm from the previous evening. "You were lucky," he said. "There was a tornado 12 miles south of there at about that time."

Before leaving town, I phoned my workplace from the station's pay phone. While coworkers were again covering my responsibilities, we had decided that I'd check in periodically to advise on any editorial snafus. Gladly, there were none. I reported my emergency room visit, which raised some concern, but I was feeling surprisingly well now and said so.

Beyond Haswell, the sun finally burned through, so that by the time I reached Eads, the temperature registered in the high 80s. With a population of about 900, and sitting at the crossroads of a state route and a federal highway, Eads was big enough to have a laundromat, so I stopped to wash my clothes.

Afterward, I ate lunch at a place labeled a "family restaurant," which during my visit, proved to be a euphemism for "bad service." From the moment I walked in, the waitress made it clear that waiting on me was an unwelcome intrusion into her own plans. This young woman stood talking to two women of similar age, neither of whom was working or dining there. I sat at the counter, and she kept right on conversing with her friends. Finally, when it became clear that I wasn't going to leave, she ambled over, stuck a menu in front of me, and without giving me time to read it, asked what I wanted. I'd already noticed a daily special, touted on a chalkboard on the wall, stating its availability from 11:30 to 1. It was now 1:15, but I thought there might be some left. "Can I still get the special?"

"No," she snapped, so I let her stand there while I read the menu and made a selection. She turned in my order and returned to her friends. Moments later, I saw my plate appear on the sill of the cook's window. The waitress, however, was too engrossed with her companions to notice. Eventually, one of the two left, which prompted my server to glance toward the window. She delivered my meal, immediately laid down my check, and wandered back to her remaining friend. After several minutes, an older woman stopped by and refilled my ice tea, but the original waitress never checked back at all. Good thing I didn't want dessert, I thought. I paid my bill and left without tipping, something I seldom do.

I beelined for the Kansas border. The next communities were little more than clusters of houses around grain elevators beside the tracks, and I whizzed through them all until Sheridan Lake, the final Colorado town offering a café. I stopped for supper, but even more because of a boil-soreness developing on my derrière.

With my well-broken-in leather saddle and usual comfortable riding shorts, I seldom have such a problem. But I'd been low on clean clothes when I'd dressed that morning, and had climbed into my only pair of padded cycling shorts. Despite the padding, these shorts never seemed as comfortable as my unpadded ones. After 65 miles, the padding now burrowed into the skin of my rump, making sitting in the saddle an ordeal. In the café restroom, I slathered petroleum jelly on the affected area and changed into unpadded shorts. I threw the offending pair away.

On a long-distance ride, a blistered bottom raises serious concern. World-class Olympic cyclists have had to drop out of competitions because of saddle sores, and the possibility of infection, especially in the less-than-perfect-hygiene conditions of camping out, is very real.

With 30 miles still to go, I winced back onto the bike and headed for Tribune, Kansas.

An hour later I crossed the Colorado-Kansas line, entering Greeley County, named for Horace Greeley, the 19th-century New York newspaper editor who had championed the working people of the plains. All three towns in the county also pay tribute to him. The small community of Horace lay just north of my route. Whitelaw, nearly on my route beyond Tribune, bore the moniker of an editor-friend of Greeley's. And Tribune, of course, so named for the New York newspaper Greeley founded in 1841 and edited for 31 years. Ironically, Greeley never lived in Kansas.

As I neared Tribune, the sky to the north darkened. Moments later, lightning streaked to the ground a few miles away. Before my trip, friends asked me if I was afraid about riding alone on low-traffic roads miles from "civilization." They envisioned problems from muggers, bandits or worse. Frankly, those things didn't worry me. But I confessed what did: tornadoes and lightning — at least when I was in their path. Seeing the latter now added urgency to my pace. Though 90 miles had already rolled under my wheels since morning, I surprised myself at how much energy I could still muster, evidence that my body had adjusted to the daily riding. I raced over the final five miles to Tribune.

The lightning and the probable storm with it convinced me that this was not a night for camping out. Instead, I checked into Tribune's lone motel. Once I dismounted, the saddle sores blazed with pain. Even the normal rub of the buttocks against each other as I walked hurt. Once in my room, I soaked in the bathtub. Afterward, using the full-length mirror to examine the damage, I was dismayed to observe twin rows of bright red blisters marching up my buttocks. Hoping for the best, I applied a fresh layer of petroleum jelly and went to bed.

The expected storm raged through town about midnight. Grateful that I was not in my tent, I turned over and resumed my slumber.

———◆◆———

The ointment helped some. By morning, walking no longer sparked pain, but sitting in the saddle all day would be another matter. After breakfast in a nearby café — where the storm from the night fueled the conversations around me — I headed for the drugstore and explained my problem to the pharmacist. He agreed that the petroleum jelly was a useful stopgap, but suggested that for riding, zinc oxide offered greater protection. And because of the possibility of infection, he recommended using an antibiotic cream at night. I purchased those products, returned to the motel, and layered on the zinc oxide.

Mounted up, I noticed twinges of pain, but not nearly as bad as the day before.

After an hour, I crossed into Wichita County and the Central Time Zone. On a bicycle, entering a new time zone always seemed momentous to me, a reminder that I was covering major chunks of America. Moments later I passed a train idling on a siding (a mile and a tenth long, according to my cyclometer) and recalled that the railroads were responsible for the adoption of America's time zones. Prior to the Civil War, communities ran on "solar time," but since that varied greatly, depending on where one was sighting the sun from, the nation consisted of a mind-boggling mishmash of local times. For every 13 miles west, sun time became a minute earlier. Wisconsin, for example, had 38 different time zones, which made issuing a schedule for train arrival times a nightmare.

After the British standardized their time on that of the observatory in Greenwich, an American professor, C. F. Dowd, proposed four time zones for this country, calculated from the Greenwich Mean Time. In 1883, the railroad industry adopted Dowd's plan, and soon communities began setting their clocks by "railroad time." Congress finally made the whole arrangement official in 1918.

In general, each time zone spans 15 degrees of longitude, but the borders often bend to conform to political boundaries. Given that, I could think of no reason why Greeley County and the slice of state north and south of it were not in the Central Time Zone with the rest of Kansas.

In any case, I set the clock in my cyclometer ahead one hour. Some riders don't bother with timepieces on tours, welcoming the journey as an escape from the tyranny of schedules and relying instead on the rhythms of nature and the signals from their bodies for when to eat and sleep. I've never felt that way about clocks. I don't worry about the time for deciding when to eat, but knowing the hour of the day helps me to estimate whether I have enough daylight and energy remaining to push on to the next community, which may be a couple dozen or more miles away.

Dry desert ranges gradually gave way to greener farmland, and more of the towns, though still widely spaced, thrived. Occasional stockyards dotted the roadside now, and the stench blowing off them encouraged me to pedal by rapidly.

I still rode Highway 96, the route I'd joined at Pueblo. It would convey me all the way to the middle of Kansas. Since

Tribune, it bore a bit more traffic than previous stretches. The road's mile markers interested me. Here in Kansas, they appeared with regularity each mile, numbering upward from the state's western border. According to my bike's odometer, each marker was planted accurately, seldom more than one- or two-hundredths of a mile off the mark. In eastern Colorado, however, the markers appeared to have been set by a wino on a three-day binge; many were missing, and when one did occur, it was never an even number of miles from the previous one.

This Kansas land unfurled even flatter than eastern Colorado. I seldom shifted gears. For most of my way across the state, the wind blew from the south or southwest. (Appropriately, Kansas is named for a branch of the Sioux Indians called the Kansa or Kaw, which means "people of the south wind.") This south wind meant that I never had a tailwind while crossing Kansas, but no headwinds either, except when the TransAmerica Trail occasionally stepped southward. The challenge of cycling now came from neither mountains nor wind, but from distance itself. Each day's journey defined itself by how long I could stay on the bike.

I rode under a remarkable sky. Neither trees nor man-made structures interrupted my view to the horizon over the full 360-degree circuit. The unmarred sky above was pure blue, and the only clouds were small cotton puffs just above the line where earth and sky met. It was as if a giant, radiant-blue bowl with small, white Wedgwood ornamentation on the rim only, had been inverted over the land.

As the sun moved across this matchless sky, I couldn't help but recall some words from the 19th Psalm:

> The heavens are telling the glory of God; and the firmament proclaims his handiwork ….
>
> In the heavens he has set a tent for the sun, which comes out like a bridegroom from his wedding canopy, and like a strong man runs its course with joy.

> *Its rising is from the end of the heavens, and its circuit*
> *to the end of them; and nothing is hid from its heat.*

While the absence of trees in western Kansas meant that I, too, could not hide from the daystar's heat, on this beautiful day, I understood how the psalmist could liken the movement of the sun across the sky to a strong man running his course with joy. For me, the sky sang with gladness.

Of course, the lack of shade made my rest stops less comfortable, but with the temperature only in the 80s, stopping in sunlight proved bearable. Finding a *place* to stop, though, required flexibility: For all the open space, remarkably little of it was not given over to one use or another. The narrow shoulder of ground immediately adjacent to the highway sprouted gravel. A drainage ditch lay just beyond that, and crops or plowed fields started at once on the other side of the ditch. I usually rested by standing on the shoulder.

The rail traffic continued unabated in western Kansas until I reached Scott City. Although the tracks continued beyond the town, I saw nary a train after that. Later, I learned that the SP-UP Railroad had shut down operations on that line. The woman who told me this clearly disapproved of the decision. Her comments recalled those of the railroad truck driver I'd talked to in Arlington, Colorado. He'd also had reservations about the wisdom of rail-line mergers. As I continued my ride, I passed a number of stranded grain elevators beside the disused tracks. I wondered if they'd be able to carry on with truck service.

My saddle sores, while less fiery today, still made their presence felt. At midday, in the restroom of a small-town Catholic church, I reanointed the pertinent areas with zinc oxide.

By Dighton, I'd ridden nearly 75 miles. There was enough daylight left to push farther, but the town looked inviting, and I figured an early stop would benefit my rear end.

Like many towns in the Midwest, Dighton permits cyclists

free camping in its city park, as well as use of the community swimming pool and the pool's showers without charge. I set up my tent near the large picnic shelter — always a prudent idea in country where storms arise with little warning. I'd learned that the storm that had lashed Tribune during the night had then pounded east and mauled Dighton as well. A citizen walking by as I made camp commented that a cyclist who'd camped in the park the previous evening had apparently been forced from his tent to the shelter by that downpour, "although I don't know how he stayed dry even in there," the man added. This remark puzzled me. The shelter was huge — at least 40 feet by 60 feet — and in good condition. Surely the rain wouldn't have penetrated to the center of that area, I thought. But I was later to learn firsthand that even a solid roof overhead does not guarantee shelter from Kansas storms.

After a shower in the pool house and dinner at the bowling alley, I returned to the park, planning to read. A middle-aged couple eating sandwiches in the picnic shelter, posed the usual questions (Where was I riding from? Where to? How far each day? etc.) and then offered me a sandwich. I declined, explaining that I'd already eaten. They told me they'd arrived early for the annual Lions Club family ice-cream social and that soon many others would descend on the shelter. Wishing I'd not set up so close to the shelter, I drifted off to a table on the far side of the park.

Numerous families soon overflowed the shelter, and after a few minutes, two men approached where I sat. One introduced himself as the president of the club and the other as the past president. "And we'd like you to join us for some homemade ice cream and cake," the president said. Pleasantly surprised, I agreed immediately. Back at the shelter, the two introduced me to several other club members, all of whom greeted me warmly. One handed me a bowl, and another began ladling ice cream into it, direct from the hand-cranked freezer it had been made in. They pointed to the table covered with cakes, from which I selected something oozing with fudge. When I'd emptied the first bowl, several people urged me to have more, so I manfully accepted seconds and managed to consume all of that as well.

One of the men told me that almost every family present was involved with agriculture in some way, so between bites, I asked about some of the things I'd noticed since Tribune. Some fields appeared freshly plowed, but it was already August 1, surely too late to be just now planting crops.

"No," one man responded. "The harvest is over on those fields. They'd have had wheat, which is planted in the fall. It sprouts in early spring."

I read more about that later. Before 1870, Kansas farmers had lost a lot of crops to insects and drought. But during that decade, Mennonites migrated into the state from Russia, bringing Turkey Red, a variety of winter wheat, with them. Sown in the fall and harvested in early summer, it was already into grain bins before most of the insects and heat struck.

"I expected to see a lot of corn," I said, "but most of what I see is a crop that looks something like corn, but only half as high."

"That's milo," another explained. "We had an unusually dry spring, and the corn didn't come up. A lot of us had to plow it under. We've planted milo as a catch-up crop, so we have something to harvest." Milo, I learned, was used for animal feed.

The first man said, "We have to practice what's called 'summer fallow' here. We don't get enough moisture to have a crop but every other year. So basically we only plant half of our land each year."

"That explains why some fields I saw had no crops but weren't plowed either."

"Yes. We try to control the weeds in the off year, but that's about all."

By 9 p.m., I had the park to myself. I turned in, grateful for the unexpected kindness of the citizens of this small town.

Chapter 23

DINING

The small towns of America don't, as a rule, offer fast-food restaurants, discount stores and especially not bicycle shops, but those that are thriving at all boast a sense of "center," some locus where even a visitor can sense the verve of the community. Sometimes that hub is a grocery or general store, but more often, it's someplace that serves meals.

Depending on local custom or whimsy, these establishments may be dubbed restaurant, café, cantina, bistro or diner, but they have in common that they bear absolutely no resemblance to a seen-one-you've-seen-them-all franchise, and they serve as a gathering point for area residents.

I have seldom dined in a small-town café I didn't like. Usually untouched by interior decorators, the decor often appears to have "just growed" and may include some odd mismatches of paint, paneling and wallpaper. There's generally a serving window or simply an open door connecting the dining area with the kitchen, and you can usually catch at least a glimpse of the cook at work, especially if you sit at the counter. When cycling alone, I especially like the counter, where I can be a single patron but still sit with people and sometimes join a conversation.

Those serving the food are generally female, and not one of them begins with the cutesy "Hi. I'm Tammy. I'll be your server today." They're still comfortable being called waitresses, although more often, since all the locals know each other anyway, they are simply referred to by their names. And their first word to customers is something more welcoming than identifying their serving function: It's "Coffee?"

The menu, if not just scrawled on an erasable wall board, is a typewritten affair in a plastic pocket folder, sometimes with a handwritten daily-special sheet tucked in as well. While food selection is often limited, with some restaurants depending too much on sandwiches and fries, those that offer a wider choice generally adhere to rib-sticking basic dishes, offered at a reasonable price. The noontime $3.95 special is likely to be meatloaf with mashed potatoes and gravy and a side of baked beans or coleslaw. Homemade chicken noodle tops the preferred soup-of-the-day list, with bean and ham vying with chili for second place.

When serving the food, the emphasis is on getting it out fast and hot. Nobody pays much attention to "presentation," and rarely does a garnish clutter the plate. But there's always plenty of coffee and always, always pie. On day rides, there's enough nourishment in a café meal to wipe out the calorie-burning benefit of the cycling itself, but on longer tours, where cyclists actually burn more calories than they can consume, these meals are welcome succor.

In his now classic travel narrative, *Blue Highways*, William Least Heat Moon reported judging the food quality of diners by the number of calendars on their walls: the more calendars, the better the food. But since so many insurance agencies and grain elevators have stopped giving out free calendars, Moon's standard no longer seems reliable. Dayton Duncan, another traveler-author, looked for restaurants identified by the owner's first name, as in "John's Café." But bike routes run through towns so tiny that often there's only one dining establishment to choose from, regardless of its name. So for cyclists, the meal quality is whatever it is, which is part of the adventure. I've more often been pleased than disgusted.

But more important than savoriness and decorating scheme is that these diners serve as the hearths of their communities, gathering places much as home kitchens once were when mothers could stay home. Small-town eateries percolate with life. Breakfast brings a mix of people nursing cups of coffee and exchanging exuberant greetings and quiet small talk. Working men predominate among the noon crowd, feeling no compunction about keeping their farm caps on or raising their voices — though the volume is driven more by camaraderie than rowdiness. Families frequent the diner for the supper hour, where the sound level is again mellow. If you've ever spent a night in a one-café town, you soon learn that a perceptible energy-dissipation occurs when the place closes for the evening.

So much does a café sustain the heartbeat of a town that even if other businesses shut down for good, the community can retain the sense of vitality that marks it as a locale of hospitality and human concourse — the stuff of life itself — as long as the café stays in business.

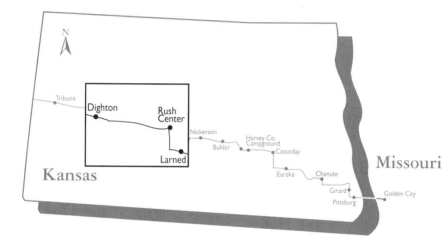

Chapter 24

WEATHER

With my gear packed on the bike, I returned to the bowling alley for breakfast. A sign on the cash register read, "If you are grouchy, irritable or just plain mean, there will be a $10 charge for putting up with you." Another, on the wall, stated, "All whining must be submitted in writing. No verbal whining accepted." And a very efficient waitress, with rings on every finger of both hands except the third finger of her left hand, cheerfully took orders and delivered meals to the customers.

A pad of blank checks bearing the name of the local bank lay beside the register. One man simply filled one out to pay for his breakfast. The waitress accepted the check willingly, without asking for identification. Another convenience of small-town life.

The pharmacist's two-ointment prescription had worked; my saddle sores were nearly healed. Though I still basted the pertinent area with zinc oxide before riding, I expected to discontinue its use soon.

But I now found it uncomfortable on the bike for other reasons. The long-distance days demanded dues, and I paid them now: My hands cramped no matter where I placed them on the handlebars; my arms, which served as shock absorbers, throbbed; my back ached from too much time spent hunched over the front wheel; the muscles of my legs felt tight; the balls of my feet hurt where I pushed on the small, clipless pedals. I swallowed some ibuprofen and pushed on.

For the first time since I entered Kansas, the land offered some modest rise and fall. I shifted gears a notch or two as I cruised over the gentle swells. Long distances still intervened between communities, and though I rode 96 miles this day to Larned, the only community of much substance I encountered in between was Ness City (population 1,800), 32 miles beyond Dighton.

Somewhere between the two towns, I crossed the 100th meridian, which is generally considered the dividing line between the semiarid high plains and the more humid lowlands. According to the bike map, the average annual rainfall west of the line is only five to 20 inches, while east of it, as much as 20-25 inches falls each year.

The day passed unremarkably as my bike devoured the miles to Rush Center, a crossroads settlement where I would finally leave Route 96. (Actually, the TransAmerica Trail traversed seven more miles of this highway, but roadwork beginning at Rush Center necessitated a detour.)

Rush Center boasted a few houses, a small park, a garage, a café and a grocery. I headed for the grocery, seeking supper. I was surprised by a sign in the window reading "NO BIKES," the first such prohibition I'd seen anywhere across America. I left my bike parked directly below the sign and walked by another that stated, "Bicyclists not to loiter." Inside, I bought and microwaved a sandwich, and felt no hostility from the clerk. I wanted to ask her what the story was behind the signs, but a string of customers kept her too busy for small talk.

The entire route to Larned ran through open country; there were no towns in between. Turning south, I now faced 19 miles into the teeth of the wind. I'd been dreading that all day, and the actual ride proved to be as tiring as I expected. Like other times when I found myself slogging along on a road made difficult by wind or grade, I recalled a bit of wisdom I'd learned from my father: Beware the path of least resistance — for it often leads in the wrong direction. Since I was clearly headed in the way of most resistance, I knew I must be going the right way! Of course, my dad was referring more to life choices than to highway directions, but the aphorism seemed to fit.

Given what happened next, though, I would have gladly swapped this difficult passage for an easier one. About an hour after leaving Rush Center, I noticed the sky behind me beginning to darken. I hoped it would stay behind me as I plodded on.

When I'm alone, late afternoon under a dull sky sometimes affects me unlike any other combination of time and atmospheric conditions. It strikes a chord of loneliness within me; it withers my confidence and calls into question the wisdom of current endeavors. As I continued riding now, the combined power of waning day and darkening sky clamped me with a nameless despair.

It didn't last long, however, for a more immediate concern soon replaced it. Each time I glanced over my shoulder, the darkness above seemed to have crept closer. The surface winds may have been against me, but the winds aloft were clearly flowing my way.

Finally completing the southern run, I again swung east, heading directly for Larned on Route 156. This meant that the gray firmament was no longer behind me, but to my left. Soon I saw lightning streaking to the earth from the furious clouds. Sometime in the next minutes, the cloudbank bridged the highway, skyrocketing my anxiety level as lightning now bolted groundward on my right as well. Surrounded by this frenzy, I lost all concern about aches and weariness and pushed the pedals fast and hard. Highway 156 bore a moderate amount of traffic, including semi-trucks, so in the growing darkness, I turned on my flashing taillight. As I passed Fort Larned State Park, a park ranger waved me over to his vehicle. "We've got terrible weather coming," he said. "You better get off the road."

"Gladly. I'm trying to get to Larned." The map showed nothing closer.

"You've got six miles to go. Hurry!" he urged.

In the next minutes as I rode wildly, lightning began jumping from cloud to cloud, a display I'd have enjoyed from safe shelter. I now smelled ozone in the air. Numerous vehicles passed me, including several pickup trucks with empty beds. Given the ominous sky and my obvious vulnerability, I was rather surprised that no one offered me a ride. One pickup, in its own race for safe harbor, even ran me off the road, the driver blasting its horn angrily as it roared by.

Ironically, the most comfort came from the one driver with too small a vehicle to take on a bike and rider: a young man on a motorcycle. As he passed, he tooted and gave me the thumbs-up signal, which I somehow found immensely encouraging.

Still feeling like a rolling lightning rod, I finally reached Larned, where several people gazed uneasily at the sky. Bypassing the attractive town park where camping was free, I hurried instead to a motel.

Fifteen minutes later the storm pummeled the town furiously. Rain, seemingly like the flow of Niagara Falls, hit us at the same time as did a high-speed gale. Looking out, I saw roof gutters, business signs, tree limbs and assorted other flotsam whiz by in midair. Although a six-foot-wide overhang projected beyond the front of my room, water, driven horizontally, beat relentlessly on my window. Just as the town's tornado sirens began wailing, a mighty clap of thunder and a flash of light erupted nearby and the electricity died. I began to wonder where I'd go if the storm suddenly lifted the roof off the motel. Moments later I heard emergency sirens and spied the reflection of red-and-blue flashing lights. I could not remember ever being in a worse storm.

Nature's fury lasted perhaps 45 minutes, and when it ended, we denizens of the motel emerged with flashlights and candles lit. The entire town was without power.

The emergency vehicle lights still flashed nearby so I rounded the motel to find out why. An electric company line-man in a cherry-picker bucket was aloft severing a power line to an adjacent house, around which firemen worked, removing siding with axes and crowbars. "The house was hit by light-ning," said a middle-aged man standing beside me. "I saw it happen from my motel room. It hit the pole, traveled right around the house on the wiring, and set the place afire."

I started to ask a question, but the man launched again. "I figured I'd better check it out. So I ran over and knocked. A lady called out for me to come in. She was 90 years old and stuck in an electric recliner. With no power, she couldn't get it forward and get out of it. I carried her out."

"Good thing for her you saw what happened," I offered.

"Yep. 'Course, since I served three tours of duty in Vietnam, I don't get rattled easily. It's all in a day's work."

As he spoke, I caught the smell of beer on his breath. He'd done a good thing in rescuing the woman and was enjoying the chance to retell it. We walked back to the motel and he point-ed at the pickup in front of his room. "The storm dumped a limb on the windshield. Cracked 'er right down the middle."

"Too bad."

"No problem. I got insurance."

Just then, a couple in their 30s came up. "Are you the cyclist?" the woman asked. When I said I was, she said, "We passed you riding into town, and I wondered if we should offer you a ride. I was hoping you made it."

"If you had, I would have accepted. But thanks."

"What happened back there?" asked the man, nodding toward the fire truck.

"The house was hit by lightning," the rescuer said. "I saw it happen from my motel room. It hit the pole, traveled right around the house on the wiring, and set the place afire. I figured I'd better check it out. So I ran ...."

At that point, I drifted away. Moments later, I heard the woman say, "Wow. Good thing you were there." The hero responded with some comment about Vietnam. Later, he and the pair sat in front of the couple's room, drinking beer the rescuer had retrieved from his truck. He had an appreciative audience, and I could hear snatches of his story being retold.

With the town still in darkness, I went to bed and slept soundly.

Awake before 7, I found the town still without electricity, but by the time I'd packed, the power came on. Aftermath of the storm littered the town. Smashed restaurant signs lay shattered in the road along with roof shingles, twisted pieces of metal and broken glass. Major limbs had been wrenched from nearly every tree in sight.

In the grocery where I ate breakfast, a local woman, seeing my biking attire, inquired where I'd been during the storm. (Four others sought the same information before I left town.) I asked her if such storms were typical of the area. "Not at all," she replied. "I haven't seen one this bad in years."

As I rode out of the motel lot, I happened to glance at the rescuer's pickup, which I'd been unable to see clearly the night before. The items in its bed summoned immediate recognition. The truck was the one that had run me off the road the previous evening.

I laughed heartily as I rode out into the new day.

Chapter 25

DOGS

There is something in the nature of many dogs that makes them think they must attack, or at least threaten to attack, anybody who rides a bicycle past their home ground. Perhaps it is an admirable instinct to protect the master's property that impels a canine to challenge a cyclist, but to the rider, who is posing no threat to the property, it seems like the dog is picking a fight. My theory is that domestic dogs live fairly boring lives and view cyclists as an opportunity for a little "fun."

Cyclists have developed numerous defensive strategies. The earliest bike/dog encounter I recall occurred when I was 12, riding with my friend, Jimmy. It was a hot day, so we'd taken canteens of water along. Jimmy happened to be swigging water out of his canteen when a large, ferocious-looking dog charged us, barking fiercely. Jimmy spit a mouthful of water on the dog's head, and the animal immediately ran home with his tail between his legs.

There are additional weapons. The usual first line of defense is shouting. What you shout is not important, so long as you shout fiercely and loud. This will frighten or confuse some dogs, who will give up the chase. The shout may also alert the animal's owner to call the dog back.

A variation on this tactic is a small foghorn attached to a gas canister, which emits a frightful sound when the release button is pressed. I carried one of these for several months, but the first time I really needed it, all the gas had leaked out. Doggone!

Speed is another weapon, but it's mostly effective against small dogs with short legs. In a short stretch, the big bowsers can outrun a bike, even the lightweight, skinny-tire, multi-speeds we ride today.

When riding with another cyclist, your position in relation to the other rider has a bearing on how much you're bothered by untied dogs. The safest place is in the lead. When a dog spots you, he charges, but by the time he reaches the street, the second rider has arrived on the scene, while you are pulling away. Most of the time, the dog will turn his attention to the closer bike. Of course, you'll have to offer your companion some noble-sounding reason for always wanting the lead position.

Yet another weapon is the tire pump most cyclists carry. Trying to swing this at a dog while keeping your bike upright, however, is quite a feat.

My choice is a small spray can containing a pepper spray that stings the dog's eyes, but does not harm him. (Postal carriers use this same stuff.) Unfortunately, this doesn't work well when the wind is blowing the wrong way. When you do manage to squirt it anywhere near a dog's eyes, he usually stops abruptly, with what I can only describe as a confused expression. But I have encountered a few big dogs who seemed unfazed even by direct hits.

Occasionally you can head off a problem simply by giving up the race. You stop riding, get off the bike, and walk past the ground the dog is defending. (It's wise to keep the bike between you and the dog.) The animal will likely keep barking, but with some dogs, it seems that when you are no longer moving rapidly, all the fun is taken out of the chase, and the continued barking has a "and-see-that-you-don't-come-back-again" ring to it.

For those mutts who continue to, well, hound cyclists no matter what, there isn't much defense. It's part of the risk of the sport. And being bitten is not the only risk. A cyclist friend of mine broke his arm when he swerved his bike and fell off trying to avoid hitting a bunch of friendly puppies who swarmed around him.

There are also a few dog owners who will stand in their yard and watch, without even calling their dog, while the animal chases some hapless rider. It makes you wonder who ought to be tied up.

On one ride, I labored up a long hill. Near the top was a hedge. As I passed it, a huge, brown dog hurtled out of the hedge; the sneak had been lying in wait for me. Before I had time to even reach for my can of spray, the brute plowed into me broadside, sending me crashing onto the road. He then ran off.

At that point, a woman, hearing the commotion, came out of the house and called the dog, saying "Here, Goliath. Here, Goliath." She made a big fuss over whether the dog was hurt. (He wasn't.) Only belatedly did she ask if I was okay.

Dogs are a lesson in "acceptable risk." For all the times I've been barked at in four decades of riding, I've never been bitten. Others have, of course, but on balance, the barked-at-biker to bitten-biker ratio is quite small. And the very qualities that make dogs a threat to cyclists — loyalty to their masters and a passion to protect the homestead — are what endear them to their owners. I wouldn't want those qualities eliminated to reduce the threat to me, the cyclist, even if it were within my power to do so.

Dogs and their threat remind me that no journey is totally without risk, but when the risk is generally manageable, riders are poorer who let the *possibility* of trouble deter them from the trip.

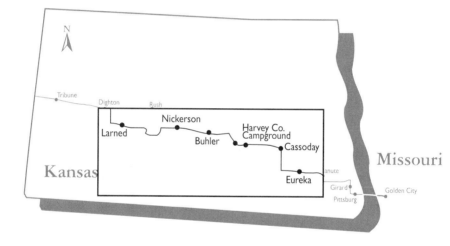

Chapter 26

COMPANION

L arned is almost halfway across Kansas, in the region of the state that receives more abundant rainfall. East of Larned, trees, which had been almost nonexistent in the western part of the state, appeared regularly, sometimes in significant copses. And the landscape became even more verdant the farther I traveled. The route for the day followed a series of county roads.

After 20 miles, I stopped at an intersection to snack from my supplies. A couple of minutes later, another cyclist with loaded panniers pulled in behind me. "Hi. I'm David Barnas," the tall, slender, young man said.

I was delighted. I'd not seen another cycle-tourist since my brief encounter with Harrison at Royal Gorge, Colorado. David said he'd seen no riders since Colorado either.

Since David was also coming from Larned, we naturally compared experiences of the storm. David had arrived in the town in midafternoon under sunny skies, camped in the park, and swam in the pool. As the skies began to darken, a lifeguard from the pool told David of the forecast and invited him to spend the night in his home. The two hurriedly threw David's bike and equipment into the lifeguard's truck and abandoned the park. Good thing, too, David said. He'd heard that the park had been especially hard-hit by the tempest.

"Want to ride together for a while?" David asked.

"Sure," I said, "but since I'm older, you might find me holding you back. If you do, don't feel you have to stay with me."

"I don't think it will be a problem," David said generously.

David was 23, the same as my oldest son and less than half my age, but he exhibited none of the frenetic know-it-all-ism that characterizes some young adults. As we pedaled on, David's story emerged. After graduating from high school, he'd had no idea what he wanted to do next, so rather than go to college, he'd taken a warehouse job and began saving money from each pay toward a cross-country bike trip. It had taken him a few years to accumulate enough, but this year he'd been ready. He'd taken a train from his family home in Buffalo, New York, to Oregon and began riding from there. Like me, he'd been following the TransAmerica Trail, but he planned to leave it in Kentucky and strike northward through Ohio and Pennsylvania to Buffalo. He hoped some clear direction for his life would surface from this journey.

"Has it?" I asked.

"Not yet. It's funny. Here I've been able to do this trip, which is something hard, and stick to it, but I haven't been able to find anything I want to stick with for the rest of my life."

"Maybe you're thinking about too big a period of time," I suggested. "A lot of people don't stay with one career forever. Try to find something that satisfies you now, but don't go into it thinking you can't change directions later."

"That might help," David said.

We stopped in Hudson, a tiny town on the railroad, for lunch. David was a vegetarian, he explained, and being on a small budget, had been preparing most of his own meals, but he went in the café with me. While I ate a dinner from the menu, David made peanut butter and jelly sandwiches from his supplies, ordering only a drink.

Apparently David had originally been a day or two ahead

of me. I'd overtaken him because of the longer-mileage days I'd been riding. Since David had no time limit on his journey, he hadn't felt my need to go as far as fast. He was the author of the "stack of pancakes" quote I'd noticed in the Ding's Café log in Colorado. And he was also the biker who'd slept in the Dighton park shelter the night before my arrival there, the one the Dighton citizen had mentioned and wondered about how he'd stayed dry in the storm.

"I didn't stay dry," David said. "You saw how big that shelter was, but the wind blew the rain in from every direction. Everything I had got soaked. Finally I wrapped all my stuff in a tarp, ran to a house, and asked if I could stay there until the storm ended. When it was over, they loaned me a dry sleeping bag and I returned to the shelter and spent the rest of the night on a picnic table. The people in the house had my stuff all dried for me in the morning when I returned the bag."

David spent the next night in the community park of Rush Center, the town where I'd seen the "NO BIKES" sign. He learned the reason behind it. Apparently a previous cyclist, in the absence of showers at the park, performed a sink wash in the grocery's restroom, messing the place up in the process.

We got so involved in conversation that I forgot to refill my three water bottles before I left the café. I still had some water left in one bottle, but not enough to carry me to the next town. David freely shared his with me, but soon we were both out. Fortunately, houses appeared more often now than in western Kansas, and though we found no one home at the one we tried, we were able to get water from a garden hose outside.

Moments later, we encountered a westbound rider, Jon, who was about David's age. The three of us exchanged route information, and I made note of a couple places Jon recommended for overnight stops.

As we rode on I looked at David's bike. From its distinct geometry, I now realized that it was a mountain bike, not a road bike. I hadn't noticed this at first because the bike had the standard, curved, "drop" handlebars common to road and racing bikes. Mountain bikes are usually equipped with straight handlebars. I asked David about his arrangement.

"I've got a road bike at home," he explained, "but this one is a higher-quality bike. I thought it would be more durable for this trip. Of course I put road tires on it."

"And you switched the handlebars, too. Right?"

"That's right. I wanted the additional options for placing my hands."

I knew exactly what he meant. The straight mountain bike bars encourage riders to sit in a fairly upright position and hold on either to the handlegrips at the ends of the bar or somewhere along the bar closer to the stem. That's far from ideal on a long-distance ride. If forced to steer constantly from the same position, riders' hands become stiff and numb.

Road bars, however, provide six options for placing my hands, and each puts my entire upper body in a different position, providing overall relief. The most prone position is with my hands in the bottom of the handlebar curls (called, in bike parlance, "riding in the drops") with my knuckles pointing down toward the pavement. Next, I can move my hands slightly forward to the point where the bars begin curling upward. There my knuckles point at about a 45-degree angle toward the road. The third option places my hands in the front of the drops with my fingers curled around the brake levers and knuckles pointing straight ahead. In either of these postures, my body presents a low profile to the wind. A fourth choice is to rest my hands on top of the brake-lever hoods (which are mounted on the front of the down curls). To go higher yet, I can grip the top of the curls themselves. And finally, the most upright position: holding the straight part of the bar near the stem.

In practice, I've found that my physique has a bearing on which of these positions I use the most. Since I have more stomach than I'd like overhanging my waistband, riding down in the drops for too long is uncomfortable and restricts my breathing. Thus I tend to favor the three upper positions. Still, it's useful to be able to drop down for occasional relief or when battling a headwind.

I have seen tourists riding bikes with mountain bars, but almost without exception, they have added bar-end appendages to the handlebars to provide additional hand-grip alternatives.

David and I ended the day in Nickerson. Entering the town, we found ourselves briefly on Route 96 again. Somewhere after Rush Center, it departs from its easterly course and angles southeast toward Wichita. We set up in Nickerson's city park, but this one had neither pool nor showers, so I washed up using the sink in the restroom, but made sure I didn't leave it messy.

The day had been hot, and I'd ridden a stretch without sufficient water. Now, since arriving in town, I experienced some nausea, similar to what I had undergone in Colorado. I recalled that the printed discharge instructions from the Pueblo emergency room described a "fluid replacement mixture" I could concoct myself: one teaspoon of sugar and one-half teaspoon of salt dissolved in one pint of water. In Nickerson's convenience store, I used a soft drink cup and the sugar and salt packets to make this cocktail. After drinking it, I felt somewhat better, so I mixed and swallowed another. Almost immediately all the nausea fled.

The clerk declined my offer to pay for the sugar and salt. Feeling hungry now, I purchased a sandwich and took it to the park, where David cooked his supper on his portable stove.

Although usually preparing his own lunch and supper, David had been starting each day dining out, so in the morning we headed for a café. I watched in near astonishment at how much this trim young man ate. We both ordered pancakes, which proved to be three platter-sized disks a half-inch thick. In addition, David ordered the largest cinnamon roll I have ever seen. At least six inches square and three inches high, this enormous pastry was mounded with white frosting.

My stomach registered full after eating two of my pancakes, so David added my remaining one to his stack. After downing all four, he turned his attention to the cinnamon mountain. We had maple syrup remaining from the pancakes, so David poured it over the pastry. He ate every bite.

As we rode on that morning, we compared notes about our respective journeys. We'd enjoyed many of the same places and both had memories of the same tough climbs. David had taken an alternate route through Idaho, so had missed White Bird, but when I mentioned the Richland butte, where Scott and I had walked a large portion of the grade, David recalled the difficult incline immediately.

David had gotten sick not long before that, in Baker City, Oregon, and had ended up in an emergency room, where, like me, he'd been given intravenous fluid. He'd stayed on in the town's campground for a couple of days to recover.

I learned that while journeying across physical geography, David was traipsing an inner landscape as well. Having been unable to connect the rote presentations of his Catholic upbringing with real life, he'd committed himself to read the holy books of each of the world's major religions. He had the sacred text of the Hindus, the Bhagavad-Gita, with him, and he explained a little of what he'd learned from it.

Had he read the Bible yet? I asked. He hadn't, but planned to eventually. I offered some ideas for how to navigate the Scriptures when he got to them, suggesting the portions most likely to grip the attention of someone unacquainted with the book and which best related the Bible's primary message. Sections such as Leviticus and Numbers, which detailed ancient minutiae, I said, could easily wait till last.

We both had sandwich makings with us for lunch, but we

had not bought bread, planning to pick it up fresh in Buhler. But this was Sunday, and when we arrived, we found every business closed and the downtown virtually deserted. The next community was 20 miles away. While we sat in front of the closed grocery considering our options, I noticed a couple using the ATM machine outside a bank. We hustled over and inquired if there were any place open where we could get food.

"No," the man said. "There's a pretty big Mennonite population here, and they don't open anything on Sundays. We just moved here about a month ago and we're just getting used to it ourselves. But we could probably make you a sandwich."

"Actually, we've got the makings, but if you could spare the bread, we'd be grateful."

"Wait right here," the man said as the couple got in their car.

After they were gone, David asked, "Who are these Mennonites?"

Because my home area also has a sizable Mennonite population, I knew part of the answer. "They're a Christian group that formed in the Netherlands and Switzerland during the Protestant Reformation. Some of their views didn't agree with other religious groups, and they were persecuted there. They migrated to Russia and later here, to the Midwest. They believe in practicing their faith in their daily lifestyle, which, I suppose, is why there are no stores open here today."

Later, I read some more of the Mennonite story. They had immigrated to Russia at the invitation of Catherine the Great, and settled in the Ukraine. By 1870, they numbered more than 45,000, many involved in raising Russian wheat, which dominated the European market. The ascent of Czar Alexander II, who demanded "one czar, one language and one religion" ended the Mennonites' peaceful existence. Many moved to the United States, settling in lands of the Midwest that the railroad was then making accessible. The Russian wheat seed they brought revolutionized the agriculture of the region and helped to make the Midwest "America's breadbasket." Ironically, 100 years after they left Russia, the wheat the Mennonites grew here was part of what saved the Soviet Union from famine. It was shipped over under a contract supplying the Soviet lands with American wheat.

Moments later the man who'd offered the bread returned with several slices for each of us in plastic bags.

The town's name, Buhler, reminded David of the movie, *Ferris Bueller's Day Off*, a comedy about a playful, streetwise high-school student who decides to cut school for a day and enjoy himself in downtown Chicago. David commented, "My generation all saw the movie and thought it was great. We were the same age as Ferris was supposed to be." That set me thinking about what movie defined my generation. Perhaps it was *The Graduate*, with its feckless young man who finally finds focus in his love for a young woman, or *Easy Rider*, about two quintessential hippies who undertake a motorcycle trip across the country to find the "real America" and their place in it.

Although *Easy Rider* featured travelers on two wheels, the drugs and the counter-culture lifestyle of the protagonists were too far removed from my world for me to identify with it. For me, a defining movie was *Lilies of the Field*, the friendly story of a man touring America in a station wagon, who ends up building a chapel for a small group of desert nuns in the Southwest. The travel without itinerary, the chance adventure and the off-the-beaten-path location all conspired to hook me.

Sometime during our first day together, David asked me what I did for a living. I answered, truthfully, that I am an editor. But I didn't elaborate or mention that I am also an ordained minister. From long experience, I've learned that the quickest way to foul up a budding relationship is to inject this "M" word before the person has gotten to know me. If I identify myself as clergy too soon, usually one of two things happens. Either the person shuts down, figuring a minister will be a drag, or they elevate me with some unrealistic expectations and cease to behave naturally.

But while we were in Buhler, David asked about places to camp free when he got to Ohio. I mentioned country church-yards. When he wondered aloud if he'd be at ease on church grounds, it seemed natural to tell him about my experience with the church and my career in it. I also explained why I hadn't told him this earlier.

"Boy, I'm glad you didn't," David said. "I'd have probably just moved on instead of riding with you."

"Are you okay with it now?"

"Well, I'm sorry for swearing around you."

"Don't apologize," I said firmly. "That's exactly why I'm not always forthcoming about being a minister. It tends to make people uncomfortable about who they are. I'm not sitting in judgment."

David breathed a visible sigh of relief. Then he grinned and said, "Yeah, I'm okay with it."

A hot, dry wind blew from the south all day as we spun the pedals, bringing elevated temperatures with it. The wind gust-ed powerfully, making our one short southern run of the day — to reach Newton — exhausting. By the time we arrived at the Harvey County campground a few miles beyond Newton, we were whipped, despite covering only 58 miles since breakfast. The temperature remained high all through the evening, but now the wind that hampered us on the road helped to make the heat bearable.

Earlier, David had suggested that he cook supper for both of us on his stove, so we'd shopped in a Newton grocery. At the campground, David expertly prepared spaghetti, but because we had only his small, one-person-sized cooking pot, the process took quite a bit of time. We had no other plans for the evening, so this presented no difficulty.

The steady wind blew the area free of flying insects, so for the first time this trip, I slept outside of my tent, falling asleep under the star-filled sky.

———•—•———

About 6:30 in the morning, I jerked awake as raindrops plopped on my face. Immediately I scurried into my tent, while the precipitation changed to a gentle drizzle. David called over from his tent, "What's your policy for rain days?"

"I ride if at all possible. I have only a limited number of days to complete my trip. What's your policy?"

"I usually lay over, but I'd like to keep riding together, so if you want to go on, I will, too." We agreed to take our time packing up, hoping the sky would clear.

It did, sort of. At least the rain stopped for a while, and some blue peeked through to the west. We, however, were heading east, where gray still dominated the sky, and we pedaled out under it.

Throughout the morning, rain fell on and off, but only halfheartedly. We were dampened, but never soaked.

I'd grown up depending on radio and television to receive weather forecasts, but I'd decided that this trip was an excellent opportunity to learn about weather changes from direct observation. I'd brought a weather book, and had been checking the clouds I saw against its descriptions and noting what sort of weather they portended. During one of this day's no-rain intervals, we noticed some low cloud formations directly overhead that I'd not seen before. They looked as if a giant cauliflower had been suspended upside down, only dirty gray instead of white. There'd been little question about what the clouds that escorted me to Larned had in store, but these didn't seem that angry. Later, checking my weather book, I decided the clouds must have been "stratocumulus," which "do not produce rain but sometimes change to nimbostratus, which do."

Fortunately, this time they didn't. By noon, the sky cleared.

Jon, the westbound rider we'd met a couple of days before,

had recommended the café in Cassoday, where we'd be around lunch time. The sign outside read, "Good Food and Gossip — Established 1879." David decided to forgo his usual peanut butter and jelly sandwich and join me for a café meal. We both chose the "all-you-can-eat" lunch buffet. After David's third plateful, I asked if he still had room for the included desert. He replied that he was operating on "David's buffet rule": "Eat until you are full; then keep eating."

A waitress took care of customers, but an elderly man in a 10-gallon hat shuttled fresh china to the buffet as needed. In between, he sat at a corner table drinking coffee with buddies of similar vintage. On the walls around the café hung photos of a cowboy working a trail drive. After a while, I spotted a familiar expression and realized that the subject of the photos was the old man in younger days.

When we eventually waddled out, it was to face a 17-mile southward jog, directly into a strong, hot wind. My thermometer registered 98 degrees. The ride was not fun, but to my surprise, it seemed to take more out of David than me. By the time we reached Rosalia, where we'd turn east again, David declared he needed a nap before continuing. The community's only store was closed on Mondays, but the woman operating the post office directed us to a faucet. We drew cold water to replace the liquid in our bottles, which the air had raised to the temperature of broth. We stretched out in the shade of a building, and David instantly fell asleep.

A half-hour later we pulled back on the road, climbing a gradual, but mile-long hill, the most incline I'd seen since entering Kansas. A hot but easy ride brought us to Eureka, where we planned to camp. On the way into the town of 3,500, we saw signs advertising Eureka Downs, a quarter-horse racing track. We learned later that horse racing has taken place there since 1872, and the parimutuel track is a popular attraction.

Though it was 6:30 when we arrived, Daryl and Sally,

westbound cycle-tourists, pedaled out of town just as we entered. Naturally we stopped to talk, but David and I were surprised to see riders leaving "civilization" that late in the day. Rosalia offered no amenities for travelers, and Cassoday, where Daryl said they were headed, sat 35 miles away. Surely dark would overtake them, we suggested.

"That's the idea," Daryl said. "We want to avoid some of this heat." (The nearby bank sign announced the current temperature as 97, and all four of us dripped with sweat in the humid air.) "Besides, Sally wants to ride her first century. We don't mind riding after dark on low-traffic roads." A century is cyclist lingo for a 100-mile ride.

Daryl, who could have been anywhere from 27 to 37, dressed as David and I did: bike shoes, cycling shorts, T-shirt and helmet. Sally, who might have been as old as 23, attired herself in bike shoes, shorts and a halter top. Her helmet dangled from the rear of her bike. She was embellished with rings on her hands, in her ears and through her nose, as well as with bandages on her shoulders and healing scars on her face, arms and torso.

"Are the bandages because of sunburn?" David asked.

"No. I fell. Back in Kentucky, a dog ran in front of me. My brakes had just been adjusted and were tight. The front brake locked and I went over the handlebars." She narrated this tale in a "Gee-imagine-that" tone, and the word "dizzy" sprang unbidden to my mind.

"But you're still not wearing your helmet, I see." I said.

"No. It's too hot!"

Daryl added, "She had to go to the hospital for stitches. It's been a tough trip. A week before we left, someone stole Sally's bike and we had to hurry to find her another one." Something about the way Daryl spoke told me that he'd probably had to finance her replacement.

David hadn't missed anything either. After the pair left, he said, "Daryl's got his hands full."

"I think you're right. But hey, she's bicycling across America. Some good's bound to come of that."

"Absolutely."

If this had been a few years earlier, when the idea of cyclists wearing protective headgear had originally taken hold, I could have sympathized with Sally's decision not to wear her helmet. The first "brain buckets" were modeled after those worn by motorcyclists. They were heavy and trapped heat inside. But cyclists' helmets had gone through at least three reformulations since then. Today's version, like the one hanging from Sally's bike, is a sturdy construction of styrofoam and plastic, with plenty of slots for airflow around the wearer's head. Wearing a helmet will never be quite as cool as going bareheaded, but it's now pretty close.

In my case, the helmet offers an additional protection. I'm nearly bald on top. The last time I rode an extended trip helmetless, I received a severe sunburn on my scalp that actually turned to an open sore and took weeks to heal.

By the time we got to Eureka's city park, the pool house was closed — meaning no showers. I settled for a less-than-satisfactory sink wash and then adjourned to McDonald's for supper while David cooked his in the park. Finally, at 9:45, I rode to the laundromat to refresh my wardrobe.

A large man stood inside with piles of change on a table in front of him. "Is it too late to start a wash?" I asked.

"We normally close at 10, but I'm gonna be here a while. Go ahead."

Once my load was in the machine, the man asked the usual questions about my trip, and I supplied the standard answers. He was at least 6 feet 2 inches tall and must have topped 350 pounds. He had black, curly hair streaked with gray, a generous amount of face and substantial hands. He sported a black T-shirt and bib overalls that gapped at his side where they buttoned. I judged him to be about my age and liked him immediately. I soon discovered that while he might have looked at home on the set of *Hee-Haw*, in his head hummed the mind of a businessman.

"I'm pleased that your dryers get plenty hot," I said. "When I did my laundry back in Eads, I had to run the dryer through seven cycles to get my clothes dry."

"Yeah, some laundromats turn the heat down so people will spend more money. But you'll get a 10-minute cycle here for 25 cents that will completely dry everything except for maybe your towel and cotton socks. By rights, I should only give five minutes for a quarter — the price of natural gas has doubled since I put in the 10-minute time. But this is a depressed area. People can't afford it."

"It must be tough to turn a profit," I said.

"Well, there's only so much growth room in laundry. A few new families move into town or a few home washing machines break down — that's about the only way income increases. But about then a few families move away. I own five laundries, and it takes them all to make a living."

"It must be hard to supervise that many. Do you have problems with vandalism?"

"Some. It fact, I'm getting ready to put in surveillance cameras."

As I removed my freshly dried clothing from the dryer, he added, "With margins what they are, I can't even put in new equipment. My taxes would go up if I did. These dryers are 30 years old, but I keep them maintained and they work great."

I returned to the park, uncomfortable in the muggy air. While I slept in the tent to protect myself from bugs, I left the rain fly off so that what little breeze there was could flow freely through the mesh. Even so, I didn't cool off until late in the night.

Chapter 27

REST

On any lengthy ride, I eventually need a rest break, and that's when coming upon a rural cemetery is like finding an oasis.

In a seemingly haphazard scattering, small cemeteries sit adjacent to country roads, the kind cyclists prefer. These burial places are ideal rest stops. Even in regions where trees do not otherwise abound, most cemeteries offer at least a few, providing shade where I can recline and cool off. And in many places, graveyards occupy high ground, affording attractive vistas for my rest period and a rolling start when it's over.

Many of these cemeteries started out as churchyards. With the passing years, some of the congregations have disbanded or moved to other quarters, and the church buildings have been torn down. But graveyards are not so easily relocated, and so they remain, quiet and, it seems to me, content in repose.

They are so tranquil that I've often wished camping were allowed on their grounds (for cycle-tourists only, of course — not RVs). Surely the permanent residents would voice no objections. Regrettably, most cemeteries are posted as closed between sundown and sunrise, an injunction against vandalism, I guess. And I suppose cyclists possessed of vivid imaginations might feel uneasy spending the night in a graveyard.

I doubt I'd be bothered, though. If, in any sense, the dead

can be considered the "hosts" of the property they now inhabit, the mood I sense on their grounds is not that they'd like to scare me off, but that they are no longer touched by the concerns of living. The world goes on, but the dead hold their place, immutable. What has been is gone; what will be doesn't matter. In graveyards I sense no angst of existence, nor, for that matter, any intimation of immortality. What haunts me in a cemetery are not ghosts, but the sense that in the larger scheme of things, my own time on earth is but a heartbeat.

While cooling down from my pedaling exertions, I often stroll among the old stones, reading inscriptions. The stones heading children's graves always touch me with sadness. The markers over those who lived long lives simply communicate, "I'm gone, but it's okay."

Still other grave markers bring a chuckle. In one cemetery, an older man was tending the grounds. When he saw me idly walking about reading the monuments, he directed me to a windbeaten old stone from an early 1800s burial and told me its story. Apparently before his death, the soon-to-be departed felt neglected by kith and kin and expressed his sadness in the epitaph he composed for his own headstone:

Here the old man lies.
Nobody laughs and nobody cries.
Where he has gone and how he fares,
Nobody knows and nobody cares.

After his demise, but before the stone was inscribed, his wife and brother learned of what he'd written. They couldn't persuade the stone carver to leave the inscription off, but did manage to get him to add a couple of lines:

But his brother John and his wife Emaline.
They were his friends all of the time.

I agree with something George Bernard Shaw once wrote: "Life does not cease to be funny when people die, any more than it ceases to be serious when people laugh."

Somehow I'm always a bit surprised after stopping in a cemetery that I don't come away with some kernel of wisdom or an increased understanding of the nature of life or perhaps even some resolve to live the remainder of my time allotment differently. But I don't.

I always seem to leave unchanged — glad for the peaceful, pleasant rest stop and the contemplative moments to be sure, but basically unchanged.

I'm convinced we need a few things in our world just to "be." Not to demand change, not to teach, not to urge greater effort and certainly not to engender anxiety. Just to be.

At least, that's enough for me.

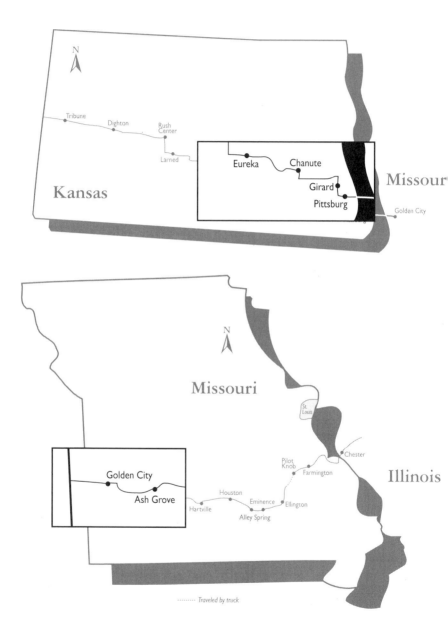

.... Traveled by truck

Chapter 28

HEAT

Most mornings, I hit the road between 8 and 8:30, but we slept late in Eureka; it was after 10 before we set out, and the sun was already high. The route took us through the tiny communities of Toronto and Coyville. In between, we encountered the Flint Hills, a minor series of swells that taxed us more because of the oppressive heat of the day than the precipitousness of the land. My thermometer registered 101 degrees, but it was the south wind that brought real misery. David described it as similar to the thermal wave that hits you when you open an oven to check a baking item. I used the words "blast furnace."

In Toronto, we ducked into a grocery store and shared a half-gallon of orange juice. We lingered, as much to cool off in the store's air conditioning as to finish the juice.

By Coyville, where we ate sandwiches in the shade of a tree, we found the liquid in our bottles as hot as the air around us. We obtained fresh water from the town's community center, but within 10 minutes, it, too, soaked up the heat.

Still we drank it, desperately needing to replace the fluids we lost through perspiration. After Coyville, shade was hard to come by. As we lay gasping in the meager shadow of a bush, I said, "Maybe Daryl and Sally had it right. I wouldn't care for riding at night because I want to be able to see the land, but this heat is doing us in."

"Why don't we get up earlier tomorrow and ride as far as we can before it gets too hot?" David suggested. "I could set my alarm."

"Let's do it."

But first we had to finish this day's trip. There was nothing exceptionally challenging about the terrain in the remaining miles to Chanute, but the heat continued to beat the energy out of us. Soon we'd consumed all of our water, hot as it was, and needed more. We stopped at a house in Benedict, where the woman filled our bottles with both ice and water. We each buried one bottle deep in our panniers, hoping our baggage would insulate them and keep the contents cold until we had finished our other bottles.

I wasn't feeling great, but David, who'd been the stronger rider earlier in the day, now bonked. His pace dropped to a crawl as we looked for a shady place to recover.

We found it in the front yard of a residence. Moments after we settled under a tree, we noticed a man walking out from the house toward us.

"Uh-oh," David said. "I bet he's coming to see what we're doing on his property. I hope he doesn't throw us off."

As the man drew near he said, "Pretty hot, isn't it? I just came out to tell you that you can get cold water from the pump back there by the house. Do you need anything else?"

"Just some rest," David said. "The heat kind of got to us."

We planned to camp in Chanute at the home of Katy Lopeman, a woman who regularly hosts cyclists. She'd been doing it for so many years that her reputation had spread on the cycling grapevine. In Colorado, John and Mary mentioned their enjoyable stay with her. David now told the man about our intended destination. Even though we were still 12 miles from Chanute, the man knew Katy, and asked us to extend his greetings to her.

Finally reaching Chanute, David, too exhausted to cook,

ate at a restaurant with me. Afterward, we asked the waitress for directions to Katy's road. Even though Chanute has more than 10,000 residents, the waitress also knew of Katy. "Oh, yes," she said, "she's the lady who rides a bike everywhere."

We also tried to phone Katy, to alert her that we were coming, but receiving no answer, we just headed for her place.

John and Mary had identified this woman as "Yodeling Katy," her bike-route sobriquet; David and I hoped to discover why.

We found no one home, but assuming she'd return, we waited. Shortly after dark, Katy, a woman near 70, pedaled in on a mountain bike with a headlight and flashing taillight. "I see I have guests," she said. "Wait just a minute until I get my ukulele." She disappeared into her mobile home while we stood there mystified.

Moments later she emerged, strumming the small instrument and singing a camp-type welcome song. Then she launched into a second number, which she laced with yodels.

"Well, enough of that," she finally said and got us some cold drinks. We were mildly disappointed when she said she no longer let cyclists shower in her bathroom. But when she mentioned that David and I were the 43rd and 44th riders to visit that summer, I realized that opening her facilities to that many would probably leave her with a lot of extra housework and a boosted electric bill for her hot water heater.

Daryl and Sally had spent a night there; Katy specifically recalled the nose jewelry. "But speaking of that," Katy said, "did you run into the other westbound group? They were decked out with rings through several body parts, but they weren't as clean as most of you are. I heard that other riders refer to them as the 'Grunge Group.'"

We hadn't seen them. There were six of them, five men and one woman, Katy thought, but she seemed a little uncertain about the gender mix — perhaps because their sartorial taste ran to baggy clothing.

They behaved well at Katy's, but after they left, she heard from a friend that the group was suspected of shoplifting where the friend worked. Unfortunately, this sort of thing gives all riders a bad name and leads to restrictions like the one in the Rush Center convenience store.

We sat on Katy's porch while she explained her involvement with cycle-tourists. "I'd been riding a bicycle myself for years for transportation — no trips like yours, but just to get around town. And I have three grown sons. If they had ever done anything like you fellows are doing, I'd have wanted someone to help them along. Back in 1981, I noticed some cyclists in a store here and bought them breakfast. They seemed to appreciate it so much that I just kept it up, only now I serve breakfast here. What time are you two planning to get up?"

David said, "We'd been thinking about 5:30, to beat the heat."

"Oh! I don't want to get up that early, so I guess you're on your own for breakfast."

David and I exchanged glances. We both wanted to know more about Katy and had visions of a hot, home-cooked meal. "We don't have to leave that early," I said.

"How about 7:00?" Katy said, and we agreed.

We set up our tents in Katy's yard for the night.

⎯⎯⎯•⎯⎯⎯

We got up at 6:30, and as we packed, Katy emerged with her ukulele and sang us the most remarkable wake-up call of the trip: "Get up you weary bikers! Get up! Get up!" Next, she set breakfast out on her porch table. It was cereal and fresh fruit, not the cooked meal we'd anticipated, but certainly acceptable. Katy asked us to bow for grace before we ate.

Katy sings for seniors' groups, visiting church youth groups and other events in the town. Her voice isn't exceptional, but her tunes are cute and her home-grown presentation no doubt entertains audiences for its uniqueness and flair.

Katy snapped photos of us and we of her, and then she sang us a goodbye song, accompanying herself on the uke. David gave her a farewell hug.

Even though we'd delayed our departure to eat with Katy, we were still on the road two hours earlier than the day before, so by the time the heat hit, we had covered about 25 miles. Due to the lighter breakfast, we ate an early lunch in Walnut. When the temperature vaulted upward, we agreed to settle for a short day and ended at Girard at 2 p.m., having covered only 46 miles.

We camped in the town park, swam in the pool, and loafed. As long as we stayed in the shade and didn't move too fast, the heat was bearable, but the temperature lingered around 102.

About 7:30, dark clouds accumulated in the sky and within minutes, rain gobbed down on the area, accompanied by frequent bolts of lightning. We retreated to the picnic shelter. We'd pitched our tents near a dry ditch that was about three feet deep. As the torrent continued, water raced through this trench, but despite the speed of the flow, the rainfall could not escape fast enough to keep the ditch from filling to the brim. Meanwhile, precipitation pooled on the ground and crept inexorably toward our tents. Running to them, we found neither leaking, but both taking on moisture as the ground water overwhelmed the tent floors. We hurriedly hauled our belongings into the picnic shelter, getting drenched in the process.

The deluge continued for about an hour, dropping three inches of rain. Shortly before it ended, a clap of thunder sounded deafeningly nearby as lightning assassinated a transformer on the top of an electric pole a half-block away.

There was no hope of sleeping in the tents. Instead, we hung them over the rafters of a nearby pavilion to dry while we slumbered on picnic tables in the shelter house. I fell asleep thinking about storm frequency: This was my eighth night in Kansas; three of them had been marked by very bad storms.

We arose at 5:30 and packed in the dark. At daybreak, we ate a quick breakfast in a Girard café and hit the road early. An hour's ride brought us to Pittsburg, which had borne the brunt of the same tempest that had driven us from our tents the previous night. According to a police officer we questioned, no actual tornado had been sighted, but "whatever's next worst" had waltzed through the community. The officer directed traffic around a two-block segment of the main street where a wooden electric pole lay smithereened on the pavement. Power lines draped the scene haphazardly, and the roof from a nearby building angled jauntily in a tree a block away.

Five miles farther on, we entered Missouri. Almost immediately, I discerned a subtle change in the environment. Somehow the landscape seemed less tamed than the tidy fields of Kansas. Land here was farmed, but the fields were smaller. Clumps of forest loomed less distantly than in eastern Kansas, and more uncultivated greenery adorned the vistas. Road kill littered the highway more frequently than in previous states as well. I had the notion that if the area were suddenly abandoned by humankind, the whole sector would revert to a wild condition within weeks.

The road loped along with an easy rise and fall. For several miles neither of us spoke. Suddenly David said, "I don't remember the last few minutes. I think I fell asleep."

I, too, had been yawning and nodding. The uneasy sleep on the picnic tables hadn't been enough. By now, we approached Golden City, the first community since crossing the state line 28 miles back. After refueling our bodies at a supermarket, we parked in the shade of a churchyard tree, stretched out, and napped for about 45 minutes.

Getting ready to mountup afterward, I couldn't find my riding gloves. I recalled pulling them off before entering the grocery, but couldn't remember seeing them since. We checked back at the store, and there they were, lying on the sidewalk in front, right where my bike had been parked.

I was relieved to have them back. Riding gloves are a near necessity for bike-tourists. They are snug-fitting, made of lightweight material, and have finger sleeves that extend only to the first knuckle. But their most important feature is heavily padded palms. The geometry of bike frames dictates that riders lean forward while pedaling, putting some of their weight onto their hands. In this position, riders' arms serve as shock absorbers. The padded-palm gloves help prevent numbness in the hands from the pressure and also soak up some of the jarring from uneven road surfaces. In addition to those intended uses, I've also found it useful to wear the gloves while making roadside adjustments to the bike; the protection of the gloves allows me to apply extra torque when using wrenches. And lastly, the gloves also make great potholders for riders who cook their own meals.

Refreshed and re-gloved, we resumed our trek. The primary highways in Missouri bore the usual numerical identifications, but the state's secondary roads were designated by alphabet characters. We'd crossed byways identified only as "M," "Y" and "J," as though they had insufficient substance to deserve a full-word name.

In late afternoon we pedaled on "A," which, when intersected by Route 97, changes to "Z." The riding-from-A-to-Z pun was not lost on us. A farm implement dealership squatted at that intersection, and we stopped there to guzzle cold drinks from the store's pop machine. "Which way are you riding?" the clerk asked.

"Eastbound," David said.

"Did you happen to run into a couple riding the other way a few days ago? The gal had rings in her ears and nose and had healing cuts."

David and I answered together: "Sally."

"Yeah, that was her name."

"She'd fallen off the bike," I added.

"Apparently more than once, if you know what I mean," said the clerk. "She was NOT having a good time when she passed through here, and she made no bones about it. She was chewing out the poor guy with her something awful."

Another employee standing nearby said, "The whole store knew she was unhappy. Boy, I'm glad I'm not married to her!"

Although there'd been a few more swells to the terrain since entering Missouri, the riding had required very little shifting. But about four miles beyond the implement store, we suddenly came upon a series of short but extremely steep hills, some brief portions of which had to be 11-percent or 12-percent grades. After days and days of mostly flatland riding — all the way from Pueblo, Colorado — we welcomed the challenge of climbing again and running through our range of gears. We also delighted in the gleeful glides down the backsides of the humps. Although we didn't know it at the time, these corrugations were the outriders of the Ozark Mountains.

Geologists consider the Ozarks to be among the oldest on Earth. Over eons, they've eroded and worn down, but they remain steep, albeit short, climbs. Lying mostly in Missouri, they cover about 40,000 square miles and are the state's largest land region.

Think of the Great Plains as a carpet stretching out toward the Mississippi River. Now imagine a big, playful dog bounding across this carpet until a rebuke from his master brings him to an abrupt halt. His momentum transfers to the rug, however, which slides forward on the smooth hardwood beneath it, carrying the pup along and piling up folds of carpet in front of him. Those folds are the Ozarks.

In Everton, I noticed a café-type establishment bearing the designation "diner" instead. Though that title is no doubt found on eateries in all 50 states, it seemed to me more an appellation of Eastern restaurants, and I had a sense that we'd begun to outrun the influence of the West.

John and Mary Sheldon had recommended an overnight with the Gilmores, a family in Ash Grove that hosts cyclists. I'd phoned the Gilmores from Golden City and been given directions, so we continued over the tumbling topography toward that small town. We arrived not knowing what to expect, but found ourselves treated superbly.

Dusty Gilmore first connected with long-distance cyclists in 1991 when a group landed in Ash Grove during a storm. Dusty opened the VFW hall for them, a practice he continued with subsequent riders. When his wife Jane saw how poorly some bikers ate, due to their shoestring budgets, she started feeding them as well. By the time David and I arrived at their door, they'd set aside a room for cyclists in the Victorian home the family was restoring, and all three of their teenage children — Jacque, Tyesha and Jim — helped with hosting responsibilities.

Once we were ensconced in the guest room, Tyesha collected our dirty laundry while Jane baked supper. Because nearly 200 riders a year now overnight with the Gilmores, the family keeps frozen casseroles on hand, including vegetarian meals for nonmeat-eaters like David. All of this was freely given, compliments of this generous family. Invited to make ourselves at home, we bathed, chatted with family members, petted the cats and the dog, and generally relaxed.

The room had only one bed but plenty of floor space. David unrolled his sleeping bag on the floor, insisting that I, as "the older man," take the bed. Before dozing off, we both penned appreciative comments in the Gilmores' bike log. Looking over previous entries, I spotted one from Sally. She mentioned how much she'd enjoyed being able to have a tub bath for a change.

———◆———

The dog woke me in the morning by pushing the door open and prancing in, nails tapping on the hardwood. Pulling on a T-shirt from the clean laundry pile, I inhaled a faint but pleasant aroma. Simply fabric softener, no doubt, but this morning it was the sweet scent of hospitality.

Dusty was away at school during our visit, and Jane had already left for work. I wandered into the dining room, gazing at Jane's large collection of unique salt-and-pepper shakers that filled several shelves on one wall. During supper, I'd asked her how long it took to dust that many items, and Jane replied, "About a day." Jane worked two jobs, Dusty attended college out of town, and the family welcomed cyclists who often arrived unannounced. Yet the house looked well cared for and was scented with the clean smell of soap. I was not surprised when Jacque hugged her mother and called her "super mom."

No one had mentioned breakfast the night before, but just as I concluded that we'd need to eat out, Jim appeared from the kitchen with a serving plate full of waffles and a jug of syrup.

The meal was my last with David. His plans included a week's layover with an aunt and uncle in nearby Springfield. He had invited me to travel there with him, assuring me that his relatives would welcome me, but my remaining riding days were dwindling fast. We agreed, however, that David would stop at my house when he rode through Ohio on his way home.

As we dug into the waffles, I realized that I would miss David. He had been a cheerful riding partner, easy to get along with and enjoyable to talk with. In the six days we'd ridden together, he had become a friend.

We finished breakfast and loaded our bikes. I took a picture of Jim standing in front of his family's large home. Then David and I rode together to the edge of town, where our routes diverged. We stopped, and still straddling our bikes, shook hands, and then both hesitated awkwardly. Finally I said, "Well, I better get going ...."

"Yeah, I guess I should, too ...."

With a final wave, we rode off in separate directions.

Chapter 29

SHIFTING

I rode out of Ash Grove pondering a caution Jane had mentioned the evening before. According to tales she'd heard from other cyclists, a problem town lay ahead. An account circulating on the grapevine had it that at Hartville, some local teens had rolled tires downhill onto the tents of sleeping riders and had run through the encampment with ropes stretched out between the attackers to knock over bikes and tents. Rumor also had it that a cyclist's gear had been stolen in that town.

But none of this information came from firsthand sources. Nobody knew exactly how long ago the alleged incidents took place. Still, on the basis of the hearsay, some cyclists, according to Jane, made a short day of it after Ash Grove, stopping in Marshfield to avoid camping in either Hartville or Houston, which had a similar reputation.

I didn't care for the idea of cutting the ride short. I had too few days remaining for my journey. Hartville sat 75 miles from Ash Grove, a decent day's ride. I'd have to take my chances.

The Ozarks bobbed out ahead of me, miles of roller-coaster hills that alternated swooping downgrades with knee-crunching climbs. The latter, while short, often included brief segments with double-digit grades. I never walked any of these hills in its entirety, but occasionally their midportions became so vertical that I dismounted and pushed the bike for 50 feet or

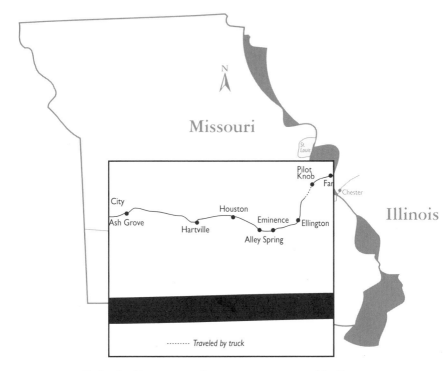

so until the incline returned to a more manageable 9 percent or less. David, with his stronger performance on upslopes, would no doubt have pedaled all the way, but I wanted my half-century-old knees to serve me for several decades yet to come.

As I stopped throughout the day for rest and eating, I found myself withdrawing, avoiding unnecessary contact with others. Where I lunched, I made no effort to talk with the people who shared the counter with me. In a store, I made my purchases, but hurried out before anyone asked questions about my ride. At length, I concluded that David had been shielding me from loneliness. I normally enjoy time by myself, but I wasn't in the mood for solitary cycling today.

Entering Fair Grove around noon, I asked a girl of 8 or 9 on a small bike if the town had any place to eat. "I'll show you," she said, and took off on her bike. She led me up a side-street hill to a café. I ordered a double cheeseburger and pota-to salad, a combo priced so reasonably that I assumed the sand-wich would be about the size of a fast-food double-decker. The two meat patties that arrived, however, must have been a half-pound each, stacked together with ample cheese on Texas toast. The sandwich stood about five inches high. "Wow. That's pretty big," I said to the waitress when she slid the loaded plate in front of me.

"Yeah, we don't mess around when it comes to hamburg-ers," she replied. For the first time on the trip, I was unable to finish my meal. I took half the sandwich with me and ate it later, feeling mildly guilty about the amount of beef I was con-suming. At home, Jeanine, looking out for my best interests, usually chides me when I'm tempted to indulge in large quan-tities of red meat.

Seeing a fellow patron at the counter reading a newspaper, I was struck by how much my focus changes while tour-riding. At home, I'm something of a news hound. I usually watch a TV news program while sipping my morning tea. I scan *The Wall Street Journal* at my desk before work hours. I listen to news analysis on the radio while driving home. And I some-times buy a weekly news magazine to get a more in-depth view of the world's happenings.

But when traveling by bike, my world-view is narrowed to the ribbon of geography I'm pedaling through. The road pro-vides enough stimulation that days go by without my even thinking about world events. The news I want has to do with road conditions, the location of services and what the weather is going to do. On the road, I seldom buy newspapers, and when I stay in motels, I rarely turn the television on. It never takes long to catch up on the news when I return home, but while I'm biking, I'm in a realm that fills my senses and occu-pies my mind to the exclusion of the larger world.

The roads I traveled in Missouri had no shoulders, and after Marshfield, they carried a moderate amount of traffic. Passing vehicles had seldom been a problem in Kansas, where most drivers were courteous. If they could not immediately pass, they waited patiently until the highway cleared. But not so in Missouri. Here they raced past me, either barely moving over at all or swinging around me recklessly even when hills or curves blocked the view of oncoming traffic. As a group, Missouri drivers were an impatient lot.

In Kansas, I'd seldom needed to shift gears, but on Missouri's corduroyed topography, I shifted constantly. My bike derives its 18 gears from combinations of the six multitoothed gear rings affixed to the hub of the rear wheel and the three chainrings on the crank. The highest gear results when the chain runs on the biggest chainring and the smallest gear ring; the opposite arrangement yields the lowest gear. All the other gears, of course, are in between.

I move the chain through the gears by means of two levers, one for the rear cluster of gear rings and one for the chainrings. The levers are attached by cables to shift mechanisms, called deraillers, which actually pick up the chain and lay it on the next ring.

Newer bicycles have an indexing device designed to place the chain precisely, but my older system, called "friction shifting," relies on feel and ear. When I shift to a different ring on the back wheel, for example, that changes the angle at which the chain runs from the front ring, making it rub on the cage of the front derailler. The resulting chain rattle alerts me that I need to make a tiny adjustment in the position of the front derailler. This process of keeping the two deraillers synchronized for each gear is called "tuning the shift."

It occurs to me that life has its share of shift tunings as well — that every advantageous adjustment in one facet of our lives requires a counteradjustment in some other facet. My career change, for example, showered advantages: better salary, home ownership (instead of living in a church's parsonage), more freedom on weekends. But the move required that we give up the quiet of small-town life and move away from friends we had been a long time making. I did not regret the change, but I was aware that one does not shift life gears without some necessary adjustments to deal with the rattles the changed situation brings. Life has no indexing device.

I knew that quite a few foreigners ride the TransAmerica Trail. David had ridden briefly with a couple from the Netherlands, and I heard about some Australian riders somewhere along the way. Several miles beyond Marshfield, I met two young Englishmen churning westward. One rode a bike equipped with a wheel size not commonly found in the United States, and he'd had a tire go bad. Unable to locate a replacement along the route, they'd arranged for a specialty shop to ship one to Marshfield. Meanwhile, they were making do with the problem tire. After my tire failure in Montana where I had to hitchhike to a bike shop, I took to carrying a spare. That sounded even wiser for someone riding nonstandard equipment.

Otherwise, though, the pair appeared well equipped. Both wore camel-pack hydration systems, water bladders worn backpack style with a drinking tube routed over the shoulder for convenient sipping while riding. The product was developed for racers so that no time would be lost reaching for frame-mounted bottles, but I assumed these systems would be a nuisance when touring. These two liked them, however.

I rolled down a steep hill into Hartville, breaking the posted 35-mile-per-hour speed limit. The city park accepted campers, but provided neither water nor restrooms. Camping was also permitted on the courthouse lawn, an all-too-public area in the midst of a busy town center, but again, with no facilities.

Jon had recommended a bed-and-breakfast establishment that had an unfinished room cyclists could use for only $15 a night. Since that also included breakfast, it was a deal. I found the Sackett House near the town center. Mike Sackett and his wife Chris welcomed me warmly, installed me in the room, and invited me to eat supper with them as well. The delicious roast beef meal now made the $15 a terrific bargain.

Mike and Chris, who came from a town in Ohio where I once lived as a child, had landed in Hartville after a decision to find a place to open a B & B and live a quiet life. They were restoring the old house and had one room ready for paying guests. The upstairs chamber where I encamped would eventually become the second finished room, but they had additional space and talked of keeping somewhere open for cyclists. They'd even phoned Adventure Cycling Association, the TransAmerica Trail developers, and asked to have their house noted on the map addendum as a regular stopover.

Had they heard about the tire-rolling incident? I inquired. "Oh, that happened in Farmington, not here," Chris said.

Following a full, cooked breakfast, Chris handed me a plastic bag full of homemade chocolate chip cookies for the road. That $15 now seemed a paltry sum for all that I'd received in return.

All across America, I noticed a wide variety of items lying beside the road: nuts and bolts, broken shock chords, a zillion beverage containers, fast-food wrappers, articles of clothing, towels, wash cloths, disposable diapers, tools, license plates, car parts and numerous other belongings. I often wondered what stories lay behind these objects. Did the screwdriver I found mean someone had broken down on the highway and attempted a repair? What problem did the person have later when the tool was discovered missing? Did the apparel strung out over a mile mean that someone had tossed articles from a moving vehicle in the midst of an argument, or had a suitcase tied on the top of someone's car popped open?

A magazine on the road shoulder beyond Hartville provided fodder for another batch of scenarios. It lay back cover up but looked in good condition, so I stopped. It was a like-new copy of *Playboy*, but it had been issued four years earlier. How did it get there? It was the kind of puzzle a short-story writer would relish. I envisioned a bride, full of dismay as she discovered her new husband's collection of "girlie" literature, driving down the road tossing issue after issue, but since I passed no others, that possibility didn't hold up. Maybe it fell off a truck moving a printer's unused inventory.

Or try this one: Four years earlier, a teenage boy purchases the magazine. He's driving the family car and hides the issue under the seat so his mother won't see it. The next day, before the lad can retrieve his guilty purchase, his dad sells the car. The new owner, who drives the vehicle only as a work car, never bothers to clean under the seat. But one day, four years later, he drives his wife to work while her car is in the shop. She drops her compact and fishes under the seat to find it, bringing up the magazine instead. Seeing only that it is *Playboy*, but not noticing the date, she smacks her husband with it, saying, "What's the matter? Aren't I enough for you?" and pitches it out the window. Poor hubby, of course, professes innocence, but his wife doesn't believe him. He spends the next seven nights sleeping on the couch.

In this version, the boy, now a young man, happens by a few minutes later, on foot, and spots the magazine. Because of a page corner folded down a certain way, he realizes that this is not only the same issue he'd lost, but the very same copy. Not one to question fate, he sticks the magazine in his back pocket and strides off, whistling a merry tune.

No doubt an experienced novelist would come up with something better, but the puzzle occupied my mind while I battled a headwind. Fortunately, the frequent valleys and the trees that grew in profusion provided windbreaks often enough that there were numerous periods of respite.

Fifteen miles before Houston, I bought an orange juice at a tiny gas station/grocery combination. The attendant said, "I wouldn't advise you to camp in Houston. I heard that some kids rolled tires down onto some bikers' tents there."

"Thanks. I'll be careful." Later, I heard that the event had occurred 10 years earlier and that the offenders had been punished by the local law. But which local law? No matter what town I visited, people always said the incident took place in some other town. Such is the power of an oft-told tale. Probably there was a single attack on cyclists somewhere in the state, but now towns all across Missouri are smeared by the legend.

I stopped for lunch in Houston, which, I learned from a sign at the city limits, had been the home of Emmet Kelly, the famous "Weary Willie" circus clown. The sign also announced the dates of the annual clown festival. With such a heritage, I found it hard to imagine the town as a problem place for cyclists. Still, I took the usual precautions — primarily leaving my bike where I could see it while I ate.

I carried a cable and lock, which I installed on the bike at night to protect it while I slept, but I seldom bothered during the day, since there was no way I could lock up the panniers. Aside from keeping the bike in view when possible, I mainly relied on people's goodwill. I also assumed that those inclined to theft or vandalism needed a little time to organize their mischief, so when forced to leave the bike where I couldn't watch it, I seldom left it there for long. On my entire cross-nation ride, no one ever touched my bike.

Nearing Summerville, I met two more of the TransAmerica Trail personalities. In front of the home of Peter and Phyllis Lowe hangs a sign reading "Bicyclist's Rest." Beside it, an old bicycle with a dummy rider greets visitors. But the most prominent object is a large plywood cutout of a dragon, painted red. This explained Mrs. Lowe's bike-route nickname, the Dragon Lady. (Jane Gilmore told me that Phyllis Lowe really didn't like that appellation; she preferred the "Lemonade Lady.")

When I rang the bell mounted on the gate, two dogs, one as large as a small pony and slobberingly friendly, came running to greet me. On their heels, Peter Lowe, a bare-chested man with a Moses beard and bald head, came to open the gate. "Lemonade or ice tea?" he asked in British-accented English.

Inside, I met Phyllis, the Lemonade Lady herself, who said, "Ah, a mature rider for a change." The Lowes appeared to be my seniors by at least 15 years.

"Are most who stop young people?" I asked.

"Generally, although we've had some in their 60s as well."

In addition to the usual log book, the couple also maintains two packets of material, one for eastbound riders and one for westbounders. Each is full of information cyclists shared for the benefit of riders heading the opposite way. For example, the eastbound envelope told of an alternate route between the Illinois towns of Chester and Carbondale, and also restaurants in Kentucky with all-you-can-eat buffets. I contributed information about the Sackett House to the westbound file.

"Did you happen to meet Daryl and Sally?" Peter asked. When I said I had, Peter continued, "They stayed overnight here. We have a small trailer out back for a guest house. Sally was ... uh, unusual."

"She'd fallen," I said.

"Yes, but when she was here she was, shall we say, 'hyperactive.' They arrived late in the afternoon, and Daryl appeared worn-out, but Sally wasn't ready to settle down. First she tried the unicycle we have, and then she found our old tandem bike. She made Daryl get on it with her and charged around for a while. Next she played with the ducks. When she found our paddle boat, she tried to get Daryl to go out on the pond with her, but he finally refused. She seemed on the move all evening."

Peter also mentioned an eastbound party a couple of days ahead of me. A man and his 7-year-old daughter on a tandem, and his wife on a single bike. I'd first heard about this trio from Daryl, who said they were several days ahead. I had seen their names again in the Gilmore log, which showed them with a three-day lead. I figured they were riding fewer daily miles than I was, since I seemed to be gaining on them.

The Grunge Group as well had stopped at the Lowes'. The visit had gone fine, but something in Peter's description of it suggested that the couple had been a bit uneasy while the band was there.

I asked about the tire-rolling story. Peter said, "That's been around for a while, but we don't know where it happened. But there's another story, and I'd love to find out if it's true. Apparently there used to be a family in Buhler who hosted cyclists like we do. But then the wife ran off with one of the riders."

"You can see how that would put a damper on hosting riders," Phyllis added drolly.

Another story passed from rider to rider concerned a three-legged dog in Burgin, Kentucky. A comment I'd seen in a bike log read, "Do not underestimate either the speed or ferocity of this dog." David had asked every westbound rider he met about this legendary beast, but only one — Daryl — claimed to have encountered the animal. But cyclist after cyclist reported that more dogs ran loose in Kentucky than in any other state on the TransAmerica Trail. Mary Sheldon had needed five stitches to close a bite she received crossing the state. After that, John loaded a squirt bottle with an ammonia-water mix to ward off attacking dogs. And Kentucky was where Sally had dumped trying to avoid hitting a mutt.

Peter and Phyllis walked with me to their porch, and as I mounted up, Peter yanked a rope, and the dummy on the old bike waved goodbye.

At Summerville, I picked up Route 106, heading for the Alley Spring campground in the Ozark National Scenic

Riverways. Beyond Summerville, the land changed from pasture and field to forest. A few miles farther on, I climbed a fire tower near the road. From the top, I could see an ocean of treetops in every direction, unbroken by settlements or other signs of human activity.

In the two days since leaving Ash Grove, I'd covered more than 150 hilly miles, and I arrived at the crowded but well-cared-for campground on the Jacks Fork of the Current River feeling weary. After a shower, I walked over to the amphitheater for the evening program presented by a park ranger. Her slide program covered the history of the area from the 19th and early 20th centuries when loggers harvested the forests. Alley Spring's claim to fame comes from the volume of water the spring itself produces — more than 80 million gallons daily, making it a spring "of first magnitude." Alley Spring also encompasses a cave and a pioneer mill.

But I'd been in the saddle too many hours to concentrate on the show for long. I couldn't get comfortable on the rough-hewn bench nor could I keep my eyes open. After a few moments, I gave up, returned to my tent, and fell quickly asleep.

———————

It rained during the night and still drizzled at daybreak. Inside the tent, I packed everything and then rolled the still-wet tent itself. The rain wasn't cold, but added to the humidity. By the time I rode the five uphill miles to Eminence, the precipitation had stopped. The town overflowed with campers and tourists looking for breakfast. The first eatery I spied proclaimed itself as a "family restaurant," and a line of people waiting for seats snaked out the door. This can't be where the locals eat, I thought, and continued down the street. A block away, in a less prominent location, I found Jacks Fork Café, comfortably busy, but with seats open.

A woman who looked like a younger version of "Granny" from the *Beverly Hillbillies* TV series took my pancake order, while her counterpart, who resembled "Flo" on the old *Alice* show took care of the diners at the tables. Most of these, I gathered from overheard conversation and workaday attire, were townsfolk. Their comfortable banter with "Granny" and "Flo" suggested that they were regulars in the diner.

The establishment had all the trappings of classic small-town cafés, including a stainless-steel-and-glass pie rack, a few single-serving-size cereal boxes displayed on a shelf above the coffee pots and a cigarette smoldering in an ashtray at the end of the counter. As in most cafés, nobody ever actually smoked this cigarette. One of the waitresses must have lit it, but while I was there, both were too busy delivering food and refilling coffee cups to bother with it.

The pancakes arrived promptly and tasted great. Both "Granny" and "Flo" checked a couple times to make sure I had enough tea. By the time I finished, I felt so good that I doubled the tip.

On the TransAmerica Trail, the Ozarks' biggest upheavals bunch between Alley Spring and Centerville, 47 miles hence, and I spent the morning and afternoon puffing up one after another, stopping only for lunch in Ellington. Unlike the mounds I climbed earlier, these were major rollers that continued upward, sometimes for miles. The map stated blandly that for eastbound riders, "the route seems all uphill." It did.

At the top of the final big climb I met a westbound cyclist who told me he'd eaten lunch in Centerville with two eastbounders, a young man in his 20s and one in his 60s. The latter had blown out one knee but was determined to make St. Louis. It seemed likely I would overtake them.

Although the Ozark "plateau" supposedly ends near Centerville, I still encountered some moderate climbs for a few miles afterward, and rain fell again. Because I wasn't carrying much food, I needed to make Pilot Knob by evening, where I could buy a meal. But by 6 p.m., my energy began failing fast and I worried that the daylight wouldn't last.

Moments later, a van pulled alongside me, and a middle-aged woman called to me from the passenger window. "Have you ridden with a young man named Jason?" she asked. "He's our son, and we've been trying to find him to surprise him."

"No," I said, "but I just learned that there's a young rider a little way ahead of me, riding with an older man."

"Yes!" she said joyfully. "That's him." Then before they pulled away, she asked, "Do you need anything?"

"No, thanks." I waved them on.

Soon afterward, as I started up another hill, I was overcome with a sense of weariness, so much so that this hill, no worse than others I'd climbed in Missouri, suddenly seemed insurmountable. The dreary rain, coupled with the early darkness in the forest around me, clamped me with a sense of futility. After several weary strokes, I slowed to a crawl, then dismounted and started pushing the bike slowly up the grade while doubts flooded my head. What was I doing out here? Who was I to think I could get by without the creature comforts of modern times? How far would I have to ride in the gathering dark? Had I finally exceeded both common sense and my physical abilities?

Before I reached the top, a small pickup truck passed and then braked to a stop. A white-haired man emerged and said, "Do you want a ride? This rain's pretty miserable." After only a second's hesitation while I considered and rejected the notion that I should pedal every mile no matter what, I accepted his offer. The two of us tossed my bike into the pickup bed.

Inside the cab, I said, "I've ridden my bike all the way from the West Coast, and you're the first driver to ever offer me a ride. Thanks."

"Well, folks around here are pretty good-hearted," he said.

We drove over only a couple of hills before the terrain flattened out and the rain ceased. Had I persevered, my final miles of the day would have been easier, but I still doubted I'd have had enough daylight. I watched for the two riders the west-bounder mentioned, but never saw them. They had probably headed into Johnson's Shut-Ins State Park, which we passed not long after I accepted the ride. I hoped Jason's parents had thought to look there.

The driver was an auto worker, heading back to his job at a Ford plant in St. Louis from his country home where he spent his weekends. In just seven weeks, he would retire and leave St. Louis for good, he said. He didn't usually return from his weekend home by way of Pilot Knob, but learning that that was my destination, he adjusted his route and dropped me in the town. He'd driven me about 18 miles.

Too tired to camp, I took a motel room. Later, in the dwindling light, I walked around the nearby Fort Davidson Historic Site, the location of an 1864 Civil War battle. Although badly outnumbered, a Union garrison held the fort against Confederate attackers. Finally, slipping out at night, the Yankee troops exploded the fort's powder magazine. All that remains of the fort for today's tourists are the earthen walls and a deep crater where the magazine had stood.

Once again I ended a day of riding as the recipient of a stranger's good-heartedness.

Chapter 30

PUSH

My whole body protested as I eased out of bed in the morning. I had bruises on my left palm from jarring while gripping the handlebars. My butt also bore bruises, beat from the saddle. My back hurt. The muscles around my knees were squeaky tight, poison-ivy rash encircled one ankle and one finger, and mosquito bites adorned my legs.

Otherwise, I was fine.

I started out gingerly but soon achieved a rhythm that switched my focus from body gripes to the pleasure of bicycling. Sixty-five miles lay between me and the Mississippi River, and I anticipated the crossing as a major milestone in my journey. The big river was the boundary that, once crossed, would truly place me "back East."

My notes for this day are sketchy, for though I covered the miles, the journey was unmarked by meetings with other bikers or local people. I interacted briefly with store clerks when buying food, but only to the extent necessary to complete the transactions. The terrain offered standard challenges — all but the 10 miles of flood plain that abutted the river proved to be hilly — but few of the hills angled as sharply as the Ozark humps. And nothing in the landscape captured my attention sufficiently to make a note about it. I did manage to excite a few dogs as I rolled past their domains, but none pursued me

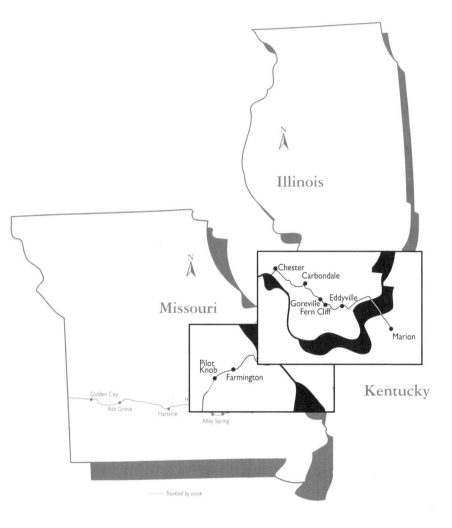

past the perimeters of their masters' homesteads. It was simply a day of good riding.

At a Farmington gas station, I used the air hose to top up the pressure in my tires. All bike tires lose a little air over time. Although I had tested my tires daily by feel, I hadn't added any air since Frisco, Colorado, where I initially pumped them up to 100 psi. When I checked them with a gauge now, I found the front tire still at 85 psi and the rear at 65. I had no flats at all on this leg of my trip.

The "bi" in bicycle, like that in bifocal, biplane or bicameral, means "two." In "bicycle," of course, two refers to the number of wheels. And to the uninitiated, the wheels on most bikes probably appear more or less identical. Both employ the same size tires and generally have the same number of spokes. Mine has 36 in each wheel, and it still strikes me as remarkable that a few thin bits of steel successfully carry a full-grown adult and all his gear.

I wasn't surprised to find less pressure remaining in the back wheel, for the performance required of it is quite different from what's expected of its rolling companion. One physical distinction reveals itself even on cursory visual examination: The right side of the rear wheel is "dished" to make space for the gear cluster. This is accomplished by installing slightly shorter spokes on the right side.

The stresses on the rear wheel are greater because of the way bikes are engineered. The geometry of bicycle frames dictates that the larger percentage of the rider's weight falls on the back wheel. Also, because the chain drives the back wheel, and then from one side only, the torque on the hub distributes itself disproportionately through the diameter.

I've ridden my current bicycle more than 10,000 miles and have never done anything more to the front wheel than occasionally tune the spokes. But I've broken several spokes on the rear wheel and finally had to have it rebuilt by hand with heavier-gauge spokes.

Beyond Farmington, the route prowls through hilly farm-land, which ends abruptly when the highway drops from plateau to flood plain. At the bottom of the final hill, I ped-aled over a levee, wondering if it were one that held during the massive flooding of the Mississippi during 1993. Many levees had given way.

The flat land beyond the levee was heavy with crops, mostly corn. If this land had been submerged, it seems to have recovered.

The last miles toward the Chester bridge over Old Man River were on a busy highway with no verge. I pulled over sev-eral times to give semis the right of way. This was no problem on the road, but the bridge had neither sidewalk nor shoulder, just a single traffic lane in each direction. I had to ride direct-ly in the traffic path, which was dangerous because the approach to the bridge curved; vehicles couldn't see me until they were actually on the structure. I had hoped to linger on the bridge, perhaps taking a photo of the river. Instead, I ped-aled across as rapidly as possible, fearing that at any moment a tractor-trailer would plow into me, having not seen me soon enough to slow down. Fortunately, I seemed to have caught a lull in the traffic, and I landed safely, if somewhat anxiously, on the Illinois side.

Popeye greeted me as soon as I arrived. Chester had been the home of Popeye's creator, Elzie C. Segar, and the commu-nity had erected a statue of the cartoon sailor in a small park adjacent to the bridge. The bronze-metallic statue stood about six feet tall and had been in the park without incident for near-ly 20 years. Two days before my visit, however, vandals had pil-fered Popeye's pipe after breaking it loose from the sculpture.

Appropriately, Chester is the home of the official Popeye fan club, which is headquartered in Chester's Opera House, (circa 1875). During the silent film era, Segar himself worked at this establishment as a projectionist. His boss, J. William Schuchert, known as Windy Bill, was the model for Wimpy, one of Popeye's cartoon buddies. In addition to being given a rounded physique like Schuchert's, Wimpy was also created with Schuchert's fondness for hamburgers.

Chester supplied the archetype for Popeye's girlfriend, Olive Oyl, in the person of Dora Paskel, the proprietor of a general store in the town. She was tall, lanky and wore her hair rolled tightly in a bun.

Popeye himself was based on Frank "Rocky" Fiegel. Like the spinach-eating mariner modeled after him, Feigel was small and wiry, and according to local legends, possessed remarkable strength and ability to fight.

Nearly a century and a half ago, Mark Twain had viewed Chester while traveling the river as a riverboat pilot. In his later account of those times, *Life on the Mississippi*, he commented:

> *The scenery, from St. Louis to Cairo — two hundred miles — is varied and beautiful. The hills were clothed in the fresh foliage of spring now, and were a gracious and worthy setting for the broad river flowing between. Our trip began auspiciously, with a perfect day, as to breeze and sunshine, and our boat threw the miles out behind her with satisfactory dispatch. We found a railway intruding at Chester, Illinois; Chester has also a penitentiary now, and is otherwise marching on.*

If the penitentiary is still there, I didn't see it, but the railway ran immediately next to the river. Twain, of course, predated Popeye, but I suspect the irreverent, old humorist would have approved of the pipe-smoking seafarer.

Proceeding into the town of 8,000 people, I found the community park. Chester is built on hills; everywhere within its limits one is heading either up or down, and the park is no exception. I rolled down a steep hill to reach it, but once on its grounds, I found that it, too, sprawled over hill and dale. At the entrance, I checked in at the home of the park superintendent, who showed me where to set up.

A large swimming pool, built more than 50 years earlier but well maintained, dominated one area of the park. As a bike camper, I was entitled to swim free and use the hot showers. I skipped the swim but thoroughly enjoyed the shower. Darkness had fallen by the time I returned to my tent.

I awoke to the smell of fire, an odor I'd sniffed before falling asleep and assumed that it drifted my way from the midnight cookout the pool staff held on a nearby hill. But now I spotted the actual source. The area under some playground swings not far from my tent had been padded with sawdust, and a small patch of it smoldered. Had someone set it while I showered or had it been there before my arrival? I'd set up camp in the twilight, so I could have missed seeing it.

The park superintendent and a helper were working on a sign nearby, so I reported the smoke. "Darn kids," the super said as the two walked with me toward the pyre. "I've got to switch to sand under the swings. This has happened before." They drew several buckets of water from a pump and dowsed the affected area.

I mentioned that I'd not found superintendents in previous city parks, but observed that this park occupied far more acreage than the others. "It's not just this park," the man said. "I also take care of the Popeye park and the grounds of a mansion that was left to the city."

The superintendent imparted this information without any air of complaint. He'd been a carpenter before being hired by the city. Clearly he was the type of fellow who needed to work outside. Caring for the parks suited him just fine, I gathered.

I left Chester heading southeast, a departure from the TransAmerica Trail. Back in Colorado, John and Mary had given me a map they'd used for the ride from Carbondale to

Chester. The TransAm route runs northwest from Chester before turning inland and then swinging southeast. "Nobody uses that route," John had said. The map they supplied was an alternative recently developed by Adventure Cycling Association, and it actually gave me two choices. After shooting down Route 3 for nine miles, paralleling the Mississippi all the way, the route diverged where the river swung away from 3. I could either continue on the highway or follow a series of back roads that stayed near the river. Both ran over land as flat as a cookie sheet, but Route 3 offered the shortest and most direct route.

I considered my options. I had only four days remaining before I had to catch a bus for home, and I wanted to ride part of Kentucky, if possible. The shorter route would enable me get farther toward that goal, so I pulled back onto the highway. I decided on a hybrid of the two routes. I'd continue on 3, skipping the extra mileage that followed the meandering route of the river, and then jog onto the back-road route when the two drew close near Murphysboro.

Along the way, a roadside store promised a cold drink. In addition to a few groceries and bait, the establishment also offered an array of gaudy collectibles for sale. If the hangdog expression and barely controlled irritability of the man running the place was any indication, business was terrible, and no joy was to be had from owning the store. That probably explained the "For Sale" sign outside.

A couple of miles farther, a side road reconnected me with the back-road route, which skirted Murphysboro but eventually delivered me to Carbondale. A few miles before that town, I rejoined the original TransAmerica Trail.

Carbondale, one of the larger communities on the route, is the site of Southern Illinois University. I arrived on the day before fall classes were to begin and discovered the place swarming with students. Twice within five minutes, boisterous students in passing cars yelled at me to get off the road.

I searched for the "Bike Surgeon," a bike-repair shop legendary along the Trail. Word was that the owner not only checked over tourists' bikes at little or no cost, but also let cyclists stay at his house overnight. At midday, I needed no lodging, but I intended to buy a new chain. I'd noticed my drivetrain shifting had become sloppy and guessed that the chain had stretched. Under heavy-duty shifting demands such as the Ozarks, it's not uncommon to wear a chain out in fewer than 1,000 miles.

The shop squatted on a side street, elbowed next to a larger building unrelated to the bike shop. No bigger than an old-time cobbler shop and every bit as messy, the place immediately put me at ease. It was the work area of a mechanic more interested in repairing bikes than selling them. The "showroom" was merely a dozen or so used bikes on a rack outside.

At the moment I walked in, the "surgeon," a man in his 30s, was "operating" on an expensive mountain bike frame that looked quite a bit worse for wear. He had the frame locked upside down into a repair stand and had a large wrench attached to one of the cups (the metal face) of the bottom bracket. Apparently the cup was frozen to the frame, for the surgeon had slipped a two-foot length of pipe over the wrench handle. While a young assistant held the bike steady, the surgeon applied his shoulder to the pipe, levering the wrench and forcing the cup to unscrew. Then he handed the wrench to his assistant, saying, "Here, you should be able to finish it now."

As the assistant took over, the man picked up a dry, rusted piece of metal and held it out toward me. "Look at this," he said, shaking his head. "The guy who owns this bike should be ashamed of himself. He rides it to death but never bothers to check the bearings for grease. The whole bottom-bracket assembly is shot!" Then, laying the rusty remains on his workbench, he added, "But you didn't come to hear my complaints.

How can I help you?"

"I need a chain, I think."

"Well, let's check it." When he examined my chain, he agreed that it was worn-out. Many shops advise replacing the rear gear-cluster at the same time, and I asked about that. "Let's try the new chain first and see," the surgeon said. "There's no sense spending money on a cluster if you don't need it."

He placed my bike in the repair stand, which elevated the back wheel. This position allowed me to see the bottom of the rear derailler, and I noticed it was cracked — a discovery not altogether surprising when I remembered that the component had been in service for at least 10,000 miles. I pointed out the problem, and again, the surgeon did not try to sell me a part. He said, "It will probably get you home all right, but it should be replaced eventually." When I said to do it now, he produced a used part he'd rescued from a damaged bike, mentioned a ridiculously low price, and we agreed on it.

Later, when I test drove my bike with the new chain and derailler, everything worked fine, and I didn't need a new cluster.

As the surgeon finished up on my bike, a well-dressed man in his 20s came into the store. "Is my bike ready yet?" he inquired.

"No," said the mechanic, pointing to the mountain frame he'd been working on when I entered. "The bearings were completely worn-out. Here, take a look." He offered the ravaged part to the man, who glanced at it without interest and said in a flat tone, "Oh." Then, as if his lack of maintenance on the bike had not registered with him, he asked, "Well, when will it be ready?" The surgeon promised it the next day.

When I prepared to pay my bill, I found that the shop was a cash-only business. "I'd have to raise my prices if I fooled with credit cards," the surgeon explained. As he cleared a spot on the cluttered counter to write a receipt, he said, "When I was a kid, most of my friends wanted to become doctors or lawyers, but I wanted to own a junkyard. I guess I've come pretty close here."

Another young man entered the shop and introduced himself as the surgeon's partner. A young woman arrived moments later, obviously the girlfriend of one of the pair. Apparently the three spent a lot of time together. They dropped into a friendly, flippant banter while shooting questions at me about my trip. Finally, the woman produced a 1 x 10-inch board, eight feet long, upon which was scrawled a series on names, dates and comments. This was their bike log (maybe "plank" would be a better term). I added my name and the date to the list and headed out.

The route from Carbondale consisted of numerous turns, one of which I might easily have missed had the state not also signed the road as a bike trail. These byways included some mild rollers, but nothing heavy-duty.

My available time for this midnation segment of my trip would run out in a few days, but I was tiring of being alone day after day. I'd be ready to return home soon.

Actually, this surprised me a bit. I taken one of those personality-profile tests some years earlier, and it had branded me as an "introvert." Commonly misunderstood as "shyness," introversion actually refers to how a person recharges his social energy. Both introverts and their opposites, extroverts, may enjoy other people, but extroverts get pumped up by being with people, often the more the better, and they find too much solitude wearying. Conversely, introverts must spend energy to interact with people, especially clusters of folks, and sooner or later need to retreat to aloneness to regroup their inner forces. For introverts, spending lots of time with others is something like a right-handed person trying to get through a day using only his left hand; it's tiring.

Perhaps that's why both Scott and David proved to be such good riding partners. Both have introverted traits and a good sense of when enough socializing is enough.

Actually, given the right personality, I usually prefer to ride with a companion, but I suppose my introversion contributes to the peace I usually find when riding alone. But just like batteries that can become overcharged, I eventually build up an oversupply of social energy and need companionship to siphon some of it off.

Of course, cycling alone has other drawbacks. I don't have the benefit of the second opinion regarding a course of action when facing bad weather or illness. There's nobody to double-check me, to make sure I don't leave anything behind. And there's nobody to leave with the bike while going into stores or hitching back for a new tire, as I did in Montana.

Beginning to feel more alone than I cared to, I threaded past quiet lakes and forests and emerged about supper time in Goreville, population 900. It didn't take long to find the place I sought. The bike surgeon had recommended "Dad's Pizza," and I found the tiny shop tucked into a row of businesses on the main street. The sign outside read, "Lousy decor, terrible service, excellent pizza."

"Dad" turned out to be an energetic man with longish hair, not quite as old as I, who sat down and talked as I waited for my meal. I told him about the bike surgeon's endorsement. "Yeah," he said. "We've been recommending each other to cyclists for several years now, but I've never actually met the man. I guess I should drive up there someday and get acquainted." Dad also asked if I wanted to send an e-mail message anywhere. He frequented the Internet and would be happy to relay a message, he said. I worded a note for the colleagues at my office, stating that I was alive and well.

A man seated nearby, who had been listening to our conversation, asked me, "What do you do for a living?" But before I could reply, he said, "Wait. Don't tell me. I'm pretty good at guessing these things. A teacher? A lawyer? Okay, I give.

What?"

"I'm an editor."

"Oh yeah?" he said with interest. "Like for a newspaper?"

"A publishing company."

"No kidding? What do you publish?"

"Products for churches."

His curiosity evaporated. "Oh."

My food arrived, and after I sampled it, I decided the sign outside was wrong. The decor *was* lousy, but the service was excellent and the pizza was pretty good.

As I paid my bill, Dad mentioned the couple riding with their daughter on the father's tandem. He'd seen them ride through the town just the day before.

I spent the night at Ferne Clyffe State Park, a couple of miles south of Goreville. Although the park sat more than a mile off route, some enterprising planners had made it almost impossible for cyclists not to find it. First, they added bike signs to the TransAmerica Trail's traipse through Goreville. Then, beginning where the Trail cut east, they constructed a paved bike path that emptied out exactly in front of the park entrance.

The park itself was chock-full of botanical variety, including 700 species of ferns, as well as remarkable rock formations and vistas. Or so I heard anyway. I arrived in fading daylight and used the remaining time to set up camp in the primitive area. There were showers, a sign said, but when I inquired, I learned they were more than a mile away, uphill, in the Class A camp area. I made do with a cold-water wash at the pump.

Before heading for the tent, I talked a few minutes with the elderly couple in the adjoining campsite. They were using the most ancient tents I'd ever seen; heavy, old canvas veterans that looked like holdovers from World War I. I hoped for the couple's sake no rain would fall during the night.

None did, and I creaked out into the sunshine before 7

a.m.. Riding back to Goreville, I entered the café "Dad" had recommended the night before. Being an editor includes an occupational curse: I constantly spot grammar and spelling errors in printed material around me, and signs in this café tendered more bloopers than usual. While waiting for my pancakes to arrive, I pondered what a "tenderlion" steak sandwich tasted like, especially when washed down with "Mountain Due." And if I craved ice cream for dessert, I could choose between "Sundays" and "cons." I notice stuff like that, but it doesn't bother me; rather it adds to the humanity of the place. What really mattered was, Did they serve good pancakes? (They did.)

Leaving Goreville behind, I traveled a string of quiet country roads and little-used state highways and found myself in horse country. I hadn't expected that in Illinois. I passed one campground/ranch that advertised trail rides and later noticed a sign indicating that another trail-ride ranch was nearby. But the horses weren't limited to commercial enterprises. Several of the private farms along the way had a few mares and geldings in the pastures. The only downside was the accompanying horseflies that tormented me whenever I slowed my pace.

Around noon I nourished myself in a convenience store at the Eddyville crossroad. For a place with few houses, the store did a surprisingly steady business. A couple of elderly tourists lunched at one table, a trio of carpenters anchored another, and I manned the third. Outside, a state highway crew of eight munched sandwiches at a picnic table. Lots of other people came and went, some making purchases and exchanging gossip, others loitering simply because they wanted to be there. In many parts of the country, convenience stores have taken over the gathering-spot role once held by general stores in an earlier era.

From Eddyville, I ran southeast toward the Ohio River, which cuts the boundary between Illinois and Kentucky. The lightly traveled back road eventually delivered me to Highway 146, which roughly parallels the Ohio. I swung east on the moderately busy thoroughfare, passing through the river community of Elizabethtown and finally taking the cutoff to Cave-in-Rock. This peculiar moniker applies to both a tiny town and an adjacent cavern, each of which squats squarely on the river's edge.

The cave itself is 25 feet high and 55 feet wide. It gained a notorious reputation in the late 1700s and early 1800s as a hide-out for bandits who preyed on river travelers.

The highway led through town to the riverbank and a ferry landing. The river was wide, and I watched a tugboat push a string of barges downriver. The ferry, which was actually a flat barge powered by a tug, chugged back from the Kentucky side. When it tied up in front of where I waited, it unloaded about a dozen cars. Then the 10 autos on our side plus a motorcycle and my bike moved on. The ferry operates at no charge to users. A fellow passenger thought the operation was financed by Illinois state funds, but his information was vague.

The arrangement by which the tug tethered the barge was brilliant in its simplicity. The barge was rectangular. A heavy steel arm with a ring end protruded at a right angle from the middle of one of the long sides. A hook at midbow of the flat-fronted tug latched into the ring. The tug then snugged up to the side of the barge and motored it across the river's expanse. For the return trip, the tug simply swiveled around the ring and pushed from the other side of the arm. This arrangement meant that the barge itself never had to turn around — we drove straight on from the Illinois shore and straight off on the Kentucky side — and the tug always faced forward regardless of which shore it headed for.

In our age where so much of life relies on high-tech gadgetry, I take heart in discovering where low-tech solutions like the barge arm are the most effective. It pleases me that the latest cars costing thousands of dollars still use a plain, old dipstick to check the oil level and that airliners costing millions are still secured in place by a simple set of chocks thrown in front of the wheels. This attitude probably has something to do with my affinity for bicycles, for they are ingeniously simple mechanisms. Who would have thought that two wheels, a set of pedals and a chain could use human leg motion to become an efficient mile-devouring device?

I asked the ferry crewman if he'd seen any other cyclists crossing this day. He hadn't, he said, because he'd just started his shift. But the young man on the motorcycle overheard me and said, "There's a couple with a little girl ahead of you. I'm on a return trip and I passed them when I was coming this way a little while ago. The man and the kid were on a tandem bike. They can't be more than a hour or so ahead of you."

Surprisingly, Cave-in-Rock has no sister town on the Kentucky side. Instead, a highway begins right at river's edge and trundles off toward Marion, Kentucky, 12 miles away. Since there is no gate at the river end of this road, I wondered if anyone had ever unsuspectingly driven right into the water.

Because the only access to this artery at the river end was from the ferry, once the vehicles that floated across with me sped off, I had the eastbound lane to myself, and I cruised along without concern about traffic overtaking me.

All at once, however, I knew my trip was over. I actually had two more days I could ride before catching a bus home, and I'd hoped to cover a little more of Kentucky, but my body now screamed for rest. Since Frisco, I'd ridden nearly 1,400 miles in 19 days with no time off, and I was beat. Even to ride one more day, I would need to first take a recovery layover of 24 hours, and then I'd only have one riding day left before my vacation time ran out. But the bus stopped in Marion, so it made sense to pull out there.

First, though, I had to get to Marion. Although the road was moderately hilly, it wasn't nearly as tough as some of the other terrain I'd ridden in the preceding days. But my energy now fled and I crawled along, ticking off the miles more slowly than usual. When I finally made town, I rented a motel room.

After a restorative supper, I pedaled my unloaded bike to the city park, hoping to find the bike couple with the child. I located their tents and spied bike garb on a clothesline, but saw no one around. Heading back to town, however, we met and stopped to talk.

I judged the man to be in his early 40s and the woman slightly younger. The little girl, age 7, perched on the rear seat of the tandem. She held onto the handlebars to which a few toy animals had been affixed. Because daylight was fading fast, we talked for only a few minutes. Mainly, I learned that the girl was ready for the trip to end, but her father said, "It will; just three more weeks." If nothing else, the girl would have a great "how-I-spent-my-summer-vacation" story for show-and-tell when she returned to school in the fall.

Had I been continuing, I'd have probably ridden with this trio for a day or two. I would have enjoyed hearing their story, but I could not go on right now. We wished each other well and said goodbye.

On the pavement in front of my motel room, I began taking my bike apart to pack it for the bus ride home. Marion had no bike shop, so I constructed a large box using lots of packaging tape and several small boxes discarded by the town's hardware store. I have never been one to form emotional attachments to objects, but as I dismantled my bicycle, I felt a little of what horse owners must feel when they have to shoot a favorite animal that has served faithfully for a long time.

Of course, I would "resurrect" my steed when I got home — but not for this trip. My journey across America was over. I looked forward to returning home, but I wondered if I could resume my life in the workaday world without feeling like an impostor. Had the trip rendered me unfit for a life where my primary journey each day was the drive to work and back? I would have to wait and see.

The packing done, I flopped wearily on the bed. Only then did it occur to me that this date was my 51st birthday. The prospect of turning 50 had spurred me to begin this trip. It seemed fitting that the tour was ending as I began another year of life. Thinking about that, I assumed other goals would emerge to claim my attention, so that perhaps I wouldn't be an impostor after all. But whatever the years ahead might bring, I knew that this year would occupy a special place in my memory. And I would forever be richer because I'd been privileged to ride across America.

Chapter 31

GLOW

It's an autumn Sunday, and I've just returned from a bicycle jaunt through some farming areas not far from my home. I don't get out on distance rides as often as I'd like, for since completing my cross-nation journey, I've re-immersed myself in family and work. So rides like today's are a treasure.

One difference now is that I am pedaling a new bike. Throughout the 10 years that I rode my old one, I often contemplated purchasing a first-class bicycle made expressly for touring, but I always had more pressing uses for the money. Nonetheless, I imagined great benefits from a state-of-the-art vehicle, and I looked on enviously at the expensive two-wheelers sported by fellow riders. But not long after completing my ride across America, the right circumstances came together, and I bought the bike I had hankered after. It's a nice bike, and the newfangled indexed-shifting system is a great improvement over the old friction-shifting arrangement. I especially like it that the gear-shifting controls have been incorporated into the brake-lever units. That means I don't have to take one hand off the handlebars to change gears. Shifting is both easier and safer.

It has come as a surprise to me, however, that except for the improved shifting, the new bike doesn't ride much differently than the old one. Granted, I had upgraded the wheels and some of the components on my old mount, but the frame was still inexpensive steel, not the lighter-weight costly alloy of my new bike, which is a pound or two lighter. I had actually considered installing a up-to-date shift system on the old bike, but an article I read about metal fatigue convinced me that I was probably wise not to go on investing money in the old-timer. Nonetheless, as a rolling vehicle, the new bike isn't a dramatic change over the other one. Discovering that reminded me why I ride in the first place: It's not about equipment; it's about joy.

Aside from the new bike, the outlines of my daily round are much as they were before I embarked. The panniers, tent and sleeping bag have been stowed in the attic. The maps have been put away. And the trip is no longer a regular topic of conversation with family, friends and coworkers. Things are so much as they were it's almost as if the trip never happened.

And yet, journeys like mine do change those who travel them.

John and Mary Sheldon gave me their e-mail address. I sent them an Internet mail message when I returned home and shortly thereafter heard back from them. They made it all the way to Astoria and then rode down the West Coast to Eureka, California. They were temporarily with relatives in New Mexico when they responded, and indicated they were ready to head home by train. "We feel it's time to stop goofing off," they'd written. But of course, the journey was never goofing off — time out perhaps, but not goofing off.

Like any competent preacher, Scott used the trip as fodder for a sermon. On his first Sunday back in the pulpit, he referred to Abraham, the Old Testament patriarch, who spent his entire adult life as a sojourner, one who lives the impermanent life of a tent dweller. Abraham learned to value the journey, Scott said, and added that our trip taught him that there is joy in every day's journey.

David stopped at my house on his way home to New York, and with another cyclist in tow. Marv, a man nearly my age, had ridden from San Francisco and was headed for Boston. He and David met just the evening before at a campground in central Ohio. Since their route would overlap for a few days, they intended to ride together. They dined with my family, and then we three talked about our individual cycling adventures late into the evening.

Several days after David and I had parted in Missouri, he'd run into Harrison, the rider I'd eaten with near Royal Gorge. The two cycled together for a couple of days. They had gotten along okay, but Harrison had little interest in adapting himself to anyone else's schedule, David said. Recalling how Harrison left me in the dust and never looked back when I'd attempted to ride to Royal Gorge with him, I wasn't surprised. Harrison is a loner.

Although David still didn't know what he wanted to do with his life, something had resolved itself. He now had the scent of home in his nostrils and declared that he could hardly wait to get there. The next day, I rode with David and Marv halfway to their evening's destination.

For Becky too, things have changed. She's happier now and no longer dominated by the wounds of the past. The sparkle and promise of her childhood blossom daily in the maturing teen that she is. In a few weeks, Becky will be old enough to drive, and she's anticipating getting behind a wheel in addition to riding above one. We've agreed that once she has her license, she'll drive me to work with my bicycle, and I'll commute home on it. These days, when we cycle together, Becky prefers to ride her Terry bike instead of the tandem. Now that she has a bike that fits her size, she can easily outride me. Thankfully, she pauses occasionally so I can catch up!

My journey across America settled something for me as well. Some restless piece of me has been put at ease. Perhaps the craving to find out where a road goes will not be silent forever. But for the present at least, panic that I will live and die without ever satisfying the urge to roam no longer clutches me. Vagabonding coast to coast has fitted me to live again in the day to day for a while.

It would be a mistake to expect more than that, I think. Like David, many people I met across the continent were on seekers' journeys — and not just the riders. Some, like hotel-owner Jack Croly in Idaho and bed-and-breakfast proprietors Mike and Chris Sackett in Missouri, had left situations where they worked for others to become their own bosses in quiet hamlets. Tina gave up her hometown to follow her long-delayed dream. (I had a note from her the other day. She successfully completed the training and is now a full-fledged flight attendant with Trans World Airlines.)

But the cyclists, too, were pilgrims. Often what they pedaled toward could not be clearly articulated. They sensed that a radical departure from their previous lives was necessary if they were to glimpse their elusive grails. Granted, a few riders were simply on enjoyable vacations or satisfying a thirst for adventure. But more were on quests, impelled by barely focused dreams, unnamed yearnings or the hope that there was more to life than what they'd already experienced. David, the couple from California, Jim, John and Mary, even Daryl and Sally, who planned to make a new home in the West after completing their ride, were all fellow wayfarers with Scott, Becky and me.

I suspect that not one completed the trek with a crystal-clear life-course in mind. John Sheldon said as much. "Mary and I still have no idea what we'll do when we 'grow up.'" They plan to continue their careers in the meantime. But, whether the riders I met have precise plans for what to do next, like me, they will have benefited from their journey. A bicycle trip causes us to slow down, to immerse ourselves in a different way of life surrounded by new landscapes, and there to see, to taste, to sample, to feel, to struggle, and finally to arrive *somewhere*. We may not end the journey knowing precisely what we are going to do next, but something will have changed, if only the sense that life is what takes place while we carry on despite our incompletions.

Because of limited time and areas not served by the buses I relied on for returning home, I was forced to leave a couple of geographic gaps in my coast-to-coast route. (I owe Wyoming and Kentucky return visits someday.) But there are no emotional gaps. My trip *feels* completed. If I have any regrets, it is only that limited time compelled me not to linger long in any one spot. If it comes to be that someday I am in Richland, Wisdom, Fairplay, Cassoday or the half-dozen other locales that enchanted me, or if I once more climb White Bird Mountain or laze through the Snake River Canyon, I'll savor them longer. But if I do not pass those ways again — for there are new places yet to go — I'll still be glad for the quiet satisfaction they imparted to me and the smile that slides unbidden to my lips when I recall my days on the road.

On my ride across America, I tuned the shift thousands of times; in return, the journey tuned me.

Bike List

Clothes
helmet
bike gloves
sunglasses
biking shorts (4)
sleep suit
regular shorts (1)
undershorts (2-3)
T-shirts (5-6)
wind jacket
tights
long-sleeve jersey
bike shoes
bathing suit
handkerchiefs (3)
sneakers
socks (5-6)
hat
slacks
flannel shirt
wool sweater
wool socks
full gloves
scarf
stocking hat

Housing
tent
sleeping bag
sleeping pad
candle lamp and candles
matches

Toilet Items
towel
shaving kit and toiletries
toilet paper
Tums
ibuprofen
Tylenol
assorted ointments
ChapStick
Band-Aids
suntan lotion
insect repellent

General
pump
flashlight
water bottles (3)
compass
reading material
notebook and pen
bungee cords
maps
wallet
money
bike
panniers
handlebar bag
pocket knife
clothesline
camera and film
lock and cable
mink oil

Tools and Parts
tool kit
patch kit
chain lubricant
spare tubes (3)
spare brake cable
spare derailler cable
spare spokes
spare chain links
spare tire
misc. nuts and bolts

Sources

Most of the information about the areas I rode through and the historical events associated with them came from talking with residents, from tourist brochures or from the narrative on the Adventure Cycling bike map. In a few cases, I consulted additional sources as follows:

The Nez Perce
> Mark H. Brown, *The Flight of the Nez Perce* (New York: G.P. Putnam's Sons, 1967).

John Day
> Kathleen Moore, *Riverwalking: Reflections on Moving Water* (New York: Lyons & Buford, 1996).

Religion in the Northwest
> Ferenc M. Szasz and Margaret Connell Szasz, "Religion and Spirituality," in *The Oxford History of the American West*, Clyde A. Milner II, Carol A. O'Connor, Martha A. Sandweiss, editors (New York: Oxford University Press, 1994).

The Origin of the Hamburger
> Neil Zurcher, *One Tank Trips and Tales From the Road*, (Cleveland, Gray & Company, 1995).

The Fires in Yellowstone
> Dan R. Sholly, *Guardians of Yellowstone* (New York: Morrow, 1991).

Virginia's vertical feet of climbing
"TransAm Facts," *Adventure Cyclist*, November/December
1995.

Tandeming
John Schubert, *The Tandem Scoop*, (Eugene, Ore.: Burley
Design Cooperative, 1993).

Effects of High Altitude
Claudia Glenn Dowling, "Death on the Mountain," *LIFE*,
August 1996.

Standard Time
Henry Kisor, *Zephyr: Tracking A Dream Across America*
(New York: Times Books/Random House, 1994).

Shopping Malls
Kenneth Cole, "Hallowed Be the Mall," *Drew*, December 1986.

The Mennonites
Richard O'Connor, *Iron Wheels and Broken Men* (New
York: G.P. Putnam's Sons, 1973).
Donna Lynn Ikenberry, *Bicycling Coast to Coast* (Seattle,
Wash., 1996).

Elzie Segar and Popeye
The Internet Web Page of the Popeye Fan Club.
http://www.midwest.net/orgs/ace1/

Books for the Road

During the first portion of my journey, I discovered that the book I'd haphazardly chosen for evening reading did not match the mood of the journey. Here are some I've read before or since that seem to me to be better traveling companions.

Ivan Doig, *Hearth Earth* (New York: Viking Penguin, 1994).

Ivan Doig, *This House of Sky: Landscapes of a Western Mind* (San Diego: Brace & Company, 1976).

Jerry Ellis, *Bareback!: One Man's Journey Along the Pony Express Trail* (New York: Delacorte Press, 1993).

Jerry Ellis, *Walking the Trail: One Man's Journey Along the Trail of Tears* (New York: Delacorte Press, 1991).

Colin Fletcher, *The Man Who Walked Through Time* (New York: Random House, 1967).

Eddy L. Harris, *Mississippi Solo: A River Quest* (New York: Nick Lyons Books, 1988).

Mark Jenkins, *Off the Map: Bicycling Across Siberia* (New York: HarperPerennial, 1992).

Thomas Keneally, *The Place Where Souls Are Born: A Journey to the Southwest* (New York: Simon & Schuster, 1992).

Henry Kisor, *Zephyr: Tracking A Dream Across America* (New York: Times Books/Random House, 1994).

David Lamb, *Over the Hills: A Midlife Escape Across America by Bicycle* (New York: Times Books/Random House, 1996).

Jim Lilliefors, *Highway 50: Ain't That America* (Golden, Colo.: Fulcrum Publishing, 1993).

Richard Lovett, *Freewheelin'* (Camden, Me.: Ragged Mountain Press, 1992).

William Least Heat Moon, *Blue Highways: A Journey Into America* (Boston: Little, Brown, 1982).

Kathleen Norris, *Dakota: A Spiritual Geography* (New York: Ticknor & Fields, 1993).

Jonathan Raban, *Old Glory: An American Voyage* (New York: HarperCollins, 1992).

George Scheer III, *Booked on the Morning Train: A Journey Through America* (Chapel Hill, N.C.: Algonquin Books of Chapel Hill, 1991).

John Steinbeck, *Travels With Charley In Search of America* (New York: The Viking Press, 1962).

About the Author

In the course of his career, Stan Purdum has been a carpenter, teacher, minister, drama director, journalist, writer and editor. His published works include material as varied as a scholarly study of the Gospel of John, a how-to book for newsletter editors, numerous winning direct-mail campaigns, short stories, family humor columns and bicycle travel-narratives. He lives with his family in Ohio.